Search and Rescue Leadership

Figure 1 HAT Program presentation.

Preventive SAR

Teaching the Hug-a-Tree Program to elementary school children helps to prevent lost person incidents. Consider adopting a Preventive Educational Program in your community.

Search and Rescue Leadership

ISBN-13:
978-1530003280

ISBN-10:
1530003288

C. 2017.   All Rights Reserved.

Editors: Bernard Fontaine and Christy Judah.

Contributing Authors:

*Anne Brandt
Shirley Cox
George Dresnek
David Dyer
Bernard Fontaine
Christy Judah
Robert Koester
Del Morris
Allen Padgett
Anthony Somogyi
Chris Young*

Additional Acknowledgements: Thank you to *Eddie Fontaine and Silvia Fontaine* for their contributions to the layout, editing, and contents of this book. You are appreciated.

Unless otherwise indicated, photos and sketches have been provided by the authors and/or individuals noted.

Published by the Contributing Authors.
Printed in the United States of America.

TABLE OF CONTENTS

TABLE OF FIGURES XI

CHAPTER 1

SEARCH AND RESCUE FIELD LEADERSHIP 1

CHAPTER 2

SEARCH TEAM LEADERSHIP 5
Knowledge 9
Administration 9
Know your Job 9
Share Information 9
Be the Leader 10
Team Work 10
Safety 10
Leadership Theories 10
Management by Objective 11
THE SMARTER Approach 12
Situational Management 13
Participative Management 13
Incident Command Systems 14
Organization 14
Command 14
Command Staff Responsibilities 14
Operations 15
Logistics 17
Finance/Administration 18
ICS Forms 18
Briefing Form 19
ICS Form 214 19
ICS Forms 20
Summary 20

CHAPTER 3

SAFETY 23
The GAR Model 24
Technical Search Teams 24
Technical Rescue 25
Environmental Safety 25

iv

Hypothermia 25
Hyperthermia 26
Other Hazards 27
Summary 29

CHAPTER 4

MAP READING AND NAVIGATION 31

Topographic (TOPO) Maps 32
The Military Version of the 7.5 Minute Map 32
Grid Systems 32
Universal Transverse Mercator (UTM) System 33
Figure 19 Meridian/Equator 35
UTM Coordinate Numbering 35
Using the UTM Grid Reader 36
Declination 39
Using the Compass 41
Aligning the Compass 41
The Immovable Object 42
Night Navigation 44
The Global Positioning System (GPS) Introduction 44
Selection of a Handheld GPS 45
Using the GPS 45
Computer Generated Maps 46
Electronic Distance Measuring 46
Summary 46

CHAPTER 5

SEARCH TACTICS 49

Part I   Reflex Tasking 49
Reflex Tasking Containment 50
Attraction 52
Wheel Model 52
Direction of Travel Possibilities 53
Direction of Travel 54
Part II   Search Tactics 55
Strategy 55
Tactics 55
Loose Grid 56
Tight Grid 58
Search Techniques 59
Perception, Recognition and Detection 60
Foveal Experiment 60
Part III Leading a Task Force 65
Using Mounted Units in Planning 66
Summary 66

CHAPTER 6

LOST PERSON BEHAVIOR 69
Sample Scenario 71
Investigation 71
Statistics 72
Spatial Model 74
Search Scenarios 75
Scenario Lock 75
Lost Person Strategies 76
Random Traveling 76
Route Traveling 76
Direction Traveling 77
Route Sampling 78
Direction Sampling 78
View Enhancing/Cell Signal Seeking 78
Backtracking 80
Folk Wisdom 81
Contouring 81
Doing Nothing 82
Profiles 82
Tactical Briefing 82
Camper (Car camper) 83
Hiker 84
Dementia 85
Hallmark Behaviors of Dementia 86

CHAPTER 7

TRACKERS 91
Helpful Tracking Tips 92
Tracking Skill Sets 92
Use Skills According to Ability 93
Tracking Ability Levels 94
Clue Aware 94
Track Aware 96
Tracker Training 96
SAR Tracking Tasks 97
PLS Approach and Identifying Tracks 97
Moving Forward on a Track Trail and Marking Found Tracks 98
Choices 99
What to Avoid 99
Combining a K9 Asset with a Tracking Asset on your Team 100
Summary 100

CHAPTER 8

CANINES & EQUINES 105

Types of Search and Rescue Dogs 106
Live Find Dogs 106
– Non-Scent Discriminating 106
Human Remains Detection Dogs 109
Dogs 109
Cross-Trained Dogs 110
Canine Typing according to the Department of Homeland Security 111
K9 Performance Variations 111
When to Request and Deploy a Search Dog 112
Working with a Search Dog 112
General K9 Do's and Don'ts 115
Scent Articles 117
Trained, Reliable and Certified Dog Handler Teams 118
Training Standards 118
How to Find and Request SAR Dog 119
Canine Summary 120

The Mounted Unit – Using Equines in SAR 121
Equine Certification and Readiness 122
Equine Safety and Liability 122
Training Sessions 123
Responding to a Search 123
Required Equipment 123
Safety 128
Summary 128

CHAPTER 9

HAZARDOUS TERRAIN SAFETY 133
The Anchor 132
The Hardware 132
The Rope 133
The Operator 134
To Move a Crew *Down* 134
To Move a Crew *Up* 135
To Move a Crew *across* a Slope 136
Patient Transport 137
Litter Wheel in Use - Litter Carry Methods 139
Summary 140

CHAPTER 10

APPLYING PROBABILITY AND CRITICAL SPACING 143
Search Probability 143
Missing Person Report (MPR) 144
Theory 144
Statistical 144
Subjectiv Reasoning 144
Deductive Reasoning 145

Probability of Area (POA) 146
Probability of Detection (POD) 146
Critical Spacing 150
Calculating POD 151
Calculating POS 152
Summary 152
Figure 84 Assessing terrain. 152

CHAPTER 11

AVIATION 155

Task Lists 155
Air Communication Plan 156
Air Space Plan 156
Mapping the Air Space 157
What to Look For 157
Landing Zone Selection 157
Obstacles 158
Marking a Landing Zone 159
Additional Air Operations Considerations 161
Hoist 161
Forward Looking Infrared Imaging (FLIR) 164
Unmanned Aircraft 164
Summary 164

CHAPTER 12

URBAN SEARCHES 167

The Environment, Common Types of Searches, and Vulnerability Assessment 167
Vulnerability Assessment 168
Planning and Strategies 168
Investigation 169
Possible Scenarios 169
Field Operations 170
The Initial Call-Out 170
The Hasty Search 170
Attractive Nuisances 170
Institution Check 171
Containment 171
Field Team Tasking – Door-to-Door Canvassing and Interviews 171
Flyers 174
Training 174
Building Searches 174
Other Field Operations 176
Briefing and Debriefing 176
Documentation 177
Applying Other SAR Resources 177
Other Considerations 178

Summary 179

CHAPTER 13

SAR RESCUE 181
Pre-planning 183
Size up... 184
Gaining Access 185
Patient Assessment... 185
Stabilization 186
Packaging 187
Extraction 188
Recovery 190
Preplanning 190
Size up/Gaining Access and Patient Assessment 191
Investigation and Security 191
Packaging and Extraction 191
Other Considerations 192
Summary 192

CHAPTER 14

STRESS MANAGEMENT 195
Symptoms of Adverse Stress Reactions.. 196
Managing Stress during an Operation 197
Should I Request Critical Incident Stress Debriefing (CISD) 198
Summary 198
References and Recommended Reading 199

APPENDIX A 212

TEAM BRIEFING OUTLINE 212
MISSION   212
EXECUTION   212

APPENDIX B – Selected ICS Forms 215

APPENDIX C 226
Additional Leadership Guidelines, Briefing and Debriefing Information   226

BRIEFING AND DEBRIEFING 227
Briefing 227
Situation 228
Administration and Logistics 230
Communications and Command 230

Debriefing 231

APPENDIX D – Pack List 233

APPENDIX E – GAR FORM 242
Team Member Risk Assessment Worksheet   242

APPENDIX F – SEARCH URGENCY FORM 243

APPENDIX G LOST PERSON QUESTIONNAIRES 244

Missing Person (MP) Questionnaire, Interview form/guideline   250
lost person questionnaire ---Long Form   250

APPENDIX H – ROPE ANCHORS 268
Basic Dynamic Belay Commands   270

APPENDIX I URBAN SEARCH FORMS 271
BASARC Form 132 – Urban interview Log   272
BASARC Form 134 --- Clue Log   273
BASARC Form 135 --- Clue Report   274

INDEX 275

TABLE OF FIGURES

Figure 1 HAT Program presentation. ii
Figure 2 Oso, WA. xiv
Figure 3 Training for leadership. 1
Figure 4 Operations. 2
Figure 5 Searcher. 3
Figure 6 Search. 4
Figure 7 Briefing. 11
Figure 9 Command Bus. 21
Figure 10 Searching. 22
Figure 11 Poisonous Copperhead. 28
Figure 12 Potential SAR Hazards, livestock. 29
Figure 13 GPS. 30
Figure 14 Map Reading. 31
Figure 15 UTM Grid zones in the continental United States. 34
Figure 16 UTM Lines are straight; unlike Lat-Long. 35
Figure 17 Meridian/Equator. 35
Figure 18 Grid Reader. 36
Figure 19 Topo Map with Grid Reader. ....
Figure 20 UTM Protractor. 38
Figure 21 Declination Diagram. 39
Figure 22 Compass. 40
Figure 23 Compass. 41
Figure 24 Azmuth. 42
Figure 25 Navigating around an object. 43
Figure 26 Probing the Ground. 48
Figure 27 Containment area map using roads, pond, stream, trails and ridge. 51
Figure 28 Topo Map. 53
Figure 29 Direction of Travel Map Scenarios 54
Figure 30 Tight Grid Search on a magnetic track line. 57
Figure 31 Above: Loose Grid Search used when resources are minimal. 58
Figure 32 Tight Grid with linear boundary (road). 59
Figure 33 Snapshots. 61
Figure 34 Evidence Search. 62
Figure 35 Foveal Experiment 64
Figure 36 Three Lads. 65
Figure 37 Potential Missing Child. 68
Figure 38 Child Walk Away. 69
Figure 39 Searching in the Snow. 70
Figure 40 Snow search 73
Figure 41 A Typical Spatial Model Overlay. 74

Figure 42 Direction Choice. 77
Figure 43 Confusion Point. 79
Figure 44 Confusion Point Two. 79
Figure 45 Wilderness Attraction. 80
Figure 46 Typical campsite for a missing hunter. 83
Figure 47 Forest Road 84
Figure 48 Lake. 87
Figure 49 Track. 90
Figure 50 Measuring a track. 92
Figure 51 Tracker. 93
Figure 52 Shading a shoe track. 94
Figure 53 Are you clue aware? Can you spot the clue? 95
Figure 54 Tracker measuring with tracking stick. 96
Figure 55 Boot track. 98
Figure 56 Grass Track. 99
Figure 57 Sign and Clue Awareness. 102
Figure 58 Canine. 104
Figure 59 Trailing dog. 106
Figure 60 Trailing Dog on lead. 107
Figure 61 Disaster Dog, FEMA certified. 108
Figure 62 HRD Dog. 108
Figure 63 HRD dog indicates on bone. 109
Figure 64 SAR Dog working in hazardous conditions. 110
Figure 65 Air Scent dog/handler working off lead. 113
Figure 66 K9 Training with a mannequin. 118
Figure 67 Water Search. 119
Figure 69 Horse relaxed. 123
Figure 70 Horse detecting change. Sees or hears something? 124
Figure 71 Horse heads toward smell then finds bucket with source material. 125
Figure 72 Horses in Line Search...close together for training purposes. 126
Figure 73 Horse hearing from the distance...sight or sound? 127
Figure 74 Mounted and Ground Searcher 129
Figure 75 Hazardous Terrain. 130
Figure 76 D-shape and pear-shape carabiner. 133
Figure 77 Litter Handling. 138
Figure 78 Possible distance traveled based upon lost person behavior information. .. 145
Figure 79 POA Chart. 146
Figure 81 Calculating AMDR. 148
Figure 82 Critical Spacing Chart. 150
Figure 83 Assessing terrain. 152
Figure 84 K9 Air Transport. 154
Figure 85 Landing Zones. 155
Figure 86 Pilot. 156

Figure 87 Providing the pilot with a reference point... 158
Figure 88 Hazards...power lines which may not be visible to the pilot. 159
Figure 89 Brownout conditions. 160
Figure 90 Smoke bomb showing wind direction. 161
Figure 91 Helicopter Operations... 162
Figure 92 Air Operations hand signals. 163
Figure 97 Waiting for an assignment. 180
Figure 98 Handling a litter. 182
Figure 99 Patient Packaging.. 183
Figure 100 Preparing safety lines.. 189
Figure 101 Securing a scene. 190
Figure 102 SAR dog. 198
Figure 103 Finding a Clue... 281

Figure 2 Oso, WA.

Chapter 1

Search and Rescue Field Leadership

Objectives

- *To provide an overview of the purpose of this text.*
- *To provide resources to find other SAR teams in the United States.*

Figure 3 Training for leadership.

Over the years, since its advent, we have had considerable experience in implementing the ADSAR course and the SAR Tech I evaluation procedure. By virtue of this position, we know that the individual must have leadership/management skills, as well as the tactical and technical knowledge to lead a crew/team. As a crew leader/SAR Tech I, other searchers on your crew will be looking to *you* for guidance ... the person with them who will be doing the actual mission searching in the field.

Accordingly, we start with *you* and the leadership ability that *you* will need to attain the objective (finding the missing person). Safety is closely tied to leadership responsibility so it is addressed next. We have then added a section on "Tailgate Management" sometimes referred to as "reflex tasking." This section recognizes the fact that in the first hours of a search there are many "do's and don'ts" that are critically important to a successful search. We know that it takes time to mobilize the Incident Command Staff. You could easily find yourself as the only SAR savvy person on the scene initially. Your knowledge, if applied in a proper and tactful way, can make a huge difference. This text provides the knowledge to act and the techniques to lead. The goal is to provide the key link between the searchers, the Incident Commander and the Incident Command (IC) staff.

The text is written in the first person active to transmit what *we*, the authors, have learned from years of training, field experience and, yes, lessons from our mistakes.

We proceed to the tactics you will be employing in a "full blown" search. This is followed by the technical knowledge that a leader in the field needs in order to successfully accomplish your search tactics. Finally, we discuss the urban search. This "urbanization" and aging of our society has created another need for your SAR talents.

For a partial listing of SAR teams in your area, you may want to consult local law enforcement, emergency management or any other agency involved in SAR. In addition, you may consult the following web site: http://www.sarzone.net.

Figure 4 Operations.

Figure 5 Searcher.

Figure 6 Search.

Chapter 2

Search Team Leadership

Objectives

- *To list the characteristics of a successful leader.*
- *To describe several leadership theories including Management by Objectives and the SMARTER Approach.*
- *To provide the leadership needed to accomplish the search objective in a safe, timely and efficient manner.*

Leadership is an art not a science to be itemized by a bureaucrat. Most leadership descriptions include a long list of traits and principles. This chapter shall limit its application to search and rescue leadership. Styles vary according to the person and the organization but most have similarities.

The Army Field Manual 6-22 defines leadership as: "The process of influencing people by providing purpose, direction and motivation while operating to accomplish the mission and improve the organization." This definition also applies to search and rescue missions. Many of the traits, characteristics and the goals are quite similar but the situation and those being led are quite different!

Search and Rescue personnel are usually highly motivated individuals who may or may not have adequate training and physical conditioning. Military personnel are usually more disciplined and physically fit. However, they may not have the Search and Rescue training and motivation. Suffice it to say that there can be some major differences that should be recognized.

The Goal: A Good Leader

Let's describe and discuss what makes a person a leader. If you recognize, agree with, and apply these traits, you will not need to memorize a list of acronyms. Note that these personality traits all ascribe to the philosophy of "virtue is in the means." In other words, too much of a trait can be as damaging as too little. Some of the most important traits include:

Courage	Bearing	Behavior	Humility
Initiative	Enthusiasm	Integrity	Tact
	Humor	Knowledge	

Courage

Do not be timid (too little) or foolhardy (too much). Courage is standing up for what is best to address the needs of the mission in spite of adversities or the objection of others. Courage is the ability to admit error and adjust accordingly. Courage is *not* the desire to be a hero at all cost. Such a misconception can and does lead to unnecessary and unjustified risks being taken with predictable serious consequences! In summary, courage is the foundation on which we build leadership.

Bearing

It is true that many individuals will make a judgment based on first impressions. Such first impressions are hard to change! Therefore, it is important to start out on a positive note. Immediate confidence in a leader starts with the leader being properly dressed, properly equipped and most important, physically fit. Leaders should have the endurance not only to "keep up" but to put in the long hours before and after the search. It is not important that you fit the Hollywood image. Be yourself but be all you can be—and present the appropriate positive first impression.

> **Steps for Decision Making**
>
> 1. Get all the relevant information that you can.
>
> 2. Get input from subordinates when appropriate; they may have relevant information.
>
> 3. Know when to wrap up the input.
>
> 4. Make a clear cut decision (it's called judgment.)
>
> It might be to do or <u>not</u> to do— but do decide!

Behavior

Having made a good first impression, the searchers you lead may now judge you by how you act—your specific behaviors and actions. Are you decisive or wishy-washy? Be *decisive*. Being 'wishy-washy' is the single best way to lose the confidence of those you lead. Again, virtue is in the means! The means is found between the extremes of procrastinating till it is too late and making a 'snap judgment' when there is time to consider the input which may be needed to make an informed decision. In an emergency, with time being of the essence, you may be forced to make a snap decision. That is okay—if you have trained diligently for such unplanned emergency situations.

Consider the four (4) steps of decision making shown in the chart on the previous page as you make decisions. Get all the relevant information, get input from others, know when to wrap up the input and make a clear decision.

You have the courage to make this move to a leadership position. *You* look the part and *you* know how to make a decision. This is a good start. The second part of how to act is your *PERSONA* -how others see you—personality wise. We all have a *persona*—we can all improve the habits that make up the persona of a good leader. Here are some considerations:

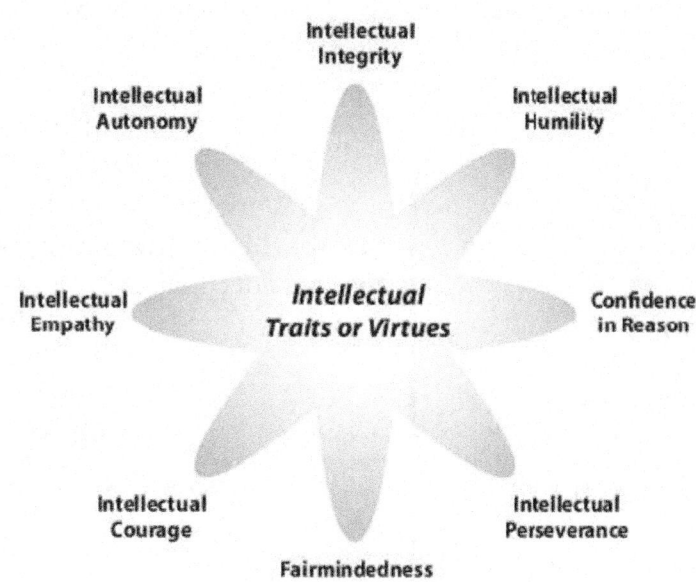

Humility

Always use "we" and never "I." Never forget this most important rule. A really good leader does not have to "blow smoke." Humility is manifested in many ways. Showing kindness and loyalty is *not* a sign of weakness. Being selfless in support of your search team will not go unnoticed!

7

Initiative

There is always room for improvement. Ask "why are we doing this" or "why don't we do that?" Think outside the box!

Enthusiasm

Obviously, if the leader doesn't have a *positive attitude* no one else will. Often, when things just go "from bad to worst" we all tend to go a bit negative. *Perseverance* is the key word—we *will* see this through! Never pass the blame in front of subordinates. Do take up problems, blunders, etc. with the appropriate staff or commander in a private setting. It is called *loyalty*, up or down the chain of command.

Integrity

Avoid any out of control ego (the excess of self-esteem). Do have the self-esteem to do what is right—it is called *justice*. See to it that justice is done.

KNOW YOUR JOB.

SHARE INFORMATION.

BE A LEADER. (LEAD!)

CARE.

USE TEAMWORK.

CONSIDER SAFETY.

Tact

Work on the habit of *thinking before talking.* Demonstrate respect both up and down the chain of command.

Humor

When all else fails, those that have experienced the extreme trauma of combat or emergency situations, etc. can attest—humor does help. Words of caution—keep it in good taste (ie: no joking about the missing person or deceased, etc.) and be aware of any cameras or friends/ family of the missing person. Expressions can be seen by many others, and boom microphones can record seemingly inappropriate conversation easily with modern technology. Be ever aware of your environment, near and far.

Knowledge

If you are not prepared, skilled and trained it will soon become apparent. This text will provide *administrative and technical/operational* knowledge needed to lead a search team in the field. No one "knows it all" but leaders are expected to keep abreast of the latest techniques and methods appropriate for the situation at hand. Remember, the most intelligent and knowledgeable people know and appreciate how much they do not know. *Train diligently!* Developing your technical and administrative knowledge and skill is an on-going process. If you don't know what you are doing, your team will soon question the wisdom of following your leadership.

Administration

Know your administrative requirements. Be prepared *before* the need arises. Start by becoming familiar with the National Incident Management System (NIMS) through the Incident Command System (ICS). The U.S. Department of Homeland Security offers online courses to provide the background information needed for this nationally standardized system. Start by taking the introduction courses, ICS 100/ICS 700; and proceed to ICS 200, 300, and 400 to complete the program.

Become knowledgeable and conversant with ICS Forms 201, 202, 203, 204, 205, 206 and *especially ICS Form 214*, the Unit Log. Prepare an *Administration Ready Pack* with applicable ICS and local forms as well as the *Missing Person Questionnaire* and other operational forms. Remember, you could be the first or one of the first persons on the scene. In that case you would initially be multi-tasked with many ICS positions!

During a search event, keep a log of events and observations—you will need it for debriefing and after-action reports. Remember, if you don't record it, it didn't happen.

Know your Job

If you are not tactically proficient *you cannot do your job* as a leader. Read, study, train and discuss operations with your peers (it is an excellent way to improve your "know-how.")

Share Information

Ideally, during a search, your team should attend daily search briefings and should be thoroughly briefed by you, the *Search Team Leader*, about the specifics that were provided to you by the ICS Planning Section Chief.

Be the Leader

Take on the responsibility. Make sound and timely decisions. Most of all *set the example.* Remember *we*; leave "*I*" at home*!*

Care

If you don't care then why should I care? That is a natural human response. You can count on it. Demonstrate your commitment for the welfare of the team before (preparation), during the search (how demanding are you?), and after the search (getting fed, rested and debriefed). These are the keys to a highly functional team.

Team Work

Know your crew and make assignments based on *ability.* Trackers, dog handlers, radio operators, compass and pace counters must all work as a team (Note: During training it pays to rotate assignments. It helps each member to understand what the rest of the team is doing and it provides you with flexibility to meet contingencies.)

Safety

Safety is the most important factor in any operation. Unsafe actions will allow you to become part of the problem instead of part of the solution! We will devote a full chapter to this most important factor but, as a leader, you must set the example. Do factor in safety when making decisions before acting. If you are unsure or have "a feeling"– then you should probably re-think what you are asking the team to do. Consider implementing a safety program. Refer to Chapter 3 and consider using the GAR Model.

Leadership Theories

There are many leadership theories. The best leaders know that it takes "different strokes for different folks." Each of the techniques listed below is valid in some situation with some team members. As situations and personnel vary, so too does the application of leadership theory. These theories are *not* mutually exclusive!

Management by Objective (MBO)

The objective (mission) is to find the lost person. Therefore, we will build our working theories around this concept. The original MBO concept was identified by the characteristics Time Referenced, Attainable, Measureable and Accountable.

This approach has been updated and improved with some changes in the approach. These changes were referred to as SMART and later as SMARTER (when the process was logically completed it added *Evaluation and Recognition*.)

Figure 7 Briefing.

11

SMARTER

Specific - Must be specifically defined and not subject to individual interpretation.

Measurable – Must have clear quantitative and/or qualitative criteria to evaluate its completion.

Attainable – Must be achievable with the resources provided.

Relevant – Must contribute towards completing the mission.

Time-bound – The objective must be achievable within the time allotted.

Evaluated – The mission must be evaluated after the de-briefing.

Recognized – In case of success, the team should be recognized for its accomplishment.

THE SMARTER Approach[1]

The Smarter Approach applies the following principles:

- It must be specific.
- It must be measurable.
- It must be laced with attainable goals.
- It must be relevant to the situation.
- It must be time-bound.
- It must be able to be evaluated.
- Participants must be recognized for accomplishment.

---

[1] For a more in-depth discussion of SMARTER see FEMA's on-line course IS 920.

This approach is in consonance with established ICS procedures and is currently being used by all emergency services. Later we will discuss the key points of the SMARTER approach.

Other relevant FEMA[2] courses include IS 240-b *Leadership and Influences*, IS 241-b *Decision-Making and Problem-Solving*, IS 242-b *Effective Communications*, and IS 244 *Developing and Managing Volunteers*. These courses offer a convenient and inexpensive method of improving your leadership abilities.

Setting team objectives allows the leader to focus on the objective by defining clear targets to reach and by measuring the progress toward those targets. It also helps to increase your team's involvement and their job satisfaction by offering them personal rewarding challenges which support individual development.

If the outcome is below expectation, a detailed review of what went wrong and how things could be improved is necessary. It is also helpful to revise the objectives. In both cases, lessons learned should be shared.

Situational Management

Situational Management simply means to remain *flexible* as the situation develops. The approach provided initially in MBO should be adapted to meet new and challenging changes in the scenario.

Time Referenced - Attainable

Leaders should be ready to apply their knowledge and use common sense. General Patton once said that *"the finest military plan begins to change when the first shot is fired."* So can the best laid SAR plan once the first crews return to debrief.

Participative Management

As the search event changes, leaders need to recognize the need to adjust. As new information becomes available, leaders must examine changes and consider the consequences of making such adjustments. Consult subordinates to:

*Gleam more useful, relevant information.
*Become aware of unanticipated consequences.

By including input from subordinates in your decision making, leaders make more informed decisions and build team cooperation and morale. This is a *motivational technique.* It will foster social acceptance of each individual while lending prestige *to the team by being a team.*

---

[2] FEMA: Federal Emergency Management Agency. http://www.fema.gov

Participatory leadership is the antithesis of *micro management*. Use your assets (members) wisely. Remember that virtue is in the means—do not be "wishy-washy" and do not be a dictatorial micro-manager.

Five Basic Functions:
Command
Operations
Logistics
Planning
Finance/Administration

Incident Command Systems

This manual assumes that the reader is familiar with ICS. The ICS courses mentioned under *administration* are a must for the Strike Team Leader in a SAR incident.

Organization

There are five major organizational functions (rather than specific persons) common to every rescue regardless of the size of the mission. We will provide a summary of the overall structure with emphasis on those operational parts of the command structure. The command functions are: Command, Operations, Logistics, Planning, and Finances.

1. Command

The Command function is obvious and functions at the top of the chain of responsibility. The Incident Commander is the person who must accept the ultimate outcome for the incident. This individual develops the overall incident objectives, strategies and manages all activities that occur on the incident. Delegation to other personnel in the various functional roles places the task completion burden on others. During small operations one person may assume responsibility for all five functions and direct the entire incident. You might

Command Staff Responsibilities

- Coordinate all tactical activities.
- Determine needs and order resources.
- Assign, brief, and debrief tactical assignments.
- Implement the tactical aspects of the Incident Action Plan and make operational work assignments based on the contents of that plan.
- Make all operation decisions to reflect and support the Action Plan and the search objectives.

be that person responsible for all on-scene activities and minute-to-minute decisions. Responsibilities include:[3]

- Assess the situation and/or obtain a briefing from the prior Incident Commander.
- Determine Incident Objectives and strategy.
- Establish the immediate priorities.
- Establish an Incident Command Post.
- Establish an appropriate organization.

- Ensure planning meetings are scheduled as required.
- Approve and authorize the implementation of an Incident Action Plan.
- Ensure that adequate safety measures are in place.
- Coordinate activity for all Command and General Staff.
- Coordinate with key people and officials.

- Approve requests for additional resources or for the release of resources.
- Keep agency administrator informed of incident status.
- Approve the use of trainees, volunteers, and auxiliary personnel.
- Authorize release of information to the news media.
- Order the demobilization of the incident when appropriate.

The Command Staff includes the Public Information Officer, Safety Officer, and Liaison Officer. They report directly to the Incident Commander.

2. Operations

Operations (Ops) personnel are responsible for transforming search objectives and strategies into on-scene actions. "The OPS activates and supervises organization elements in accordance with the Incident Action Plan (IAP) and directs its execution. The OPS also directs the preparation of Unit Operational Plans, requests or releases, resources, makes expedient changes to the IAP, as necessary; and reports such to the Incident Command (IC). The major responsibilities of the Operations Section Chief are:

- Develop operations portion of IAP.
- Brief and assign Operations Section personnel in accordance with the IAP.
- Determine need and request additional resources.

---

[3] http://www.uta.edu/campus-ops/police/docs/EM%20ICS%20Job%20Duties%20and%20responsibilities%202009.pdf

- Review suggested list of resources to be released and initiate recommendation for release of resources.
- Assemble and disassemble strike teams assigned to the Operations Section.
- Report information about special activities, events, and occurrences to the IC.
- Maintain Unit/Activity Log (ICS Form 214)." [4]

A group supervisor, working under the Operations Chief, can manage up to five Single Resources, Strike Teams or Task Forces, each operating under different functional area on the incident. Bear in mind that the span of control drives the organizational structure. The use of Strike Teams and Task Forces is encouraged whenever possible, to maximize the use of resources, increase the management control of a large number of single resources, and reduce the communications requirements. To clarify, a few commonly used terms are listed below:

- *Single Resource.* A *Single Resource* is the smallest unit which can operate independently. This could be a helicopter, a search dog with handler, an ambulance, tracker, etc., each of which can be assigned as a primary *Tactical Unit*. A resource is the equipment plus the required individuals to properly use it.

- *Task Force.* A *Task Force* is any combination of resources which can be temporarily assembled for a specific task or objective. All resource elements within a Task Force must have common communications, and each Task Force must have a Leader. A Task Force is established to meet a specific tactical need and subsequently demobilized as single resources or reorganized into another Task Force configuration.

- *Strike Team.* A *Strike Team* is a set number of resources *of the same kind and type*, which have an established minimum number of personnel. A Strike Team will always have a Leader and will have common communications. Strike Teams can be made up of search crews, search dogs, or any other kind of resource where the combination of single resources of the same kind becomes a useful tactical unit.

- The *Staging Area Manager* also works under the Operations Chief. The Staging Area Manager is responsible for all activities that occur within the staging area. There *are four status conditions:*

    1. Responding/enroute,

---

[4] https://www.osha.gov/SLTC/etools/ics/ops_chief.html

2. Available (on 3 minute standby),
3. Assigned-operationally committed not available, or
4. Out-of-service crew and resting, mechanical deficiency, etc.

The ***Staging Area*** should be established as soon as possible to ensure that:

- the LKP/PLS is protected and
- the Command Post can operate without the interference of a continuous stream of new arrivals.

3. Logistics[5]

All incident support needs are provided by the Logistics Section, with the exception of aviation support. Aviation support is handled by the Air Support Group in the Air Operations Branch. The Logistics Section is managed by the Logistics Section Chief, who may assign a Deputy. A Deputy is most often assigned when all designated units (listed below), within the Logistics section, are activated. Six units may be established within the Logistics Section:

- Supply Unit
- Facilities Unit
- Ground Support Unit
- Communications Unit
- Food Unit
- Medical Unit

The Logistics Section Chief will determine the need to activate or deactivate a unit. If a unit is not activated, responsibility for that unit's duties will remain with the Logistics Section Chief.

4. Planning

The Planning Section is responsible for:

- Collecting, compiling, evaluating and disseminating all incident information.
- Investigation.
- Maps, records, photographs, and meteorology.
- Preparing an Incident Action Plan.
- Developing a strategy - "Think Tank Function."

---

[5]http://www.uta.edu/campus-ops/police/docs/EM%20ICS%20Job%20Duties%20and%20responsibilities%202009.pdf

- Resource information management; including inventory of all resources and their status, maintenance, deployment, recall and use. (All searchers should be sure to report in as your team arrives on scene.)
- Documentation and demobilization.

Of particular interest to you and your team is to:

a. Have a standing intra-team communication plan for call up and responding.
b. Ensure that all team members have adequate directions to *the staging area.*
c. Ensure that all members *always* adhere to the staging area sign in and sign out procedure.
d. Ensure that the readiness status assigned (previously defined) is maintained.
e. Upon signing in at staging area, ensure that your team status is reported to the Resource Unit.
f. Become familiar with the area of operations map, weather, incident mission (ICS 204), etc. The more you learn and know while on standby status, the more prepared you become to complete your mission.
g. Read the entire Incident Action Plan (IAP), if available.
h. Identify the briefing location and daily briefing schedule.
i. Delegate team members to find quarters (resting areas), mess (food supplies), latrine (restrooms) and other essential support facilities.

5. Finance/Administration

The finance section monitors all costs which are incurred as a result of the search. It encompasses procurement of any materials and supplies, all accounting, time records and cost analysis of the final expenses.

ICS Forms

Incident Command Forms may vary from region to region but they basically all contain the same information. These are readily available on the internet from multiple sources and easily downloaded to your computer for field use. Some versions may allow you to save data as it is put onto the form prior to printing the form. Those forms may include:

Briefing Form

This is your primary operation directive form. It is normally prepared by the Resource Unit of the Planning Section and is provided to you when you are briefed for a specific operation by the Operations Section. Be sure that all entries are correct. Ensure that the assignment meets the requirements of the SMARTER concept as delineated earlier. Briefing is the time to correct any errors, omissions, invalid assumptions or ambiguities. Do not leave the briefing until all is perfectly clear. If possible, allow the entire team to attend.

(Note: Additional information on Briefings and Debriefings are contained in the Appendix.)

ICS Form 214

This is *your* Unit Log Form. Fill in the initial entry data (Items 1-7) as soon as possible. Fill in each activity or incident as it happens (if possible).

Example: Left CP (Command Post) at 0730 hours, dropped off at 1836/7741 at 0727....T. Jones received abrasion while descending steep slope at 1832/7711, bandaged and continued search.

You will need this form upon returning to CP. Debrief your team, correct any errors or mission and then use this form to debrief the Situation Unit of the Planning Section. In addition, leaders need to become familiar with all the applicable ICS forms including:

● Form 201	Incident Briefing	Section Chief
● Form 202	Response Objectives	Section Chief
● Form 203	Organization Assignment List	Resources Unit
● Form 204	Assignment List	Section Chief, Staff
● Form 205	Incident Radio Communications Plan	Communications Unit
● Form 206	Medical Plan	Medical Unit
● Form 208	Site Safety and Control Plan	Safety Officer, Staff

• Form 209	Incident Status Summary	Resources Unit
• Form 210	Status Change Card	Staff
• Form 211	Check-In List	Staff
• Form 213	General Message	Staff
• Form 214	Unit Log	Staff
• Form 215	Operational Planning Worksheet	Staff
• Form 215a	Incident Action Plan Safety Analysis	Safety Officer, Staff
• Form 215a Instructions	Incident Action Plan Safety Analysis Instructions	Safety Officer, Staff
• Form 217	Radio Frequency Assignment Worksheet	Resources Unit
• Form 218	Support Vehicle Inventory	Ground Support Unit
• Form 219-2	Resource Status Card (Crew)	Staff
• Form 219-4	Resource Status Card (Helicopter)	Staff
• Form 219-6	Resource Status Card (Aircraft)	Staff
• Form 219-7	Resource Status Card (Dozers)	Staff
• Form 220	Air Operations Summary Worksheet	Air Operations Unit
• Form 221	Demobilization Checkout	Resources Unit

ICS Forms Available Online.[6]

A quick internet search of ICS forms will lead to several web sites which provide downloads of ICS forms which are "fillable on line." Since all events are expandable as the situation/search grows, the use of ICS forms increases as the incident expands.

ICS courses 300 and 400 will assist the incident command staff to become more familiar with the use of all forms and procedures as recommended by the Department of Homeland Security.

Summary

It is a life-long journey striving to *continually* improve personal leadership traits and techniques. Good SAR leaders constantly review leadership traits and characteristics. Have the *courage* to assume the leadership role. Look and *act* like a leader (bearing). Be *decisive;* do not waiver. Do not show excessive ego and work in tandem with your fellow team members.
Perceptions of you by your team and by your superiors in the chain of command are, in fact, reality. Therefore, your *persona* is important. Listen to other ideas whenever possible. The *procedures* discussed have been developed from input by many leaders with many years of experience. These procedures can and will serve you well as a crew leader.

---

[6] ICS forms available at: https://www.osha.gov/SLTC/etools/ics/ics_forms.html

Leadership Theories are developed in academia but they are applied in the real world as leadership techniques. They are interchangeable parts that are *not* mutually exclusive. Avoid being too myopic and/or set in your ways. Become the leader you admire by continually working to increase your skill and techniques. *The missing person demands it.*

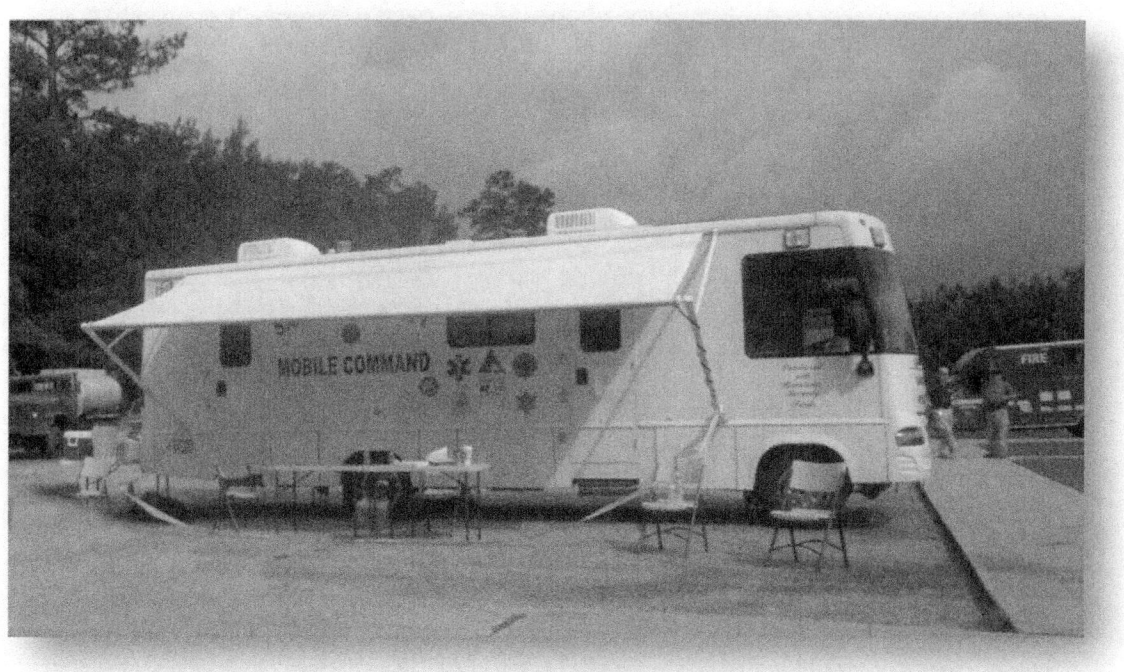

Figure 8 Command Bus.

Figure 9 Searching.

Chapter 3

Safety

Objectives

- *To provide information regarding safety practices during training and searching.*
- *To provide an overview of hypo- and hyperthermia and recognize symptoms of each.*
- *To increase awareness of safety in the field and the effects of the environment on a searcher.*

Why is it that we always preach safety then, sooner or later, we do something "stupid" and suddenly there is an accident? There are many excuses but no justification for any *preventable* accident. Too often we hear "I was in a hurry" or "I just didn't think about that" or even "we've always done it that way." In the workplace there is a legal mandate to practice safety in the work environment and while doing the work. In search and rescue we can't always demand a safe work environment but we *can* evaluate our operational environment. Some environments may seem benign at first glance but when searched may turn out to be otherwise. We *can* take many measures to significantly reduce the inherent dangers involved.

Plan Ahead

Before starting any search activity, learn all you can about where you are going. In an urban search it is wise to get some background information on the neighborhood or industrial/commercial area hazards. (See Chapter 12 for more details on urban searches which may present challenging dangers to you and your team.)

In wilderness searches you should always study the topo map before starting on a search, whether it is a rapid route search or an extensive sweep. Remember, *anyone* can get "turned around" (lost) and become the object of a secondary–and embarrassing search. Be especially wary of those contour lines that touch each other or bodies of water that have to be crossed.

Size Up

In fire and medical emergencies the very first act upon reaching the scene is a *size up.* The same rule applies to a SAR incident. We start with a *size up for safety*–can we do this safely? What do we need to get the job done safely? The short answer is to *think ahead*. For instance, if those little brown contour lines are close or touching, do we have ropes and are we prepared to use them?

The GAR Model

To provide a thorough and orderly format we suggest that the GAR Model (Green, Amber, and Red) be used. This model is used extensively by all of our armed forces–because it works! We have adapted this model for use with Search and Rescue missions. Like ICS, this model is intended to be flexible.

The GAR Model SAR Form provided in the Appendix has been developed specifically for SAR missions. No list of safety considerations can be all-inclusive–remember that. It does, however, provide guidance that will assess three important things. First, it will assist the leader and the rest of the team, to assess/size up all aspects of the mission; second, it will lead to and account for mitigating actions; and third, it will establish clear accountability for the leader and the team members.

The success of the GAR Model is dependent upon how it is implemented. Risk assessment with the GAR Model is a continuous, ongoing process. This procedure allows us to assess those risks in a set format and then adapt it as needed.

All members of the team need to be on a continuous look-out for unsafe situations. When a situation arises, and it will, the team can and will take action to STOP, ASSESS and MITIGATE, if possible, that situation. If the team cannot take action to mitigate a RED situation and make it at least AMBER then the leader must notify the Command Post for instructions on what action to take or what additional resources are needed.

AMBER conditions can be cumulative. That problem is addressed by considering a high AMBER rating suspect, requiring a second look to ensure that it doesn't accumulate into a Red (STOP) condition.

What about a GREEN rating? All is fine? Perhaps all is well but things can happen quickly and change a GREEN to RED with no AMBER warning. We therefore strongly recommend that the entire team use their searching skills to be constantly aware of the changing situation and the possibility of danger. Assess your situation as Green, Amber or Red and be aware of ever changing conditions.

Technical Search Teams

A search team leader may start out with a safe orientation but suddenly be faced with a hazard that the team is neither equipped for nor trained to handle. *Don't try to be a hero*–dead heroes are of no help–call for the technical rescue team. In the above example, if the missing person is found perched on an outcropping of a vertical rock face then it's time to call for a technical rock rescue team, or, in some circumstances both air rescue and a high angle search team. The point is, don't exceed your capabilities and endanger yourself, your team and/or the person needing help.

Technical Rescue

The technical rescue teams may include the high angle rock rescue team mentioned above, cave and mine rescue teams, and confined space teams. These are sometimes needed in urban searches. Most well-trained fire departments are specially equipped to handle all sorts of confined or otherwise hazardous environments. Rivers and white water rescues require specialized equipment and training. If you are not a fire fighter, a trip to the firehouse to learn about these capabilities is time well spent. In any case, *do not attempt to cross water that is over mid-thigh or moving rapidly*. The force generated by water is seldom respected. That lack of respect can easily lead to disaster!

Environmental Safety

Start your environmental safety preplan with the assumption that Murphy (of "Murphy's law" fame) is the weatherman, that is, "if the weather can go wrong, it will." Paraphrased in a more formal way – *be prepared*. Be prepared to meet rapidly changing weather in both the search and the rescue phase. The human body is not equipped to deal with the many environmental extremes faced in SAR so dress for the weather but prepared to adjust to change.

Hypothermia

Hypothermia (cold) is the most potentially dangerous hazard faced in SAR operations. Normal body temperature is 98.6 degrees Fahrenheit. When body temperature drops below 95 degrees Fahrenheit hypothermia starts. First there is a cold feeling and unusual shivering; then there is a loss of muscle coordination which progresses rapidly to sluggish thinking and talking. If these symptoms start – act immediately to provide warmth in whatever way is available. Exercise increases circulation, especially to the extremities. Remember that just the opposite occurs in water. Get the person out of the water as soon as possible and replace wet clothes with dry. In case of severe hypothermia (below 90 degrees body temperature) do not attempt rapid re-warming in the field. Re-warming from such a low temperature requires professional medical personnel and facilities. Move this victim as soon and as smoothly as possible. As above, do remove any wet clothes as soon as possible and replace with dry clothes, blankets or a sleeping bag.

Hypothermia Chart

If the water temperature (F) is:	Exhaustion or Unconsciousness occurs:	Expected Time of Survival is:
32.5	Under 15 minutes	Under 15-45 minutes
32.5 – 40.0	15 – 30 minutes	30 – 90 minutes
40 – 50	30 - 60 minutes	1-3 hours
60-70	2 to 7 hours	3 – 40 hours
70 – 80	3 – 12 hours	3 hrs - indefinitely
Over 80	Indefinitely	Indefinitely

FROSTBITE

It's serious, it's painful and it's easy to achieve!

Proper attire from head to toe is the best preventive medicine.

If frostbite occurs, avoid movement of the affected body part (don't let the victim walk on frost bitten feet or toes!).

Warm area as soon as possible but do avoid warming in the field if cooling and refreezing can occur.

Also, victim will usually experience severe pain as the re-warming occurs.

Avoid rubbing, twisting or other harsh movement of the body part If the ears or nose are affected, warm gently.

Hyperthermia

Hyperthermia (or heat exhaustion) is the second most likely environmental danger—the heat related illness. Localized heat cramps and whole body heat exhaustion are the most common heat related ailments. They are an omen that heat stroke is just around the corner.

Address heat cramps and heat exhaustion as soon as they are noticed. The symptoms to look for include profuse sweating but the skin will feel cool to the touch. The pulse may be weak and rapid. Provide water and whatever cooling is available.

The real danger is *heat stroke*. At this point the body is in a *life threatening emergency*. The skin is hot, red and dry and the pulse speeds up. Cool the person down immediately. In the field, the most likely means will be drenching the person with water; then fan the wet areas especially at the pulse points. The evaporative effect will start immediately. Then evacuate the person to a cooler environment. Remember:

Heat Exhaustion and heat cramps: profuse sweating, skin cool to touch; pulse weak and rapid; moist clammy skin; pupils dilated; normal or subnormal body temperature;

Heat Stroke: skin is hot, red, dry, and pulse speeds up; pupils constricted; rapid heartbeat; high body temperature;

The best medicine for hyperthermia is preventive medicine. Carry adequate water (two liters), have well-ventilated clothes, and a wide brim hat, take your salt tablets, and most of all slow down because it is hot out there.

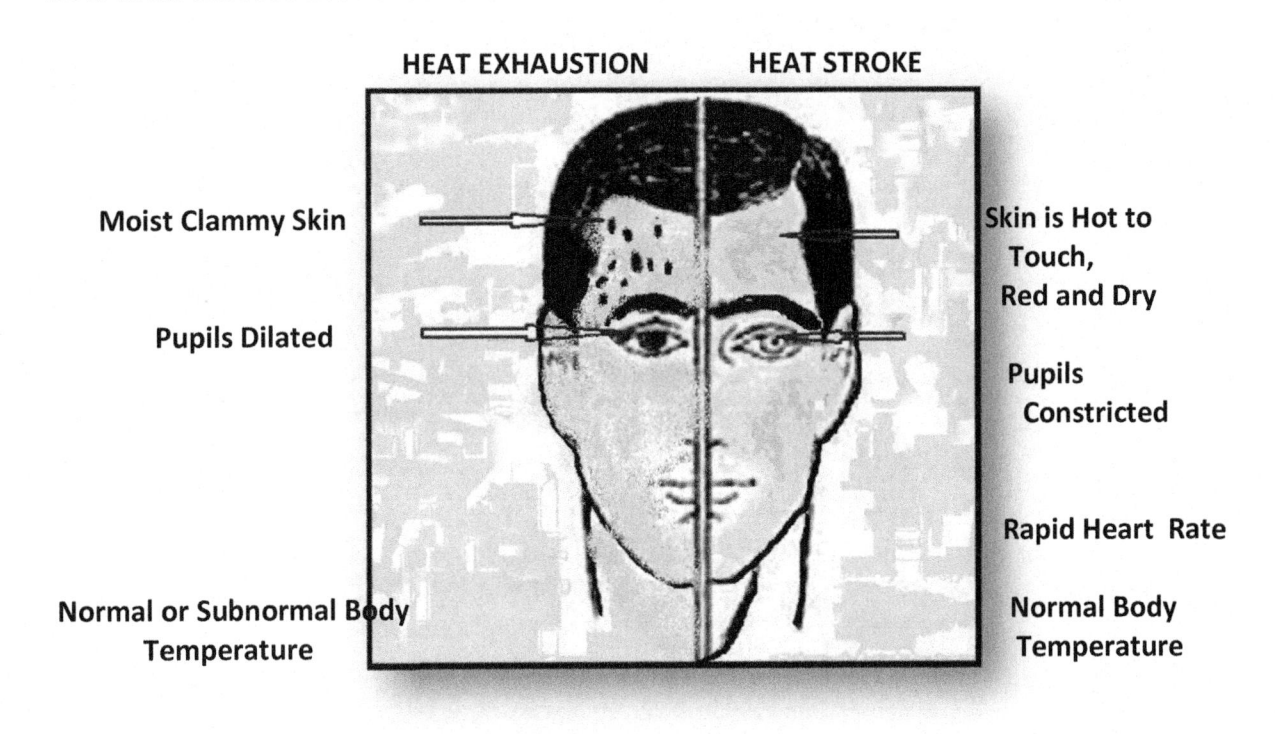

HEAT EXHAUSTION   **HEAT STROKE**

- Moist Clammy Skin
- Pupils Dilated
- Normal or Subnormal Body Temperature

- Skin is Hot to Touch, Red and Dry
- Pupils Constricted
- Rapid Heart Rate
- Normal Body Temperature

Other Hazards

Other hazard may include poisonous snakes in your area. One of the most venomous in the United States is the rattlesnake. "The Rattlesnake is easily identifiable by the rattle on the end of its tail. They are actually a part of the Pit Viper family, and are capable of striking at up to 2/3rd of their body length. The Eastern Diamondback in considered the most venomous species in North America. Surprisingly, juveniles are considered more dangerous than adults, due to their inability to control the amount of venom injected.

Most species of rattlesnakes have hemotoxic venom, destroying tissue, degenerating organs and causing coagulopathy (disrupted blood clotting). Some degree of permanent scarring is very likely in the event of a venomous bite, even with prompt and effective treatment, and can lead to the loss of a limb or death.

Difficulty breathing, paralysis, drooling and massive hemorrhaging are also common symptoms. Thus, a rattlesnake bite is always a potentially fatal injury. Untreated rattlesnake bites, especially from larger species, are very often fatal. However, antivenin, when applied in time, reduces the death rate to less than 4%."[7] Be aware of what animals are potential dangers in your primary search areas. It could save your life.

There are many other hazards encountered in search and rescue. A SARTECH I certification requires emergency medical training– preferably wilderness emergency training. In any case, it is prudent for at least one member of the search team to carry an emergency medical kit. They are readily available.

Figure 10 Poisonous Copperhead.

---

[7] Listverse. Animals. Top 10 Most Venomous Snakes. Lakhovas, March 30, 2011. http://listverse.com/2011/03/30/top-10-most-venomous-snakes/

Figure 11 Potential SAR Hazards, livestock.

If the searcher comes upon a scene like this they should go around it. The bull shown above weighs about 2400 pounds and is protective of his "family." If there is an injured person or child in the pasture the search team should send a searcher to the far side of the pasture to distract the bovines while the search subject is rescued (bovines are normally quite curious and will investigate a distraction). Like most animals, they can run faster than the fastest searcher."

Summary

This focus of this chapter is for you, the leader, to become more *safety conscious.* Know your basic topography where you commonly search and what critters and hazards may confront you. Bugs, snakes, ticks, and a host of other dangers lurk in almost all environments. Simply insect spray with deet may be wise before every search. Tuck your pants into your boots. Tuck your shirt tail into your trousers. Wear appropriate boots. In flooding situations or other disaster scenes even more dangers can be present. Pay close attention to safety briefings. Preparation and knowledge is critical to your safety. Always use the GAR model and ensure that *all* team members receive a thorough safety briefing *before* proceeding on a search mission".

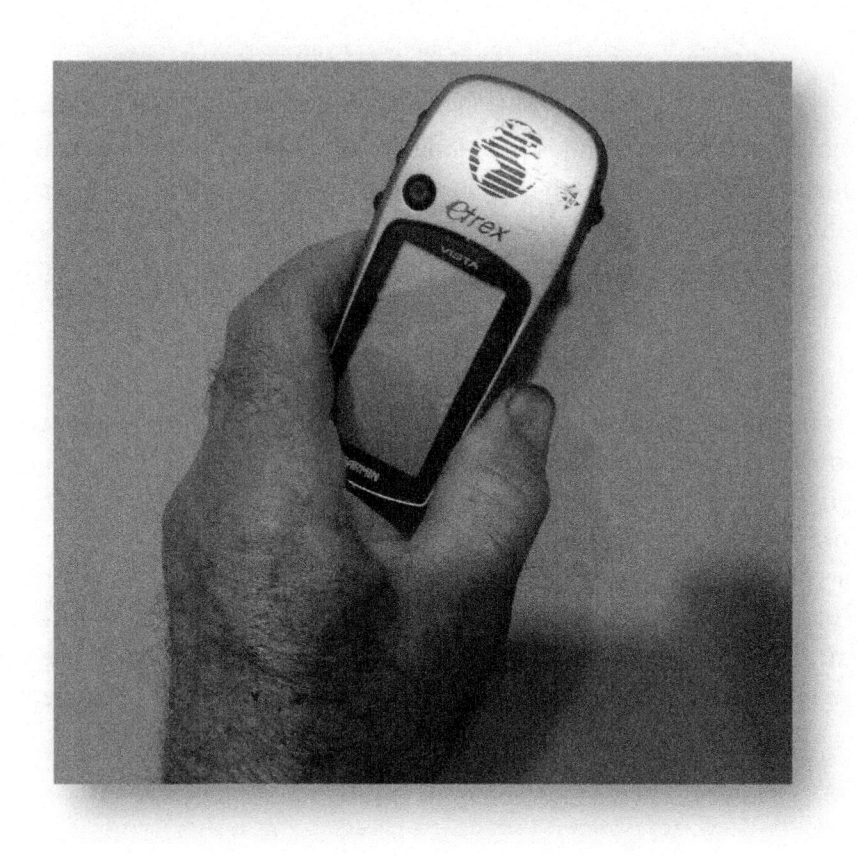

Figure 12 GPS.

Chapter 4

Map Reading and Navigation

Figure 13 Map Reading.

Objectives

- *To provide an overview of map reading.*
- *To describe operational techniques for the application of map reading skills in the field during a search.*

This manual assumes that the reader has the working knowledge of map reading attained through the FUNSAR (Fundamentals of Search and Rescue) manual and has attained the proficiency needed to successfully pass the SARTECH II exam. That said, many searchers do not use maps often enough to instinctively remember such nuances as declination adjustments, etc. Others depend on newer technologies such as the global positioning system (GPS) and on-line topographic maps that can now be displayed on a cell phone. Such technology is very useful but it does *not* replace the skill needed to do a sweep search on a given azimuth. It would certainly be embarrassing to end up searching in the wrong segment! We have also added a section on using the GPS and other electronic devices to *assist you* in navigation.

Topographic (TOPO) Maps

The topo map is the map most often used for wilderness searches (Other maps often used for urban searches, will be discussed in Chapter 12). Topo maps are normally provided in the 7.5 minute (1:24,000) scale; that is, about an 8.6 square mile representation of the Earth's surface – an ideal size for an on-foot search operation. These maps are available from the United States Geological Survey (USGS) but, as the printing of this manual, most jurisdictions now obtain their topo maps on-line and use a large size (typically 12" X 18") print for the command post and the 8 1/2" X 11" standard print for field use.

The Military Version of the 7.5 Minute Map

The USGS map is similar to the Defense Mapping Agency 1:25,000 scale map with the Universal Transverse Mercator (UTM) grid always overprinted. The scale is slightly different but these maps can be used in the same manner as the USGS maps.

Note: Your grid reader may have an error of 1:1000.

Grid Systems

The Geographic Coordinate System is commonly known as Latitude/Longitude. *Longitude i*s represented by a system of imaginary lines running from the North Pole to the South Pole of the Earth. *Latitude* is represented by a system of imaginary rings encircling the Earth perpendicular to the north-south lines. Latitude can be defined as angular distance, in *degrees*, relative to the equator. Latitude provides the north south component of a geographic position. Longitude is defined as an angular distance, in *degrees*, relative to the prime meridian. Longitude provides the east/west component of a geographic position.

The *Equator* represents 0 (zero) degrees Latitude and the *Prime Meridian* which runs through Greenwich, England represents 0 (zero) degrees Longitude.

These are the starting points for "lat/long" positioning. Latitude can range from 0 degrees, at the equator, to 90 degrees N, at the North Pole, or 90 degrees S, at the South Pole. Longitude represents divisions of a circle (the equator), so its range is theoretically 0 degrees to 360 degrees. In actuality, we use the longitude line directly opposite of the prime meridian as a limit for east or west location. This longitude line is referred to as the *International Dateline*. Since the prime median is 0 degrees, the *International Dateline* is 180 degrees. Therefore, longitude can range from 0 degrees, at the prime meridian, to 180 degrees East or 180 degrees West at the International Dateline.

Coordinates are expressed numerically as angles and divisions of angles. For example: 35⁰ degrees, 44' minutes, 30" seconds. You may remember from geometry that angles are divided into minutes and seconds, such as 1 degree equals 60 minutes, 1 minute equals 60 seconds. In some cases, coordinates are expressed in degrees and decimal minutes instead of degrees, minutes, and seconds. For example, 35 degrees, 44.50 minutes.

The protocol for expressing a coordinate in latitude/longitude is to indicate the position north or south of the equator *(Latitude) first,* then indicate the position east or west of the prime meridian *(Longitude) second.* A typical expression of lat/long coordinates for a location in North Carolina would read: 35° 44' 30" N, 79⁰ 39' 07" W.

Several things about lat/long are important for SAR members to remember. One important consideration is the fact that longitude (used to determine East/West position) lines grow closer together as they near the poles of the Earth. This creates problems in defining linear distance relative to angular measure. For example, 1⁰ of longitude at 0⁰ Latitude (the equator) are equal to roughly 69 miles straight line distance. At 36⁰ N latitude, which runs through the lower half of the continental United States, 1⁰ of longitude is equal to approximately 56 miles. At 85⁰ N latitude, which is close to the North Pole, 1⁰ of longitude is equal to only about 6 miles. Due to this deviation, we do not have a simple plotting device for determining longitude on maps.

Another factor affecting SAR use of lat/ long coordinates is the accuracy of plotting points on a map. This is due in some part to the situation described in the previous paragraph. In addition, a great deal of skill and a correctly scaled device is needed to accurately plot points using lat/long. If a point is plotted to 1" (1 second) of accuracy on a 7.5 minute topographical map, the point is accurate to within approximately 31 square meters, at best. This is certainly close enough for SAR use, but plotting to 1" of accuracy on 7.5 minute maps is unrealistic. Plotting a point to 15" (15 seconds) of accuracy is much more realistic and even this can be tough to accomplish, especially in the field. A point plotted to 15" accuracy will locate a point within approximately 460 square meters, which is not as close as we would like.

While it is obvious that the lat/long coordinate system is not ideal for SAR use, we do need to be familiar with it. This system is globally universal and can be used between most all types of organizations world-wide. Aircraft and marine vessels use this system for navigation, especially in conjunction with electronic guidance systems such as the Loran and GPS (Global Positioning System). There may be a time when SAR personnel will need to give a location to an aircraft crew in lat/long coordinates. As hand held GPS receivers become more popular with SAR agencies, this is becoming easier to do.

Universal Transverse Mercator (UTM) System

Now that we have a fundamental understanding of the Geographic Coordinate System, we can discuss the Universal Transverse Mercator (UTM) grid system. The UTM system is a metric system of coordinate measurement. An important characteristic of the UTM grid system is that unlike latitude/longitude, the UTM north/ south lines do not converge. They remain parallel over the entire map. This produces consistently scaled grid squares at all points on the map. Geographic points can be plotted from these grids with a grid reader which we will discuss later in this chapter.

The UTM system does not use angular measurements to report geographic position as with the latitude/longitude system. Instead, linear measurements in meters are used. The equator is the origin for the northerly coordinate component in the northern hemisphere and the termination for the northerly coordinate component in the southern hemisphere. This is to allow navigators in both hemispheres to determine northerly position by working from south to north in both hemispheres. The International Dateline (180^0 Longitude) is used for the origin of easterly position reporting. Notice we said easterly, not east/west.

The UTM system divides the circle created by the equator into 60 segments or zones. Each zone is equal to 6^0 longitude (360^0 divided by 60 equals 6^0). The zones are numbered 1 through 60 starting at the International Dateline and moving from west to east (see the drawing to the left) Therefore, the International Dateline is the westerly border of zone 1 and easterly border of zone 60.

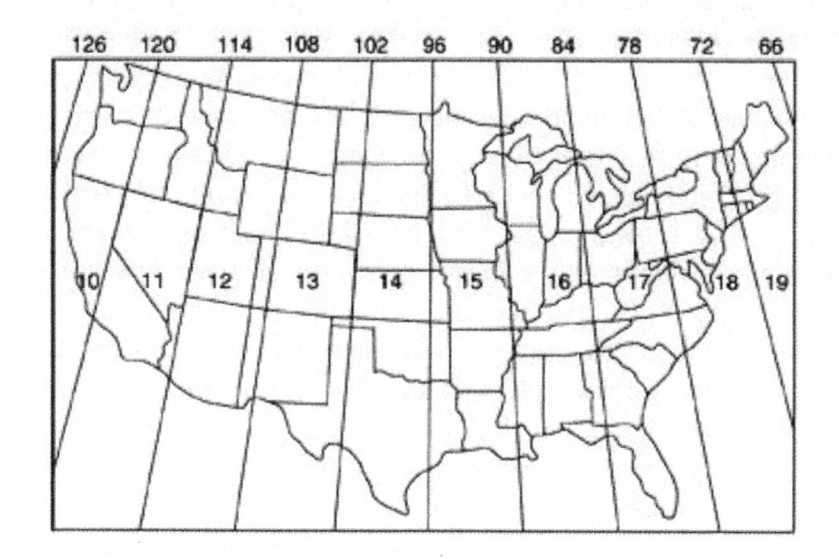

Figure 14 UTM Grid zones in the continental United States.

The UTM system uses narrow segments to minimize the curving distortion of the north/south lines (as discussed earlier) when the area is flattened and projected in two dimensions. Since the north/south curved distortion becomes the greatest near the poles, there is a limit as to how close to the poles the UTM system will work. Because of this, the zones extend to only 84^0 N latitude in the northern hemisphere and 80^0 S latitude in the southern hemisphere.

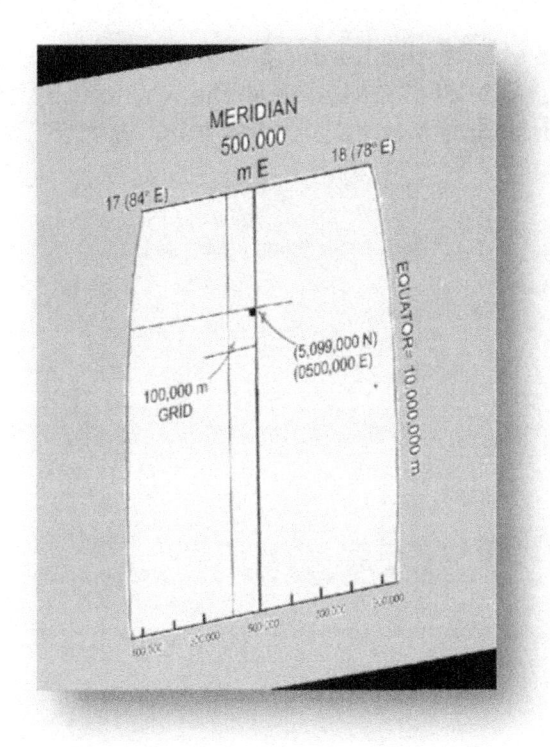

If we take a 6⁰ UTM zone, flatten it and view it in two dimensions, we notice the longitude lines that form the east and west boundaries of the zone are curved slightly. The longitude line in the middle of the zone, the *central meridian*, is straight and perpendicular to the equator. The *equator* and *central meridian* of each UTM zone are used as the basis of the UTM grid for each respective zone.

Figure 15 UTM Lines are straight; unlike Lat-Long.

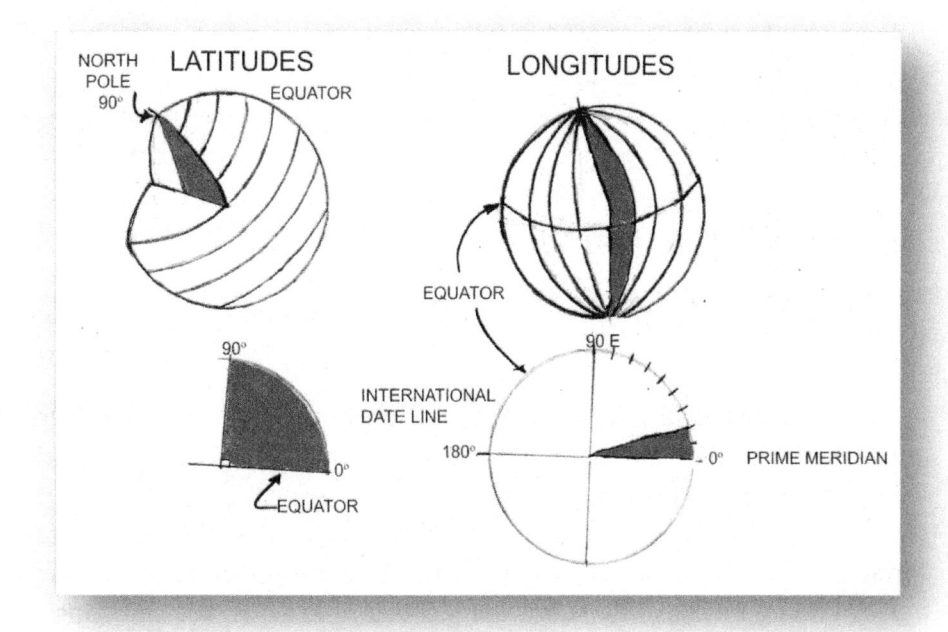

Figure 16 Meridian/Equator.

UTM Coordinate Numbering

Incidentally, the central meridian of each UTM zone is also used as the basis for the easterly coordinate numbering for that zone. The central meridian for each zone is arbitrarily given the number 500000 m E (500,000 meters). UTM grid lines *west* of the zone's central meridian will have *decreasing* numbers. The numbers decrease until they reach the border of the next UTM zone (the numbers do not necessarily reach zero). Grid lines *east* of the zone's central meridian will have *increasing* numbers until they reach the border of the next zone. This creates a numbering system that increases from west side of a UTM zone all the way to the east side of the zone. Consequently, *easterly* UTM coordinates are always read from west to east (*left to right*).

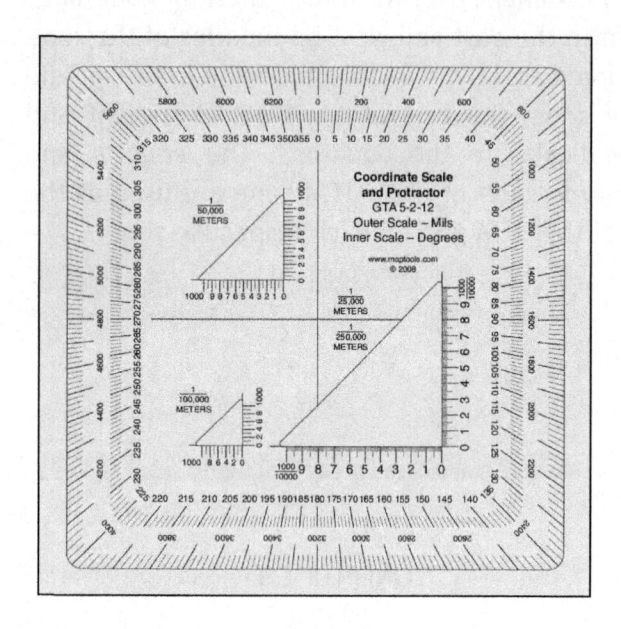

Figure 17 Grid Reader. 1:25,000 scale grid reader is shown.

Using the UTM Grid Reader

Always read left to right at the bottom first. Then read up. Disregard the two digit superscript – these tiny numbers indicate the 100K and 1,000 K grid. Place the grid reader on the map object to be located.
The United States Geological Survey incorporates the UTM grid system into their topographical maps. The 7.5 minute topo maps have 1 kilometer grids, which are easily subdivided using a grid reading devices. By subdividing these map grids, we can consistently plot a position on a map to within about 20 meters (65 feet) or closer with ease; even in the field. This obviously makes the 7.5 minute topo map and the UTM grid system ideal for SAR use.
If you have a USGS map that does not have a 1000 meter grid, you can add the grid by using a straight edge and fine point pen. Simply connect the blue tick marks along the edges from side to side and top to bottom.

You now know how the grid system was derived, how the grids form zones and why we use the UTM grid. Do you remember how to derive UTM coordinates and how they are read? If not, go back and review the above discussion. Now you are ready to determine an eight digit (about 10 meters) location. With current technology the Operations Section can now plot your exact location on their map based on the UTM coordinates that you call in from your map or GPS/cell phone.

GN 4* 59'

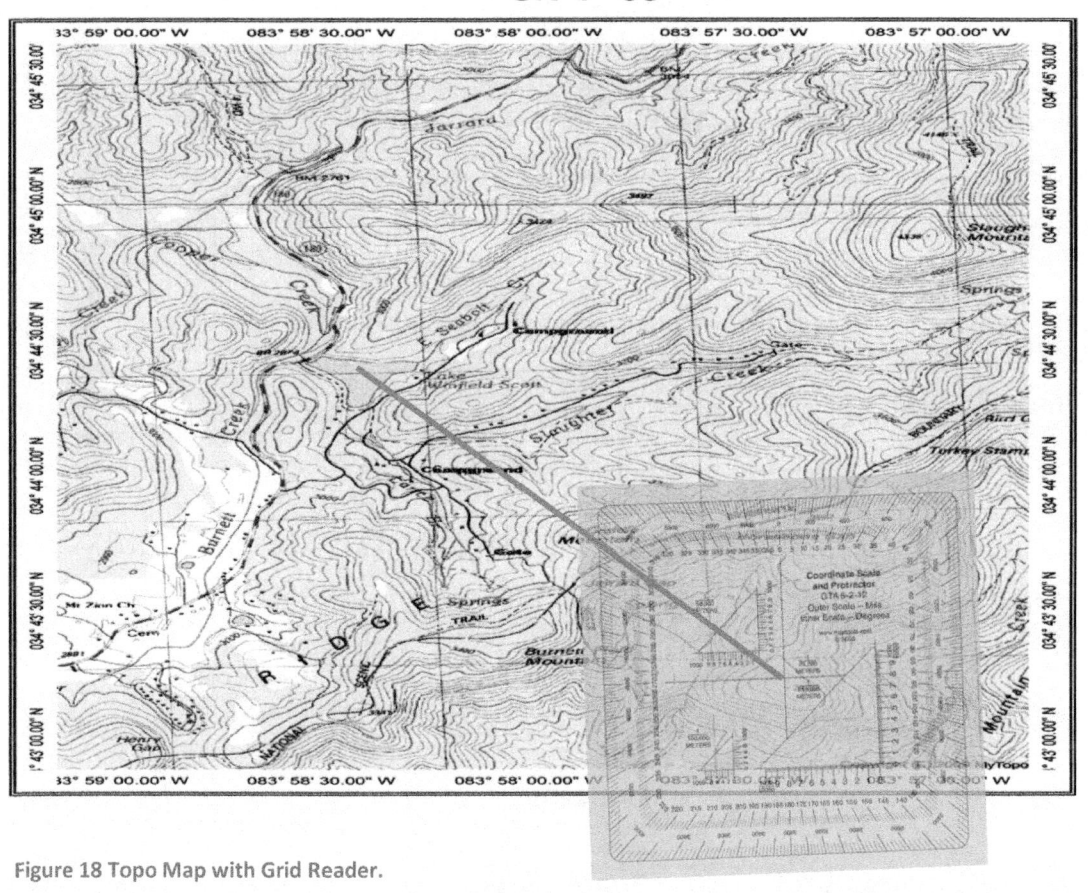

Figure 18 Topo Map with Grid Reader.

The Grid reader and topographic map shown are parallel to / even with the grid lines. The Grid Azimuth is 308 degrees.

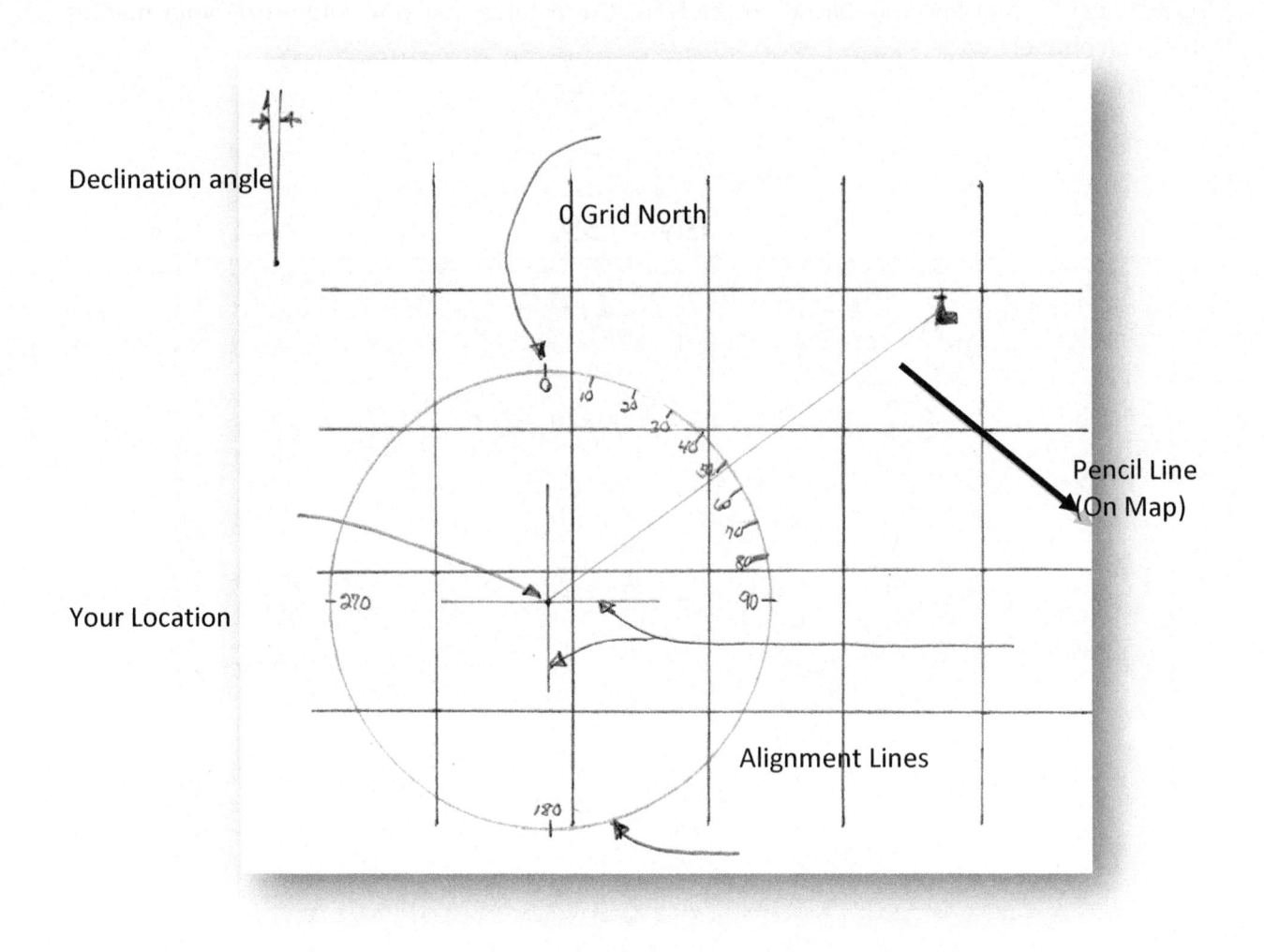

Figure 19 UTM Protractor.

1. Lightly draw a fine line between your location and the church.
2. Place protractor on map ensuring that alignment lines are parallel to the map grid lines.
3. Read degrees on the protractor (52 degrees GN); adjusted for declination show in top left. So the magnetic azimuth will be 56*59' or for all practical purposes, 57 degrees magnetic.

Declination

Many people treat setting the declination like going to the dentist–they either disregard it or treat it as a real pain! If one happens to be on the zero declination line that's okay–but do you know where that line is located? Of course not! Does it change? Yes, it does! As an individual moves further and further from the zero degree declination line the error is compounded and thus can put you into another search segment! A chart has been prepared to assist you in going from map to compass and vice-versa.

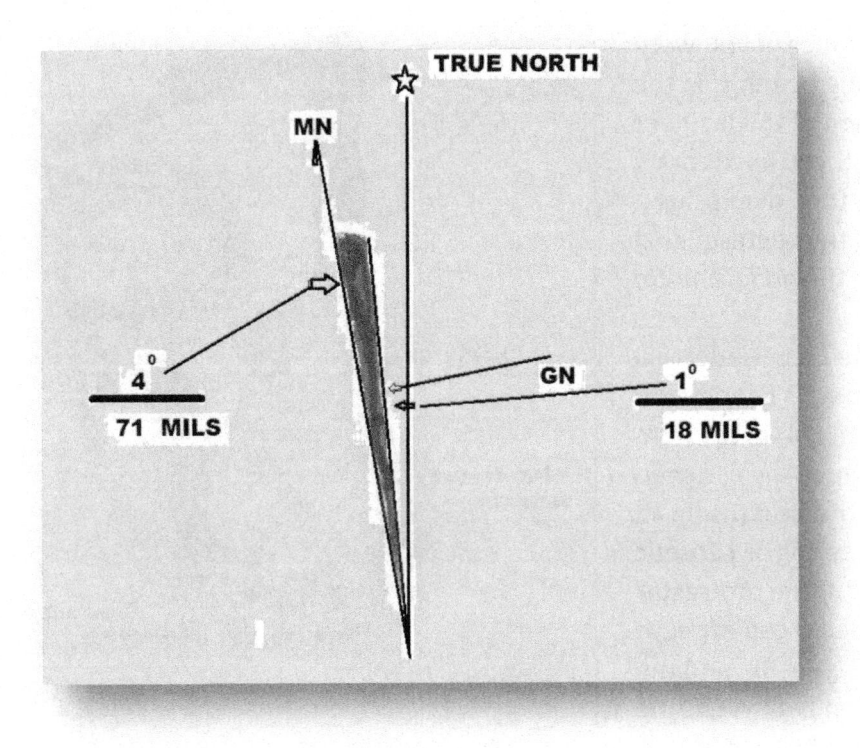

Figure 20 Declination Diagram.

The 308 degree grid azimuth base on the chart below, becomes 312 degrees magnetic azimuth.

Declination Chart

	WEST (left)	EAST (right)
GRID > MAGNETIC	ADD	SUBTRACT
MAGNETIC > GRID	SUBTRACT	ADD

For instance, if you were plotting track line bearings in the Planning Section of the Incident Command post, you might draw a line on the topo map using a protractor and thus determining the *grid azimuth*.

The crew leader will need the *magnetic bearing* (on the ICS Form 214) to perform the area sweep in the assigned segment in the field (using an Orienteering or Lensetic compass). If the protractor provided a grid azimuth (bearing) of 32^0 and the declination is 4^0 WEST the magnetic bearing is 36^0. Reverse the procedure going from compass to map. A declination setting chart aids is shown.

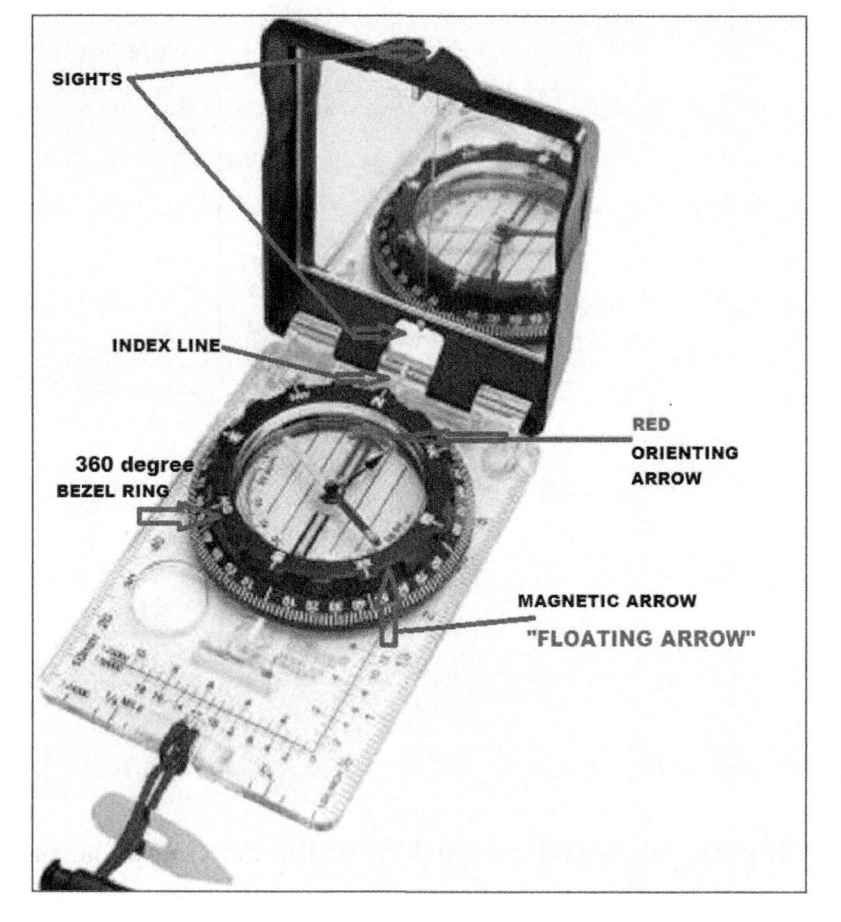

Figure 21 Compass.

Using the Compass

To properly orienteer on the map and on the ground you will need an accurate grid scale with a protractor (for the map) and an accurate *aimable* orienteering compass with a mirror or a military type lensetic compass.

Having attained the proper magnetic bearing (adjusted for declination), it now becomes a matter of technique and skill. We will discuss technique but you will have to practice, then practice some more to stay on a magnetic bearing up the hill, down the hill, over a boulder or around a pond.

The technique is not difficult. First, move all metal and electronics well away from the compass. If you have an upscale compass, check to be sure it is properly adjusted for the local declination. Now point your body toward the direction of travel (your toes and the compass travel line should be in alignment). Hold the compass in a comfortable position and *turn the whole body* to attain the desired azimuth). Do *not* use wrist and arm movement. Do ensure that the compass is level and the magnetic needle is free to move. Set the outer bezel ring to the desired azimuth. Now turn the entire body until the magnetic needles north arrow (usually colored red) is aligned with the bezel's index line and your aiming line is on a target. You are now oriented on the desired azimuth.

Figure 22 Compass.

Aligning the Compass

Now for the hard part–that is, traveling cross-country *on that exact azimuth*. Never hold the compass at belt level and walk along keeping the magnetic arrow on or about the index line

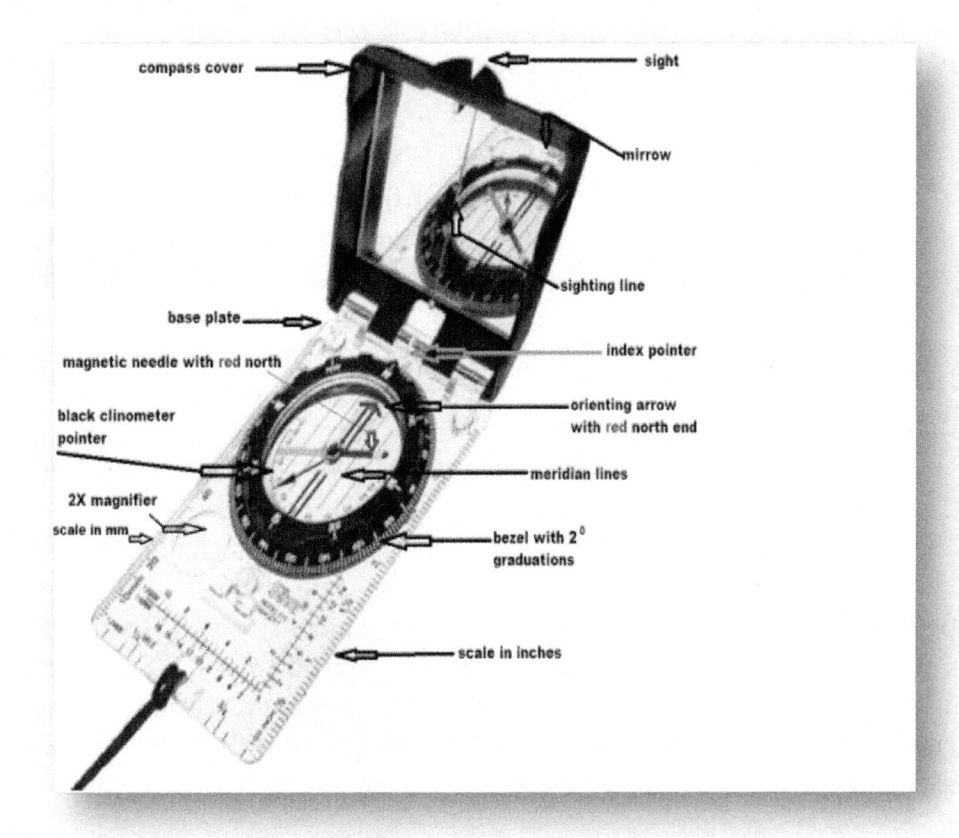

41

(desired azimuth). At eye level, keeping a good comfortable posture, move your whole body (no arm or wrist movement!) until the index line (desired azimuth) is aligned with the magnetic arrow using the mirror (or lens) and the aiming sight.

Now, pick a distinctive object in the distance at the desired azimuth. Travel to that point keeping a pace count. Sounds easy, but, which pine tree did you sight on? When you fell into the creek did you lose your pace count or did you lose sight of the object; or, there just wasn't a distinctive object to sight on? Therein lays the challenge! An alternative is to send "the point person," preferably dressed in a day glow orange SAR vest, out ahead on the azimuth. The point person is kept on or near the desired azimuth for as far as can be seen. That person concurrently does a pace count as they move to that point. The compass person moves the point person left or right until they are exactly in the sight on the desired azimuth. The point person continues on the proper azimuth until the "line of site" is no longer possible (or the destination is reached). The compass person then proceeds to the point, keeping a pace count, comparing pace counts with the point person, reaching a consensus, and recording it (beats using memory). The process is then repeated as often as necessary. On a final note, it is very easy to lose a pace count as one tumbles into an ice cold stream or other challenge.

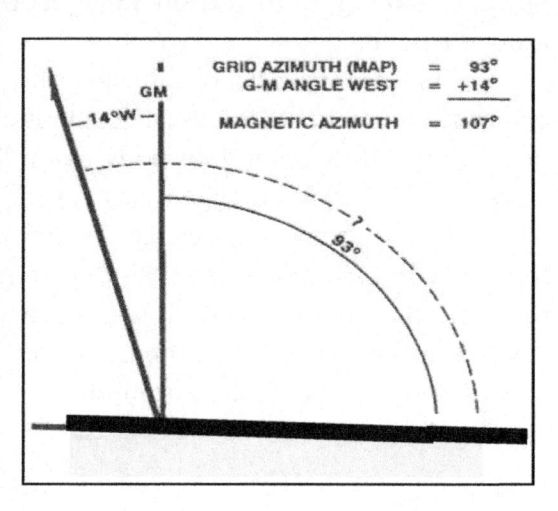

Figure 23 Azmuth.

We strongly recommend using a sports coach's counter commonly referred to as "the clicker." It could save you the heartbreak of losing a pace count!

As you move along on the correct azimuth, cross check your location on the topo map. The topography should match your map location.

The Immovable Object

The above technique works fine until you meet the immovable obstacle. The obstacle may be a pond, a huge brush pile or even a building. The technique used to work around an obstacle is illustrated. Notice that the four 90 degrees add up to 360°/0°–– or back on course. (See illustration 25.) Sounds easy but staying on the required azimuths and making accurate 90 degree turns in the wilderness can be challenging. A consideration: Use the "leap frog" method described above. If a body of water is involved and line of sight can be used, send a person around and attain an exact bearing 0 degrees on the far shore as described above. At this point, a hunter's range finder would easily complete the process. If not, use the process shown in the illustration. It may induce some minor distance error but the bearing will be "right on." In a search, distance measurement is often the same as track line measurement used by the planners to calculate the probability of detection (POD). Such calculations are not exacting and some minor distance error can be accepted. However, small errors in bearing can create a "blunder" (surveyor's term) over a long distance!

In open areas use a point person. In heavy undergrowth you may be relegated to "following the needle." A person directly in front can be helpful to open up a path and warn of obstacles. In military and law enforcement operations one may have to "follow the needle" in complete darkness (using luminous lines on the compass). Cross referencing the topography helps (*if* there is some topographical difference). This requires a lot of special operations training. If you are not trained in night navigation do *not* try this. Your light sources may fail. Stop, call in, and wait for day light–*don't* become part of the problem!

(Note: SARTECH I Evaluation requires the ability to navigate at night in a wilderness environment).

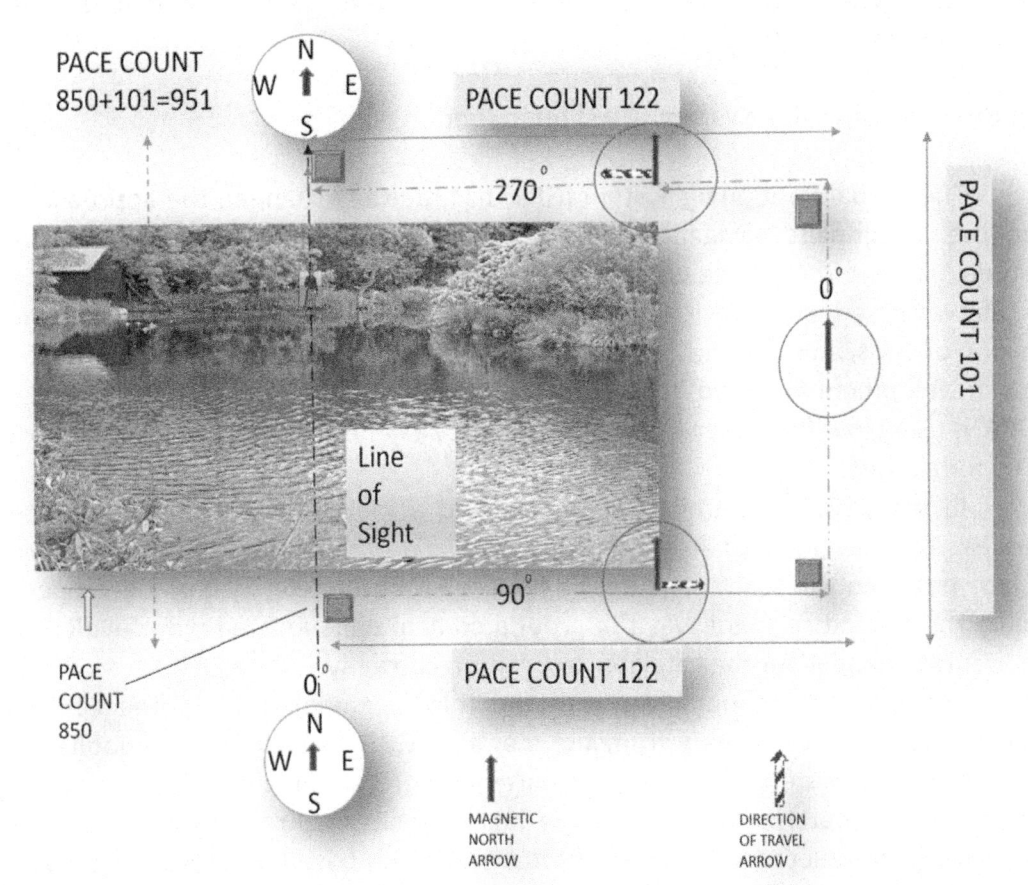

Figure 24 Navigating around an object.

Night Navigation

No one gets lost in the morning! Almost always, the call comes in the evening. It, therefore follows that we must be able to night navigate; waiting for the sun to shine may *not* normally be an option! The main difference between day and night navigation is in the technique used and the skill required.

Light discipline is not normally a factor (except perhaps in a military or law enforcement searches. Long distance sighting as in daylight is not as likely. Distances are usually shorter and sighting (aiming) while maintaining the correct azimuth is difficult. A head band strobe light can be useful. Night navigation will require a lot of "following the needle: practice. *Do not* try night navigation without extensive practice.

Electronic Navigation Aides

The review of map reading techniques and the application of navigation in wilderness searches now includes the use of electronic aides to provide a more complete and accurate navigational system. The devices described enhance the task of navigating–*they do not replace the use of maps and compasses!*

The Global Positioning System (GPS) Introduction

The Global Positioning System (GPS) has radically changed the approach used by those who use a complete navigational system, whether for military or civilian use. Originally, latitude (above or below the equator) was measured by a quadrant sighting of the angle of the sun above the equator. Longitude, on the other hand had to be measured from the celestial position of stars, adjusted mathematically to one's position based on the Earth's circumference. Early development of radios provided for improvements based on Long Range Navigation (LORAN) using low frequency signals for ships at sea and high frequency Radio Direction Finder (RDF) for aircraft.

In the 1960's the United States needed a method to track intercontinental ballistic missiles. The placement of 24 or more satellites in precise orbits 12,500 miles above the Earth's surface provided the space segment of the Global Positioning System developed to meet this need. The second segment was the ground control units located world-wide. They maintain the accuracy needed for the satellites to perform correctly.

We will concern ourselves with the third segment, that is, the GPS receiver. The receivers available today vary from the standard GPS receiver to automobile and cell phone systems. All the systems use the same parameters to obtain a position on the Earth's surface. First, location is determined from the available satellites. Three or more satellites will provide the most accurate location. The exact location is then based on the distances calculated from extremely accurate atomic clocks on the satellites. This measurement can also provide the location's elevation (if the receiver is so equipped). Based on the above explanation, you can see that we can normally obtain our location in longitude, latitude or UTM coordinates and in most cases, our altitude. This information will assist greatly in determining starting and ending points, way points, current location, etc.

Selection of a Handheld GPS

Hand held GPS's, like cell phones, are still evolving. Therefore, we recommend that you become familiar with both your SAR needs and the wide choice of devices based on both price and capabilities. Read the literature and talk to someone in SAR who is knowledgeable and reliable for recommendations on brands and features.

Some of the current features of the GPS that are useful in wilderness search include (but are not limited to) the following:

1. providing UTM and long/lat in the various map datum (North American Datum 1927 and 1983, World Geodetic System 1984, etc.),
2. providing an electronic compass,
3. altimeter readings,
4. odometer and
5. setting up a route with *waypoints* or simply one *destination*.

Using the GPS

We cannot overemphasize the need for you to practice using the device with both a paper topo map and a magnetic compass. You will need to practice the following basic steps:

1. turning on and acquiring at least three satellites,
2. setting the appropriate map datum (if working with a separate map),
3. setting odometer units (miles or kilometers),
4. setting the altimeter based on current weather at a known elevation), and
5. entering data such as : *waypoints, route, starting points* (if called for),   *destination* (if no waypoints are involved), *route reversal*, etc. (see your instruments' manual).

When you are proficient with your device (as described above) you can then practice the use of the device by setting up a small course in a known area. Set up a route with several *waypoints,* press the *GO TO* button for your device, following the "steering screen" arrow, note the distance and azimuth indicated. They should be quite close to the course you set up using your trusty compass and pace count (don't forget to incorporate the declination as described earlier). You can now run several more courses to ensure that you have confidence in your new instrument.

Remember, your GPS is one of several tools that will assist you in your search. Currently, the orienteering or lensetic compass is still the most accurate way to stay on an azimuth in an area search. The GPS can tell you where you are on the Earth's surface, can record your track line and can easily put you on a *route* to a specific point such as a trail shelter.

In summary, the GPS is a useful tool to make you, the searcher asset, more effective.

Computer Generated Maps

The use of "off the shelf" maps is rapidly being replaced by the use of computer generated United States Geological Survey topographic maps. These maps, when combined with multi-layer computer generated data provide both the ICS Command and the searchers with enhanced capabilities that can often improve the *Probability of Success* in a search. In addition, many systems are now available for cell phones at little or no cost. Through the use of "Apps" the searchers can now carry, in their cell phone, the NASAR Field Guide and the topo maps needed to initiate a search.

Electronic Distance Measuring

Distance between established GPS points can be measured and compared to the pace or track line measure. The required procedure will be found in the detailed instructions of the GPS instrument being used. "Apps" are also currently available to determine distances, typically from 10 to 1000 meters. Such measurements are quite useful, both in training and in field use to measure and/or verify courses and distances across impassable obstacles. As technology continues to advance, so will the electronic options available to searchers and command staff. Tech savvy SAR personnel should be constantly aware of new products and their application in order to take advantage of these tools, adding them to the cache of the reliable map and compass.

Summary

This has been a quick review to help you brush up on map reading and cross country orienteering. The Incident commander, your search team and the lost person will all depend on you to accurately search your assigned segment. Don't fail them by getting into the wrong segment or worse yet, getting lost! The solution? Practice, train and practice more and learn to use the tools available such as GPS units, etc. It is for the lost person.

End Note:
http://www.mappingsupport.com/p/recreation/utm_coordinates_topo_map.html

Notes:

Figure 25 Probing the Ground.

Chapter 5

Search Tactics

Objectives

- •*Understand the purpose of reflex tasks.*
- •*Define place last seen and last known point.*
- •*Describe search tactics to include attraction, containment, hasty and grid searches.*

As we mentioned in the Introductory chapter, our goal is to assist you to become the most efficient and effective Strike Team/Task Force Leader possible. All the information provided is oriented toward *how* you affect the search in the field. This chapter will be divided into two main parts. The first we refer to as the "Reflex Tasking" (sometimes called "tailgate management"). The first operational period is critically important to any search, whether small or large. We will elaborate on this in some detail.

The second part is about the tactics employed after the Reflex Tasking is underway. We will start this section with a brief discussion of the *strategy* as it is developed in the Command Post. This background is helpful in understanding why we do what we do (the search tactics) in the field. Few will admit it but the use of the terms *strategy and tactics* are often confused. This is not surprising as there is certainly some overlap and interaction between the two terms. For our purpose we will consider the *strategy* to be the domain of the ICS planners and the Incident Commander, that is, the "plan of action to achieve the over-all mission (to find and rescue the missing person(s)." The *tactics*, on the other hand, are the "specific actions used to achieve a specific purpose." (This is described on ICS Form 214.)

Part I Reflex Tasking

Reflex Tasking is implementing and assigning those tasks which should be applied immediately, by reflex. All emergency services have such tasks delineated. For instance, in the case of fire services a set protocol is followed upon arrival at the scene (i.e. Size up for safety, don the proper protective equipment and review the entire scene (wind direction, positioning of equipment as it arrives, etc.). This process is equally important for a search. *Omissions or mistakes* made at this point can easily *slow down the search* at a point when time is of the essence. The search area increases as delay occurs! It is, therefore, urgent that we implement the following measures as soon as possible.

Note: Urban Reflex Tasking is discussed in Chapter 12.

The most important first task in a wilderness search is to *secure the Last Known Point or Place Last Seen (LKP/PLS)*. *Last Known Point* – where the person was last known to be such as the automobile at the trail head parking lot. *Place Last Seen* – where a reliable witness last saw the missing person such as at a cabin on the trail.

As soon as the initial Missing Person Report is received and the LKP/PLS is determined, the immediate area should be secured in the same manner as a crime scene. Law Enforcement can best relate to and accept this concept. *Never* give out this location on the radio.

Always establish a staging area as early as possible. These two immediate actions will go a long way toward avoiding the trampling and destruction of clues, especially those used by trackers and canine handlers. Such clues are absolutely essential in the early establishment of a direction of travel. Do take note of the discussion on how to approach the LKP/PLS in the tracking and canine chapters.

While the first few search personnel establish the above, the best available interviewer should first complete the abbreviated Missing Person Questionnaire (MPQ), and then complete the full MPQ; providing key information needed for initial tasking. It should be noted that the interviewing and any related investigation should be continuous until the missing person is found. As more information is developed we increase the Probability of Success which is described in Chapter 10.

As soon as the three actions above are completed, the *indirect tactics* (sometimes referred to as "passive measures" are put in place. Some of these measures do not require skilled, experienced searchers. Others require considerable skill.

Reflex Tasking Containment

As soon as the *Initial Planning Point (IPP)*[8] has been established, the containment of the search area needs to be considered. Early action can reduce the size of the search area and enhance the *Probability of Success* (POS). Ideally the placement of volunteers at intervals surrounding the area containing the Initial Planning Point (LKP/PLS)) will create an effective containment. Often this ideal situation is not possible. Trails, high observation points, even rivers can be used–whatever works to contain the missing person. Many containment tasks require little training and can often be assigned to capable volunteers. This assignment can require the person to stay on the assigned station for many hours. Consideration needs to be given to comfort, logistics, shift rotations, etc. Someone needs to be responsible for these things so begin by assigning a capable, responsible non-searcher to ensure that the

---

[8] Usually the LKP or PLS.

communications and logistics are addressed. *Delegate* this task and focus on the search. Mature, dedicated volunteers are well-suited for this task.

A riverbank may have sandy edges which make fine "track traps." A tracker may be useful along the riverbank. Dirt and gravel roads and the dirt shoulder of paved roads should be carefully checked to "cut for signs." This is especially useful if the MPQ has produced any useful tracking information (such as size, weight of person, type footwear, etc.) The gravel road is a good area for a mounted searcher to patrol (see Chapter 7).

Note: Training is important to ensure that clues (tracks, etc.) are not destroyed.

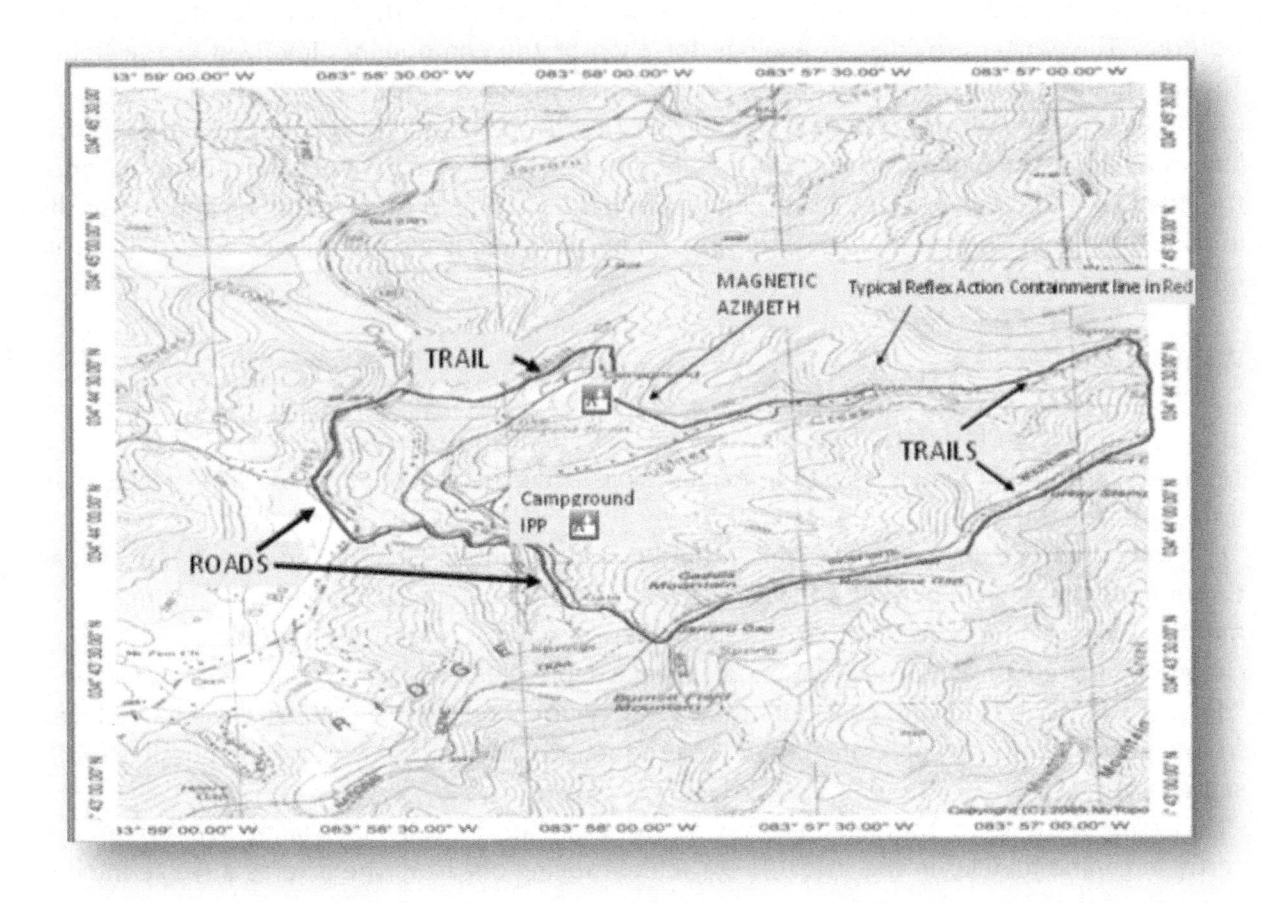

Figure 26 Containment area map using roads, pond, stream, trails and ridge.

The map shows a containment situation where many of the site factors occur.

Attraction

As soon as containment is in place, consideration needs to be given to providing attraction which may cause the missing person to move toward the light or sound produced and create the attraction needed for them to do so. Bright flashing strobe lights and air horns work best to reach as far as possible but whatever works to create the necessary attraction should be used. A word of caution: the silence needed for listening is as important as the noise created. With multiple sites emitting sounds this process needs to be a coordinated effort to work as intended. Again, this task needs to be delegated to capable, reliable volunteer support personnel.

You have now "shut the door" and provided the attraction that might, just might, guide the lost person(s) to safety. Now it is time to get into the search aspects of *Reflex Tasking.* This can best be done by use of the "Bike Wheel Model" designed by Robert Koester and Ross Gordon. This wheel provides an analogy for each of the components involved in the Reflex Tasking required during the early part of the first operational period.

First is the *hub, the Search Manager and Overhead Team*. This could be as little as one knowledgeable SAR person working off the hood of a car or the tailgate of a pickup truck (hence the title "Tailgate Management"). This one person is in charge of reflex planning and is also the initial ICS Incident Commander (IC). This person needs training and experience and could easily end up being…*you*!

Wheel Model

At this point it is important that trained, experienced personnel such as SARTEC I and II searchers, preferably searchers with managing skills and experience, begin to fill in the ICS staff. If the hub fails the wheel (search) will fail.

Next comes the *axle*. It is the Initial Planning Point *(IPP)*. This point *will not* change throughout the search–even if a Place Last Seen (PLS) develops as the search continues. As mentioned earlier, it is critical that the immediate area around the IPP (at least a 300 meter circle) is secured to avoid destruction of irreplaceable clues–the clues that would give us a "direction of travel." If one considers that, given a direction, the search area will be reduced from a possible 360^0 to approximately 30^0– a reduction of 30/360 or 1/12 of the possible initial search area.

The point is to protect the area and get the best available trained tracker and/or certified canine handler in the field. They will be moving out from the axle as a spoke moving out toward the rim. This "axle area" requires a very thorough search for clues. This applies to both wilderness and urban searches. (See Chapter 12.)

Finally, a reminder, that a careful, thorough (tight) search of the immediate area (300 meter radius) is essential. It is the most likely area to produce *clues*. We usually don't have the luxury of skilled trackers and canine handlers in the early stages of the search so what should you, the IC, do in the meantime?

Let's look at the *spokes and reflectors.* The "reflector" can be anything that would attract the missing person. For example, in the wilderness search it may be a waterfall or pond. (See Figure 43.) In the urban search it may be a park or a carnival. Volunteers can be sent to *attractions.* It is obviously helpful to have a reproduced photo of the missing person(s) as soon as one can be provided by the person/party reporting the person(s) missing.

Direction of Travel Possibilities

The following maps show three likely scenarios for a direction of travel from the Initial Point at the campground. Note that each option is identified by definable lines (1, 2, 3) and into segments A and B. These areas or segment can be assigned to search crews based on probability (see *probability of area* in Chapter 10.)

Figure 27 Topo Map.

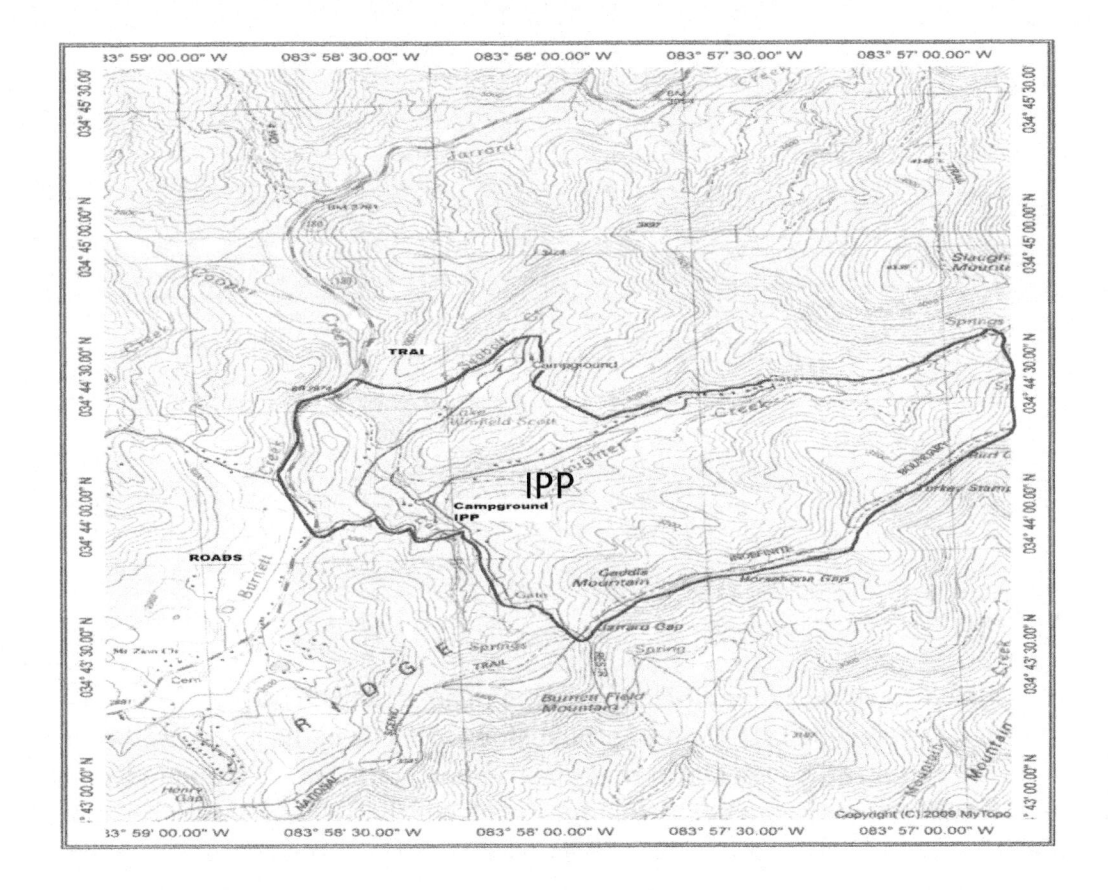

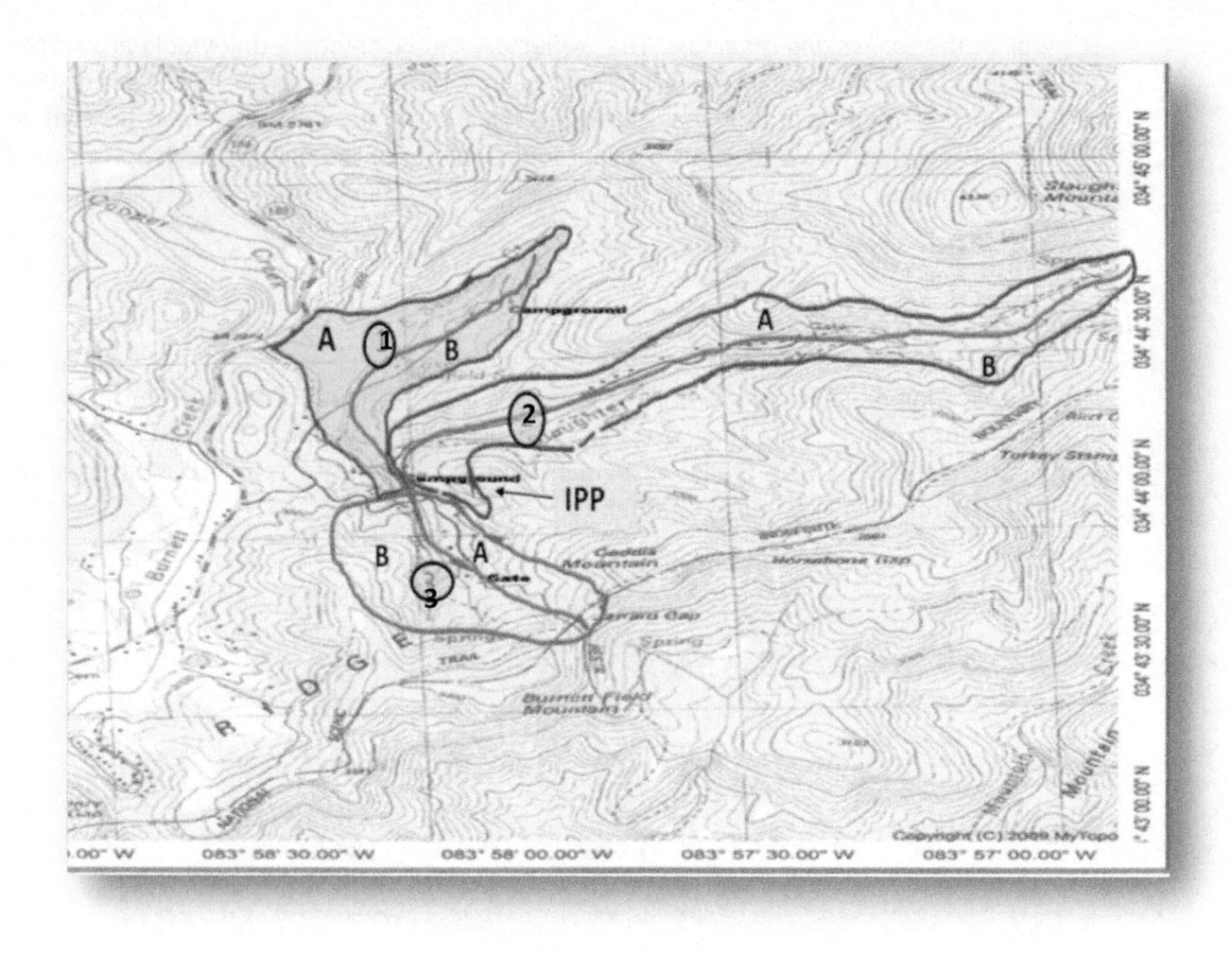

Figure 28 Direction of Travel Map Scenarios

Direction of Travel

The "spokes" could be a road, trail, power line right-of-way (ROW) or any other "path of least resistance." A detailed description of probabilities of these paths being used is described in Chapter 10. At this point we are still in the reflex action mode. The last and most important action is to form Hasty Teams and assign them to check out these likely paths. An abbreviated format of POA selection (see Chapter 10) can be used to assign priorities – especially if there are a limited number of "resources," that is, well trained, highly mobile teams who have the search experience and tracking skills needed for a hasty search. Such a team will size up the situation, prepare for the trek needed and move out at a pace that will allow the team to complete the assignment in a timely manner, yet slow enough to ensure that no clue is missed.

Any possible attraction or "point of confusion" where the trail splits or takes a 90° or more turn) will receive close attention. (See Figure 42.)

It is not unusual for animals to continue straight on such turns, leaving a well-worn path than can be mistaken for the trail being used. The well-trained Hasty Team will be careful to avoid damaging any "track traps" of soft or sandy ground along the path. In such cases a "path of most resistance" around track traps is most appropriate.

To complete the Reflex Actions requires that the initial IC provide a thorough briefing to any new IC and especially to the planning section. The second main topic of this chapter, that is, the *strategy* developed by the Planning Section on the tactics, that you will be using to implement their strategy, is addressed next.

Part II Search Tactics

Strategy

As the Planning Section becomes operational they will "size up the situation" by compiling all available information, from the initial briefing (above), to the MPQ, talking directly to the interviewer to gain all possible input needed to develop a strategy.

With this information and preparing the probability studies (see Chapter 10) the strategy for conducting the overall search will be developed. Areas (sectors) will be developed based on the probability of areas (POA). These sectors will then be prioritized into segments based on their probability of detection (POD) within each identified segment. This will provide the best probability of success (POS). The POS will then be used to provide the search assignment priority that will be provided to you, the Strike Team (or Task Force) Leader. It is now up to you to meet the required POD in the assigned segment. Next, we will address the tactics and techniques.

Tactics

Search tactics are divided into three types:

1. The **hasty** non-area linear search. It has been discussed in some detail in Part I. It can be continued into the main search effort as the need arises. As the search develops the hasty team searches may provide input (clues) that will increase the POA of a certain sector. This can occur when a new possible sighting is reported or an area or confusion point needs to be rechecked.

2. The **area search** is divided into the ***loose grid search*** and the ***tight grid search.***

Before we discuss the loose and tight grid search we need to discuss terms and techniques. First the terms:

Baseline –This is the starting line on which the searchers line up. Normally it is as perpendicular as possible to the line of travel.

Guideline -The segment of the sector being searched should have identifiable boundaries. This may be a river, road, right of way (ROW), ridge or other identifiable control line to guide on. In a large area search with few natural boundaries the guide may have to be a magnetic bearing.

Guide Person-With a linear boundary such as the road, the guide keeps the road on his *right;* that is, *guiding right.* Each person maintains the assigned critical spacing (see Chapter 10) and echelons out from the guide.

This will allow the searchers to remain in their assigned lane in the route type search. Such searches are often used in law enforcement evidence searches. See Figure 32.

Search Lane- The sweep width on a tight area search will only be as wide as the sum of the searcher lanes. In a large area doing a tight grid search, complete coverage can be attained by a multiple sweeps. By flagging the flank at regular intervals as the strike team moves forward, it can be retrieved as the next iteration of the sweep continues.

Grid Naming- To assist in describing and implementing the area grid search the Venturing SAR teams in the Northwest have developed a number- word(s)- number system. As an example, a pattern described as 5-guide right-20 would indicate 5 searchers guiding right with a 20 meter critical spacing. The word "compass" may be added to indicate that the guide line is a magnetic bearing rather than a road or other identifiable linear boundary.

Loose Grid

The loose grid search types are shown in the following figures. The loose grid may be the best approach if the assigned segment is large, the searchers are few, and the missing person(s) is/are not categorized as "high urgency" in accordance with the *Search Urgency Form* (see Appendix F). It is recommended that only experienced searchers be used because staying on a linear or compass guide is difficult. This approach does offer the flexibility of looking in and around obstacles or looking into potential sheltering by putting oneself in the mind of the missing person.

These difficulties can be reduced somewhat by maintaining a track line in the center and having each side sweep an area. In either case the sweep can be larger than the Average Maximum Detection Range (AMDR).

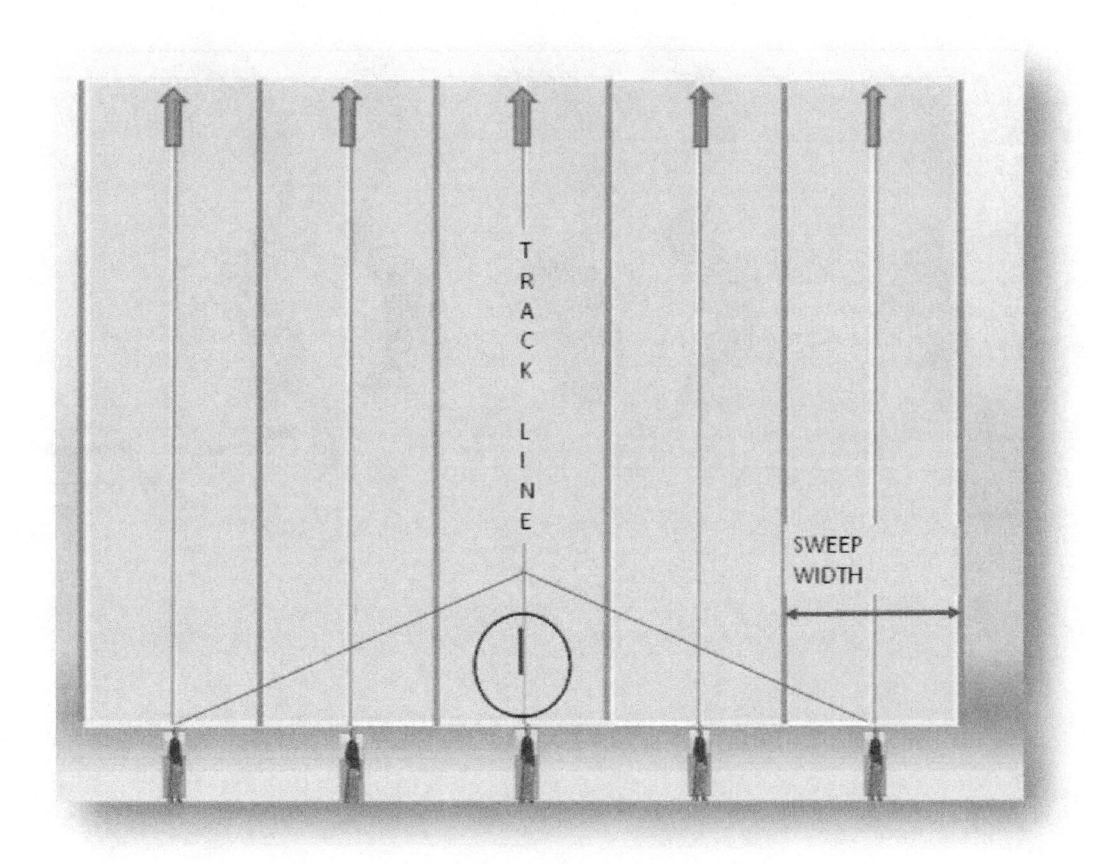

Figure 29 Tight Grid Search on a magnetic track line.

TRACK LINES

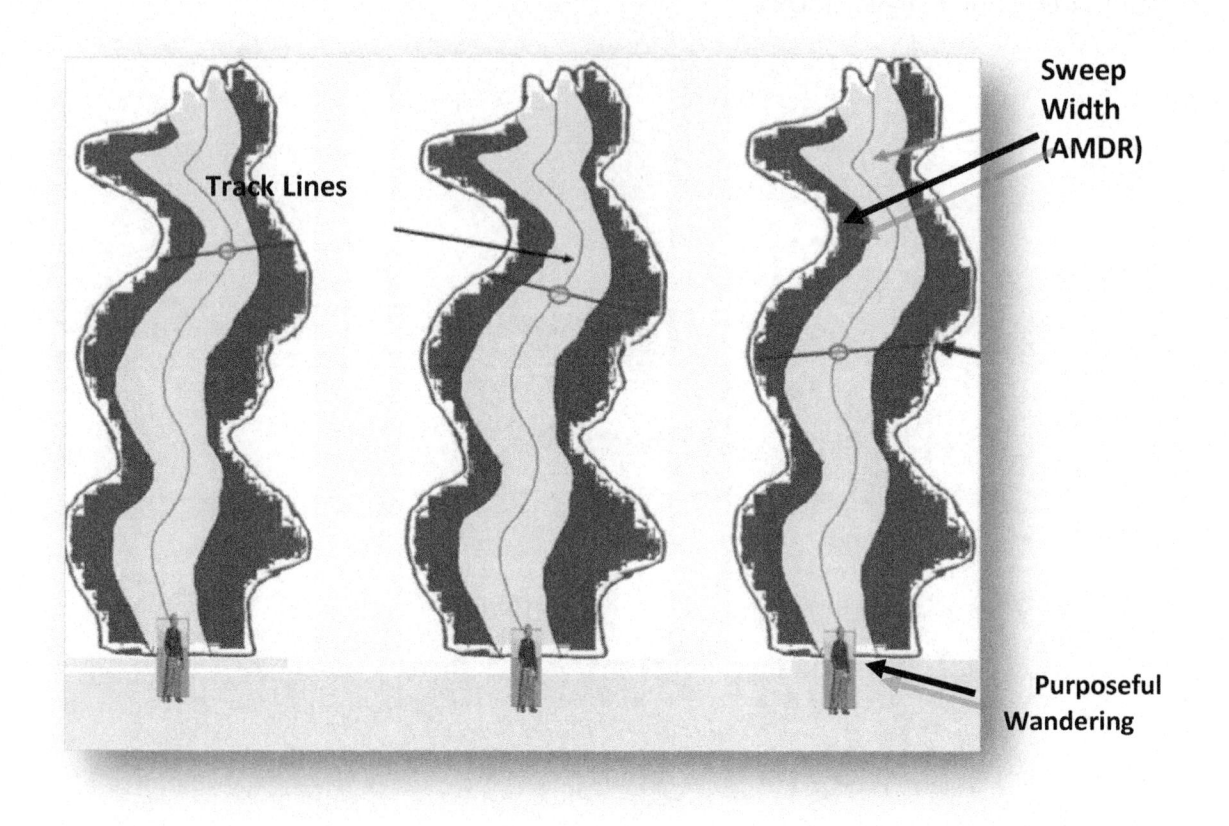

Figure 30 Above: Loose Grid Search used when resources are minimal.

Tight Grid

The **Tight Grid** search is obviously much more thorough. It is the obvious choice when there are adequate searchers; even if some are not highly qualified and experienced. This approach is called for when the urgency is high and the missing person(s) early rescue is critical. It is also used for LE searches for evidence (to include spacing of *less than* AMDR, that is, a bit of overlap in the sweep widths is used to ensure full coverage.

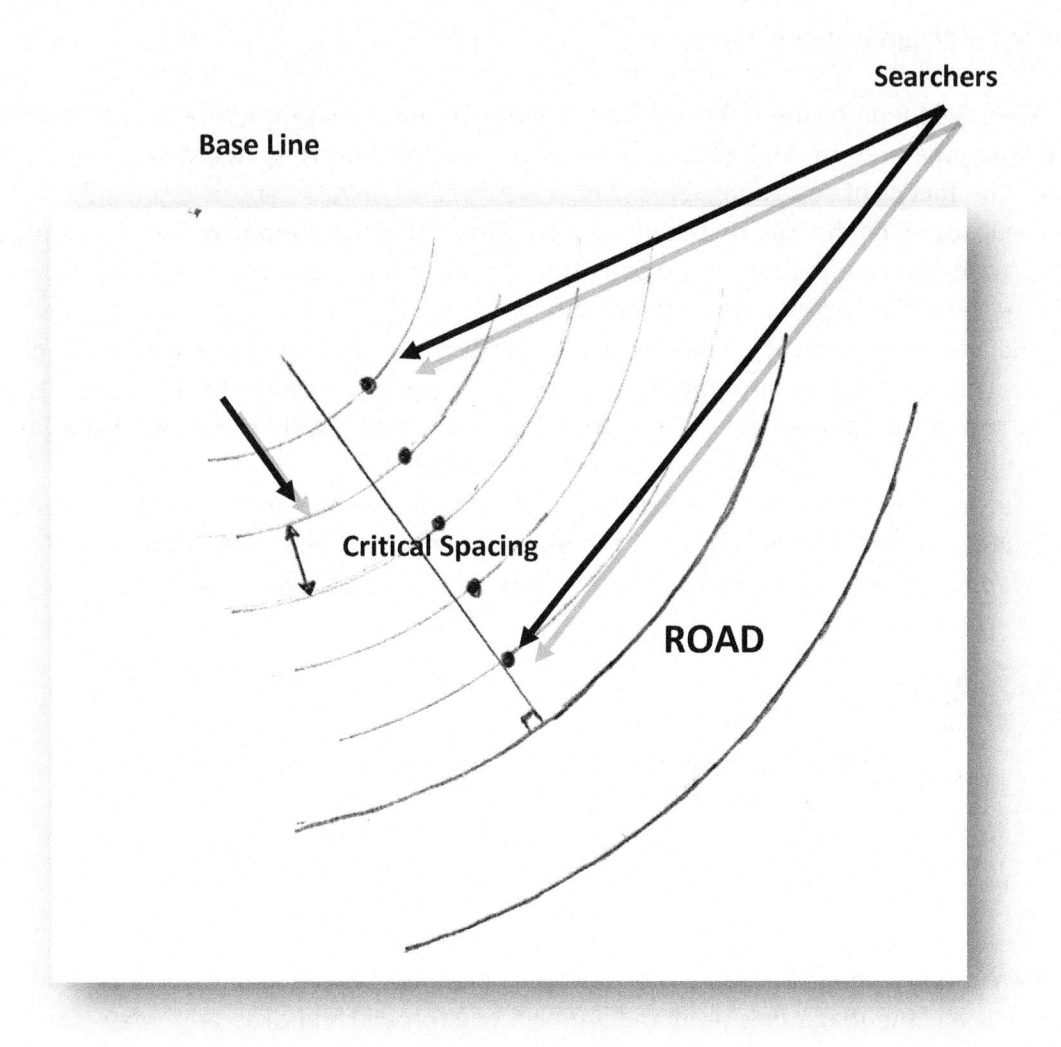

Figure 31 Tight Grid with linear boundary (road).

Guide Right on Road

The tight grid route search shows searchers slightly staggered to maintain critical spacing. With a critical spacing of ten meters, we have a five-guide-right formation shown.

Search Techniques

The techniques presented here are an overview that will suffice to give you the basics. Searching for clues requires the knowledge, training and experience of a well-rested dedicated searcher. It has been proven that search efficiency peaks after several hours and then slowly diminishes to a point (at about six hours) when the searcher loses effectiveness. That is why the assigned search task should not exceed six hours to completion.

Perception, Recognition and Detection

The *perception* of the public and untrained volunteers is simply that a search operation is when everyone lines up and goes to look for the person that they heard was lost. We have discussed the tactics of search *movement* now we need to have a serious discussion on how to detect the lost person(s). The first step is *recognition*. There are many factors to consider and train for to become effective at recognition. It all starts with the MPQ (Missing Person Questionnaire). What exactly are we looking for?

The person represents a rather large clue but many clues (such as footprints) often blend in nicely with the environment. Experienced searchers (and hunters) seem to detect what the rest of us cannot see. Their senses are not necessarily superior. Experience has taught them to detect what **doesn't belong** in the picture.

You can start **your detection training** by looking at a Fed Ex truck. We've all seen lots of Fed Ex trucks but how many have seen the big arrow on the back of the truck? *After you've detected it once you will tend to focus on the arrow whenever you see such trucks.*

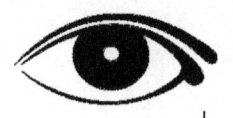

Foveal Experiment

Detection is the next factor to consider, that is, finding what you are looking for, whether it is a camouflage finished handgun or a boisterous child dressed in day-glow orange. The description provided to the strike team using the ICS Form 214 and the briefing will provide you with a preconceived notion of what to look for on your assigned mission. This preconceived notion, or *canonical perspective* as it is formally known, is a starting point but it could easily change. For instance, the child in orange may get warm and remove the orange jacket. He may even lay down in exhaustion.

The strike team leader needs to point this out and other considerations to the assigned searchers, especially if they are inexperienced. You are focused on the search and are mindful that you are looking for *any* and *all* clues that will lead the strike team to the missing person(s). We are now ready to scan the sweep widths of our search segment....or are we? Are you looking or are you seeing? To answer that question we need to understand a bit about the human eye. When we "scan" an area we are "seeing" (detecting) a large area through the eye lens onto the retina.

Snapshots

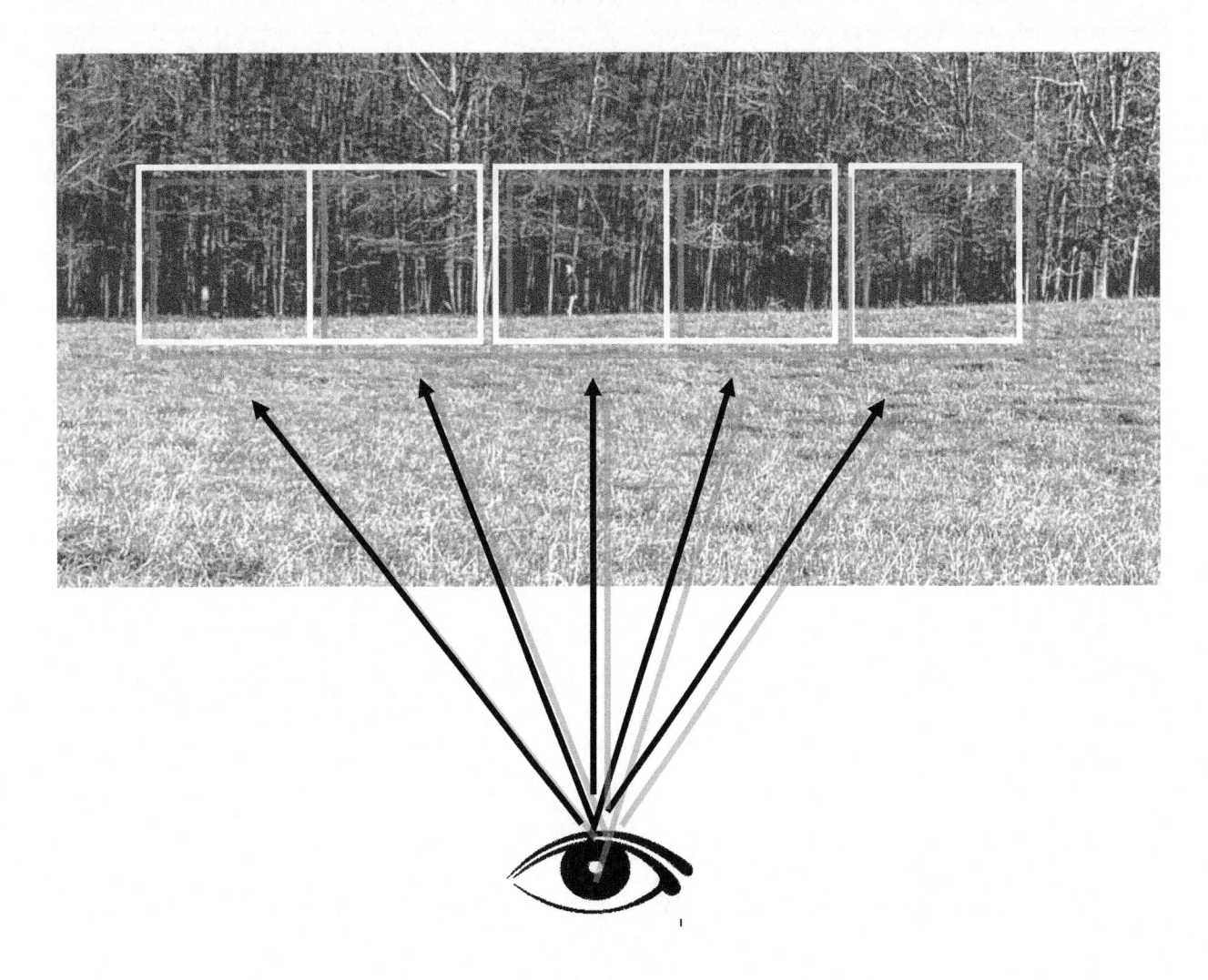

Figure 32 Snapshots.

When we "focus in" on an item we concentrate on the optic signal to the brain from a small area known as the *foveal* field. It is the area which provides the clearest image while the rest of the field of vision is somewhat less focused. If you stand this textbook at a distance of four feet (4) feet with the foveal experiment page facing you, then you will be able to read the small print inside the circle but not the larger print outside the circle.

Note that the *foveal* field is rather narrow (about 2⁰). What does all this mean? If you are searching for a small (or distant) object you need to use "snapshots" instead of scanning. Stop – Look – Move – Stop -- Look.

You will take advantage of the foveal's acuity. If you are "going back for a second look" you will likely be using the *foveal* field. In any case, snapshots will always give you a more detailed vision. Another technique to use when searching an assigned sweep width is to "circle around" to get a rearward view. Turn around distance will vary but, in a thorough tight search it is recommended that AMDR distance be used.

Figure 33 Evidence Search.

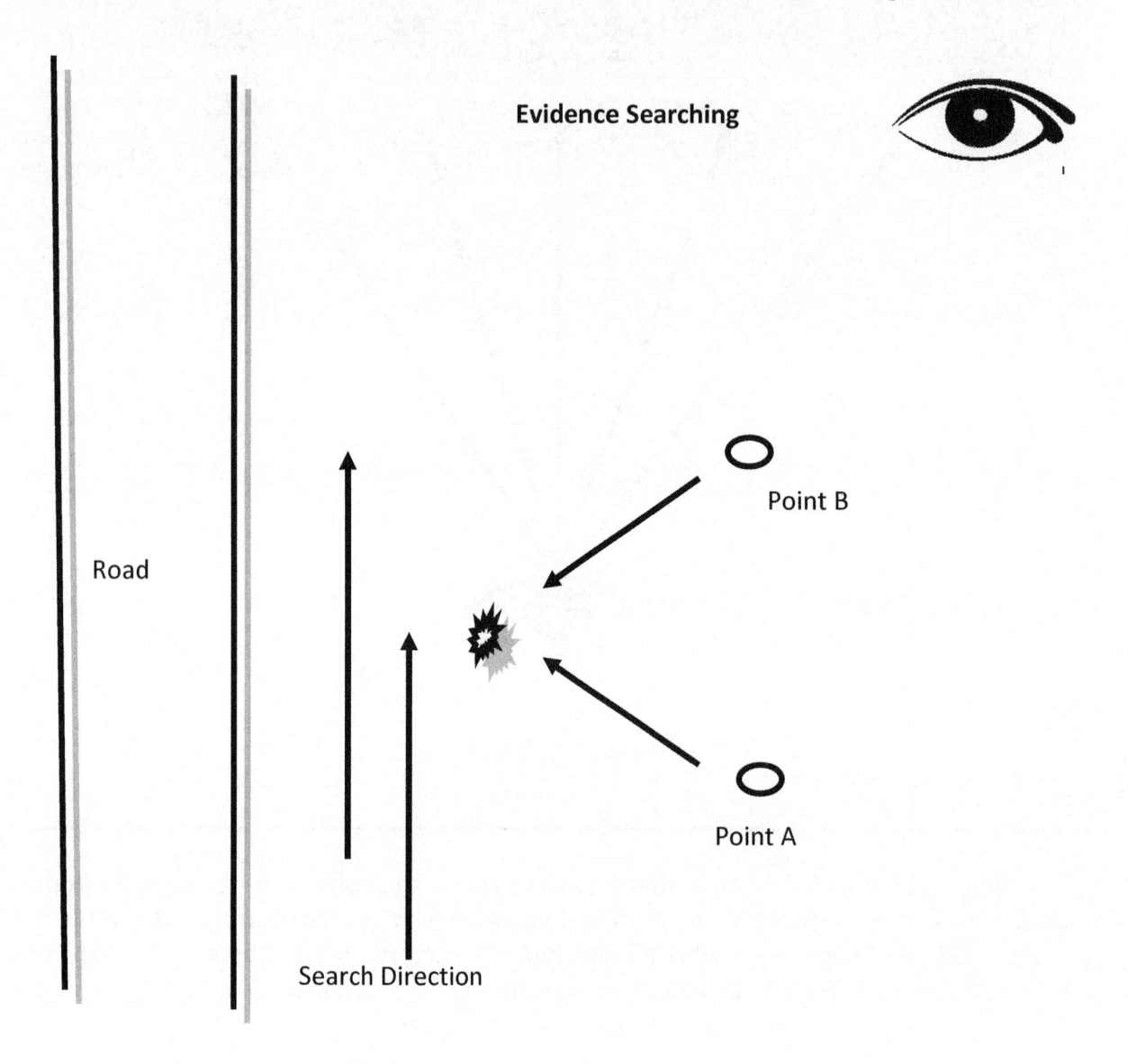

Evidence Searching

Photo A was taken from Point A with nothing visible looking forward in a tight evidence search.

Photo B (below) with weapon visible when turning around and looking behind. This was taken from Point B.

Foveal Field Illustration

****

FOVEAL EXPERIMENT

The human eye can only send a sharp focus to the brain from the foveal.

1-2 DEGREES
FOVEAL FIELD
@ 4 '

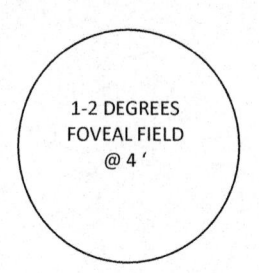

Figure 34 Foveal Experiment

Use the "snapshot technique and the circling around approach on the following exercise.

Do you see the three lads in the woods? The largest lad is the most difficult to detect as only his face contrasts with the surroundings.

Figure 35 Three Lads.

Part III Leading a Task Force

The leadership traits needed to lead a task force are quite similar to those needed by a strike team leader. One main difference is that you will have subject matter experts such as trackers, canine handlers, wilderness medicine EMT's, etc., available.

These subject matter experts should brief you, the leader, first (so you both agree on each position), and then the entire task force. It is essential in a task force that all resources work in consonance toward achievement of the goal. The best way to accomplish this is to be knowledgeable of the needs and abilities of these specialists. Toward that end we have included chapters on most of the support specialties found in search and rescue operations.

Using Mounted Units in Planning

Integrating mounted SAR into the overall search effort will most likely have a beneficial result in assisting ground units and SAR dog units to find high probability areas for search. A mounted strike team can cover a much larger area very effectively and be deployed for a longer cycle. Mounted SAR can help IC provide these resources (ground and dog) with target areas to maximize their efforts. Mounted SAR can also give IC more input as it strives to allocate its best tools over the entire search area. Consider using them wisely.

Summary

In this chapter we have taken what the Incident Commander wants (the strategy) and converted it into the "how to" of searching (the tactics). It is important to start properly. Accordingly, we start with the "Reflex Tasking," that is, addressing what must be done immediately! Identification of the LKP/PLS, direction of travel, completing the Lost Person Questionnaire, initiating containment and attraction are all items that an early, well-trained responder should have in effect as soon as possible.

The use of Koester's "Bike Wheel" is quite helpful in initiating the tactics needed to move forward in the search. The Hasty, Loose Grid and Tight Grid are also discussed. By applying all the skills discussed in this text we can proceed in a well-coordinated manner to find the subject of our search.

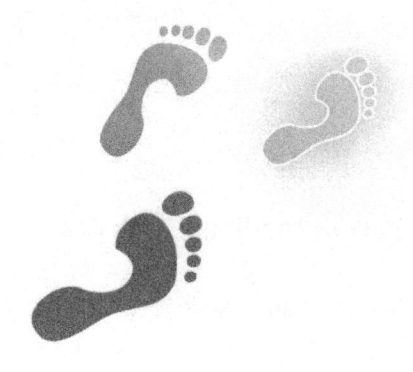

Notes:

Figure 36 Potential Missing Child.

CHAPTER 6

Lost Person Behavior

Objectives

●Understand the importance of typical lost person behavior based upon type of lost person.

●Understand the use of the Spatial Model when planning a lost person incident.

Figure 37 Child Walk Away.

What is lost person behavior? How does it affect what a searcher and a team leader does out in the field? Is it a search management issue only or does everyone play a role? A search revolves around one central question – where? At one point in time someone knew where the missing subject was – this is the basis of the place last seen (PLS). In some cases it might have been a Last Known Position (LKP) when the investigation selects a particular place that can be tied to the subject. Both of these can be used to establish the Initial Planning Point (IPP). Yet the real question remains, and where are they *now*?

Lost person behavior is not a single statistical measure, behavioral profiling, or just investigation. Instead it is the combination of different approaches and sources of information to build a composite picture of the missing subject. It is a look at the past: previous similar; it is a look at the future; what is the destination they might be trying to reach, what strategies they might employ while lost, how will the weather influence their decisions and choices? Ultimately the goal remains – where they are now. Everyone needs to understand typical lost person behavior.

The searcher can decide where to place their gaze and what locations require a more intensive search. For a team leader the responsibilities and decisions are even greater. How will the assigned search area be searched? What information about possible subject traits should be shared with the team? What areas within the search area warrant extra attention? Will shouting the subject's name be productive, counter-productive, or does it matter? How far off a linear feature should be searched? Does searching in particular geographic features propagate a better chance of making a find? These are some of the critical questions – lost person behavior can provide some of the answers.

Figure 38 Searching in the Snow.

Sample Scenario

A 21 and a 19 year-old couple were last seen at the ski lodge (PLS) at 10:00 by friends. The last electronic record of their lift ticket has them on the Moonraker lift at 13:30. The top of the lift (LKP and IPP) has access to the backcountry. They are known to ski out of bounds, but they never carry appropriate equipment. The avalanche danger is high at the higher elevations and considerable at lower elevations. Subject Category: Snowboarder. Likely Scenario: Avalanche, trauma, lost, overdue, stranded, investigative.

Investigation

The foundation of lost person behavior is good investigation. Without it nothing is known about the missing subject. Before a meaningful search may commence initial investigation it must determine two major pieces of information. As a team leader it is important to both know and brief your team on these. They include search data and planning data.

Searching data: The physical description of the subject, pictures, what they are wearing and what items they may have with them. In addition, it will provide information on what name to call and if shouting a name will be productive.

Planning data: The two most important types of planning data are the Initial Planning Point (IPP) and the subject category. In order to determine the subject category a short synopsis of the circumstances and background of the subject is typically required.

The initial investigation is enough to start the planning process and deploy teams out into the field. A team leader may be tasked before the planning staff has in-depth knowledge of the subject. However, experience has shown that the initial tasks often remain the same for the subject category, even after more in-depth investigative information is obtained. Search planning is a continuously evolving process. With additional information, even the subject category can change. Search management continues the investigative process throughout the search. The reporting party, family, friends, and professionals (doctors, pharmacist, therapist, etc.) all become sources of information. Typical SAR questions are often captured on the Lost Person Questionnaire (LPQ). The text *Lost Person Behavior,* by Robert Koester, also contains additional questions specific to each *subject category.*

The process of determining the subject category is derived from this initial investigation. It is never as straight forward as the text books describe it. In fact, on actual searches, it may be necessary to consider two or three subject categories at once. Fortunately, a hierarchy does exist to assist searchers.

> *In trouble? Lost? Kids will often be unpredictable and within moments can be out of sight if left unattended.... It happens over and over.*

The highest order of that hierarchy is the subject categories that are constrained by physical or outside forces. These include disaster forces such as earthquakes, tornadoes, mudslides, and hurricanes which may cause urban entrapment. It also includes the force of water or simply standing water. A missing aircraft must follow certain physical laws and searches for emergency beacons and also follow the laws of physics. Abduction changes the behavior from the subject to the perpetrator and is another example of an outside force. If no physical or outside force applies to the incident, then the use of wheels is considered.

If the subject is in or on a wheeled or tracked vehicle then *that* is the predominant predictor of both where and how far away the subject might be found. This hierarchical level includes vehicles (both two and four wheeled drive), snowmobiles, ATVs, motorcycles, and mountain bikes. If the vehicle is located without the subject then a new IPP would exist and the subject category would change. An important consideration would be the next level – which is the *cognitive class*.

The *cognitive level* is applied when the mental capabilities of the subject are impaired in some way. It includes Autism Spectrum Disorder, dementia (Alzheimer's), despondent, intellectual disability, mental Illness, and brain injury (a new category). While a hiker with dementia is placed into the dementia category it is still important to look at the hiker category for certain traits. If no cognitive issues exist, then the subject's age is examined next.

Children are categorized based upon their age instead of the activity. The children category is further broken into toddler (1-3), Preschool (4-6), School age (7-9), Pre-Teenage (10-12), and Adolescent/Youth (13-15). Subjects 16 or older are considered adults and classified on the basis of the activity. In the case of a group of children, the classification is on the basis of the oldest child. As before, for the older children, it is still important to consider the activity.

The last level in the hierarchy is based upon the subject's activity. Common examples include fishing, hiking, snowboarding, and hunting. While at the lowest level on the hierarchy – activity is the basis of most subject categories. The use of a hierarchy, as a set of rules or algorithm, is shown.

Once the subject category is determined it allows the search planner and team leader to take full advantage of lost person behavior. The next step is predicting what the missing person, who is the current subject of the search, might do, based upon what previous similar subjects have done in similar terrain. To accomplish this, statistics are used. While statistics come from the raw data of numbers, they tell an important story.

Statistics

Data by itself is useless. However, data can lead to information with the aid of statistics. Statistics can give us rings on a map or a better understanding. In the end it is the decisions that matter – where will I send my search teams? Search and Rescue (SAR) is an inherently a spatial problem. It is all about the *where*. With some lost subjects, the why may forever elude us. Since we are attempting to predict where our subject might be located, it is important to match the current circumstances to the database as much as possible.

The most common source of SAR statistics are taken from the International Search and Rescue Incident Database (ISRID). In 2002 a grant from the U.S. Department of Agriculture was used to create ISRID. The database grew to 50,000 SAR incidents and was the basis for the book *Lost Person Behavior*.

The information in this chapter provides highlights from ISRID but during incidents the complete text should be consulted. In 2014 an additional contract from the U.S. Department of Homeland Security allowed another round of data collection bringing ISRID to nearly 150,000 incidents. The ISRID database is organized first into incident types. Only data from actual search incidents are used for the spatial statistics. The data is then divided into Eco-region domains. At this time only the temperate and dry domain are represented. It is expected that the polar domain will be found similar to the dry domain and the tropical domain will be found similar to the temperate domain. Data from urban searches are treated as a separate domain since the landscape is dramatically altered by development. Water is also treated as a separate domain. The temperate and dry domain data is further broken up into mountainous and non-mountainous terrain. Finally, the statistics are reported by subject category. The goal of this organization is to best match the statistics to the current incident's environment.

Figure 39 Snow search

The statistics provide information that can be shown using spatial models. The best known spatial model is the distance from the IPP. This information was likely used to determine the search area, more probable locations, and ultimately a team leader's task area. Other *spatial models* include changes in elevation, time subject keeps moving (mobility), dispersion angle if a destination or direction of travel is known, track offset from a linear feature, and the find location. All of this information may be combined to produce maps as shown in the figures below and on the next page. Ultimately, all the models may be combined along with human input to produce the overlays.

Spatial Model

A Typical Spatial Model with the radial distance based upon statistical data and map scale.

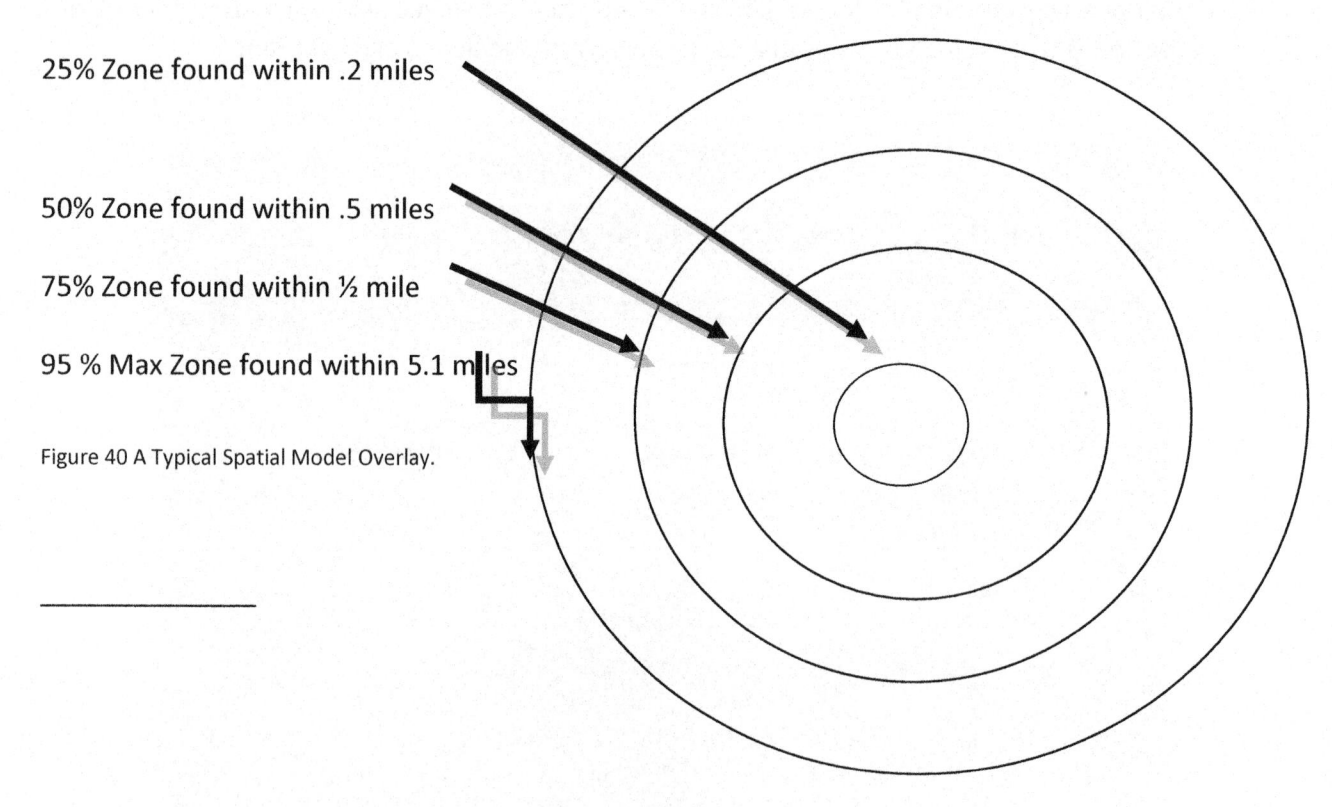

25% Zone found within .2 miles

50% Zone found within .5 miles

75% Zone found within ½ mile

95 % Max Zone found within 5.1 miles

Figure 40 A Typical Spatial Model Overlay.

Note: If radius is 1.0 mile, area of circle is 3.14 square miles.

A team leader should be most interested in *track offsets* and *find location* statistics. In addition to the spatial statistics, possible scenarios statistics give the team leader important implications on how and where to search. All of the spatial models will cause the probability within an assigned search sector to be slightly different.

Search Scenarios

Avalanche scenarios require special equipment and expertise. The criminal scenario requires knowledge of crime scene preservation, looking for locations used to hide a body, clandestine graves, and possible encounters with perpetrators while on task. The despondent, drowning, and medical scenarios are subject categories onto themselves. Keep in mind that subjects will typically move a short distance off a trail or road for medical scenarios. The same is also true for the trauma scenario. The biggest impact on field tactics would be an evading scenario. Lost continues to be the most common scenario for many subject categories. The overdue and stranded scenarios typically have the subject on or close to the intended route of travel. However in the stranded scenario safety concerns for the search team may need to be addressed.

Search team leaders, as well as planning staff, need to be aware of scenario lock as described below.

Scenario Lock

The term *scenario lock* describes a common phenomenon among inexperienced or barely experienced search planners and Incident Commanders. They tend to take the *most likely* scenario and turn it into the *only* possible scenario. Once they have conducted a search that addressed the one scenario, they are prepared to suspend the mission. This problem is usually solved once the management team has been wrong a couple of times. Hopefully, nobody dies during the learning curve. It is far better to remember that several scenarios are always possible and to plan accordingly.

Mobility and Responsiveness

Others have also reported on the subject's mobility and responsiveness for hikers, hunters, and skiers. About half of the subjects were mobile (at some point while lost) and most were responsive.

Subjects are classified as "mobile and responsive," "immobile and responsive," "mobile and unresponsive," or "immobile and unresponsive." It should be noted that classification in this category was based solely upon incident reports. All fatalities were classified as "immobile and unresponsive."

Mobile and responsive which describes a typical overdue or lost hiker, is the most common classification. The percentages of lost persons found *mobile and responsive* are higher than other categories.

The *second most common* classification is the *immobile and unresponsive* subject who is often seriously injured or dead. It may also describe a dementia subject who has stopped moving and will not respond to searchers' shouts. The *mobile and unresponsive classification* is the least common and may also be attributed to dementia, autistic, and similar subjects who are still moving but unresponsive. Other common categories associated with *mobile and unresponsive* are *despondent, mental Illness, mental retardation, and some child categories*. Of course, during the search, it is impossible to know which category the lost person will fall into (unless the search staff is talking to them on a cell phone). However, good investigation may indicate the child is afraid of strangers, the dementia subject ignores his name being called, or the subject is deaf. Even though the overall percentages differ among the various subject categories, the different outcomes can be used to make tactical decisions and help predict survivability.

Lost Person Strategies

Ken Hill conducted structured interviews with rescued lost persons soon after (sometimes during) their recovery, and conducted tests, through survey research and interviews with 120 deer hunters in Nova Scotia. Generally, persons who become disoriented will use at least one of these methods. Some lost persons may attempt several different methods. Limited data exists from dry domains; however, preliminary observations suggest cross-country travel towards a landmark is much more common. In addition, Robert Koester added contouring as a strategy based upon several incidents.

Random Traveling

Totally confused, and usually experiencing high emotional arousal, the lost person moves around randomly, following the path of least resistance, with no apparent purpose other than to find something or some place that looks familiar. Although many lost people move randomly during their initial reaction to being lost, most settle down and apply a more effective method. Only a few lost persons—such as some school-aged children by themselves—will continue to move randomly while lost. Most subjects show somewhat more purposeful behavior in their attempt to get out of the situation.

Route Traveling

In this case, the lost person decides to travel on some trail, path, drainage, or other travel aid. The route is unknown to this person, and he is uncertain regarding the direction he is headed, but hopes that eventually he will come upon something familiar. When this fails, as it often does, he rarely reverses direction on the route to go the other way. If the trail peters out, for example, he may revert to random traveling. Sometimes referred to as "trail running," this is usually an ineffective method of reorientation, shown most often by school-aged children up to 12 years of age.

Direction Traveling

Certain that safety lies in one particular direction, the lost person moves cross-country, often ignoring trails and paths leading in the "wrong" direction. Sometimes, in fact, this person will cross railroad tracks, power lines, highways, and even backyards with the conviction that he is headed the right way. Unfortunately, this strategy (which is rarely effective) often puts him into the thickest part of the woods, making him especially difficult to find. It takes considerable overconfidence about one's sense of direction to employ this tactic which is not uncommon for subjects of land searches.

Most typically, it is seen in some hunters who have come to exaggerate their outdoor skills to others and to themselves, believing there is some sort of shame in becoming turned around. While the tactic might be appropriate for trained searchers who are often given a "bail-out" compass direction, it is not otherwise a recommended strategy for lost persons. However, some lost persons try it and have been known to walk across roads and trails.

Figure 41 Direction Choice.

Route Sampling

In route sampling, the person uses an intersection of trails as a base, traveling some distance down each trail in search of something familiar. After "sampling" a particular route without success, this person returns to the intersection and tries another path, repeating the processes until all routes at that intersection have been sampled.

Direction Sampling

Direction sampling is similar to route sampling, except that the lost person does not have the advantage provided by an intersection of trails. Rather, this subject selects some identifiable landmark as a base, such as a large tree or outcropping.

From there, he goes in selected directions, always keeping the base in view, looking for something that will help him figure out where he is.

When he is just about to lose sight of the base, he returns to it and samples another direction, repeating the process until all possible directions are tried. Often, however, he does lose his base before the sampling procedure can be completed. At that point he tends to move somewhat randomly until he finds a landmark suitable for serving as a new base, and the directional sampling strategy may be started anew.

> **Direction Sampling**
>
> Three possibilities arise:
>
> He may repeat the sampling procedure, but now travels further distances on each route;
> he may choose to proceed down the likeliest trail until he comes to another intersection where he can repeat the strategy;
> or
> he may decide to try another tactic.
>
> Older children and adolescents sometimes report having tried this method of reorientation.
>
> It can be effective when combined with back-tracking.

View Enhancing/Cell Signal Seeking

Unable to find anything familiar after traveling around the woods, the lost person attempts to gain a position of height to view landmarks in the distance. This person attempts to enhance his view by climbing a hill, ridge, or tree. A knowledgeable adult with a topographic map or at least some survey knowledge of the area, surrounded by dense vegetation, might attempt reorientation by climbing a hill (sometimes a tree, if this can be done safely) and matching visible terrain features with those on the map. In fact, many subjects with outdoor experience report view enhancement as a favorite method of reorientation.

With the advent of cell phones, more lost subjects use view enhancement. However, instead of moving uphill to obtain a view, they gain elevation in an attempt to obtain a cell tower signal. Lost subjects will leave trails and other travel aids and often head directly uphill. When the strategy works, the SAR planner will know (they get a phone call); when it does not, it may complicate the search process.

Figure 42 Confusion Point.

Another example of a confusion point is shown below where the dash lines indicate the hiking trails and the dotted lines indicate animal trails. The hiker starts down the trail; trail makes a hairpin turn; animals and hiker go straight; hiker gets lost. These are the locations on a trail to check closely for signs that hiker followed the animal trail.

Figure 43 Confusion Point Two.

Figure 44 Wilderness Attraction.

Backtracking

After getting turned around, the person reverses the track and attempts to follow the exact route back out of the woods. This can be a very effective method. It does require some skill and patience to use.

Unfortunately, lost persons seem reluctant to reverse their direction of travel without good reason, believing it to be a waste of time and that safety might be over the next hill or around the next bend in the trail. They also know something bad already occurred in the original return direction (they got lost).

If a person becomes confused on a route that has numerous branches, he or she can backtrack to each intersection, and employ a route-sampling tactic to determine the correct fork. If these persons are in the woods—and competent at reading tracks—they should be able to follow their own sign back. Perhaps the effectiveness of backtracking is not captured by ISRID. If the person quickly realizes their mistake and backtracks it is not likely a search incident will ever develop.

80

Folk Wisdom

This miscellaneous category refers to the attempt to reorient oneself by using any of the numerous adages on how to find your way safely out of the woods. These adages are usually passed on by the campfire or disguised as "facts" in survival books.

The most common of these is "all streams lead to civilization," a principle that, if followed in Nova Scotia, will more than likely lead the lost person to a remote and *bug-infested swamp. In the dry domain, mountain streams often simply end as a wash in the middle of the desert.*

Staying Put

Every woods safety program stresses the importance of "staying where you are" when lost, which can be considered an excellent—if somewhat passive— strategy for reorientation, as long as the lost person can reasonably expect a search to be organized on his behalf in the very near future. Sadly, very few people apply this method of getting out of the woods safely. While it is true that most lost persons are found in a stationary position (especially after the first 24 hours of the search), this is usually because they are fatigued, asleep or unconscious.

In a review of *Overstaying,* 800 Nova Scotia lost person reports found only two cases in which the subjects had intentionally stayed in one place in order for searchers to find them more easily. One was an 11 year-old boy who had received *Hug-a-Tree* training at school. The other was an 80-year old apple picker who settled down comfortably within five minutes of being turned around, just 100 yards from where she had entered the woods.

The ISRID database contains 383 cases (28%) where the subject stayed put. So either the strategy is more common than originally thought or subject behavior may be changing.

One survey of persons with excellent outdoor experience revealed that they are aware that *staying put* is the recommended course of action. However, they may be disinclined to stay in one place for any length of time, especially during the day. As mentioned above, a popular reorientation strategy reported by these individuals was view enhancement.

Contouring

Some subjects in more mountainous terrain do not go up or down, but instead contour. This behavior is most typically seen where the terrain becomes much steeper. Therefore, climbing uphill does not seem like a good option.

Heading downhill may appear gentle but featureless. The subject wanting to be able to follow some type of feature will find if they contour they can stay oriented to the mountain on one side and the featureless forest on the other. They hope they will eventually intersect with a road or trail. They may also intersect with a significant drainage feature which might alter their plan. This strategy has been seen in adults, children, and those with cognitive issues.

Doing Nothing

While not a strategy at all for getting found, several of the ISRID databases listed doing nothing as an option. In one sense it could be viewed as *staying put*. However, the people filling out forms wanted to differentiate between the subjects who made an active decision to stay-put (and then usually attempt to signal or build a shelter) and those who did nothing at all. The "doing nothing" approach was often applied to dementia cases in which the subject simply sat down.

Profiles

The subject profile is a compilation of traits and characteristics that are common among a particular subject category. It would be rare for a subject to exhibit all of the traits. It is even possible for some subjects to exhibit none of the traits. However, most subjects are highly likely to exhibit some of the characteristics. When nothing is known about the subject and before initial investigative is completed it provides a starting point. Considering that investigation and information provided is sometimes wrong or misleading the subject profile should never be ignored.

The following excerpts of selected profiles are taken from the text *Lost Person Behavior* by Koester in order to give a sense of what the profile contains. The full profile should be consulted on actual incidents. The following subject profiles are presented:

Abductions   Campers Hikers   Children   Dementia

Tactical Briefing

During the tactical briefing, be sure to share the following:

• The points of interest such as the IPP, contact with perpetrator, assault site, murder site, body site.

• Bodies are typically concealed, 55% of the time, with materials on hand.

-Look in debris piles.
-Discarded evidence is often found along roads.
-Encounters with perpetrators are possible.
-Clandestine graves are usually shallow, close to the road or water and downhill.
-Note any changes in vegetation, colors, or the surface of the ground.
-Look for signs of passage from humans or animals.
-Be aware of any depression or pushing up of the earth or cracks in the soil.

Abductions

Searchers and search planners should be aware of perpetrators' tendency, when "dumping" the subject, to find a location that is quick and easy, typically involves a vehicle, but is also secluded.

Typical locations often are turn-outs, culverts, and sides of bridges. Remote roads with little traffic have a high probability. The subject is typically found not far from the road. Dumps and dump sites also have higher probability.

A "typical" case is an 11-year-old Caucasian female from a middle class or blue collar family with good family relations. Classic indicators of sexually motivated abductions include white female, aged five to twelve, missing from home or familiar place with no history of running away; she is described as happy, and the disappearance is unexplained. The more red flags raised, the more immediate and aggressive the response.

Camper (Car camper)

Campers are located at a campsite and may be engaged in a variety of activities around the campsite. The category can be defined as missing persons whose vehicles and gear were located at the campground. The term "car camping" would also be appropriate. If planning a hike, they would be classified as hiker. Backpackers, even if staying in a campground for the night, are also classified as a hiker. Children are placed into the age appropriate child category. Subjects with dementia have become lost in campgrounds. However, they would be classified under dementia.

While most campers become lost in the immediate vicinity (59%), several other more "urban" scenarios are possible.

Figure 45 Typical campsite for a missing hunter.

Campgrounds often have a vast network of interconnecting marked and unmarked trails that often cause confusion. In addition, miscommunication, investigative causes, evading, and substance abuse all occur. Simply being overdue from a planned activity can account for 25% of the reported incidents. Subjects are not typically prepared for the outdoors. Subjects may not have any substantial outdoor experience. Large differences in ability may also exist. Half of subjects are lost in a group. If the campsite is near water, drowning is possible.

Hiker

The Hiker category includes walkers, hill walkers / fell walkers (in the United Kingdom), day hikers, multi-day hikers (backpackers), trekkers, and trampers ("serious hikers" in New Zealand). Mountaineers have been placed into the Climber category. Children (12 and under) missing while hiking were placed into the appropriate age group. Subjects with a cognitive disability (intellectual disability, autistic, etc.) were placed into the appropriate category, even if lost while hiking.

Figure 46 Forest Road

Hikers are oriented to trails. The lost scenario accounts for 68% of missing hikers. Errors typically occur at decision points (trail junctions, obscure trails, game trails, social trails, and head of drainages). Other common errors include heading the wrong direction down a trail. At night or under limited light conditions, the color of the trail blaze (marker) can be confused. In addition, certain colors of trail blazes may be confused by those with color blindness. Errors at decision points account for 56% of lost cases. Errors can be active (standing at a trail junction and making the wrong decision after reading the map upside down) or passive (not even noticing they left the trail). All team leaders need to be aware of decision points. When encountered in the field extra effort should be spent trying to determine if the subject might have gone off the trail or taken the wrong trail. Hikers are guided by terrain to other linear features once they are lost. Many follow the path of least resistance. Poor navigators fail to notice landmarks, while good navigators make a point of noticing landmarks (both local and distant). Youths and some young adults will also cut switchbacks. This often results in missing the trail. It may result in the subject moving uphill, even up and over a ridge line.

Among hikers, 32-48% will be found uphill in relation to the IPP. A recent phenomenon involves lost subjects moving uphill or leaving trails to move uphill in order to obtain cell phone coverage. Many attempt to reorient themselves by trail running or finding a high spot. Hikers in dry domains stay mobile twice as long than in temperate domains, and typically travel farther, have greater elevation changes, and a wider dispersion angle. They are also more likely to travel cross-country. In general, around a third (30-40%) will travel at night.

Most children go missing from home. They may be attracted to animals and water. They tend not to respond to whistles or calls. Prior training may alter this, but preventative programs at this age are uncommon. They rarely walk out by themselves. They are difficult to detect because of their small size and ability to squeeze into small spaces.   They are often hiding or sleeping in a structure, which includes yards and outbuildings. They will penetrate brush to sleep or hide. Many toddlers are found asleep inside a structure or in the brush. A sleeping child may not even respond to his own parents shouting his name. Toddlers are capable of sleeping through loud noises (many parents often train children to sleep with loud noises).   Good survivability is due to a child's tendency to find shelter and typically urgent aggressive search response.

Distances traveled are generally rather limited. However, important differences exist among temperate, dry, and urban domains/areas. Statistical data tables presented may be specific to age group (1-3), a subset of all children (1-6), or for all children (1-12) depending upon the amount of information.

Dementia

Dementia includes Alzheimer's disease and several other related disorders (vascular dementia, Parkinson's disease, and dementia with Lewy bodies among others). From a search and rescue perspective there is no appreciable difference between the different dementias.

Alzheimer's disease is the most common form of the irreversible dementias and the term is included since, in common language, it is often used to represent all dementias. Regardless of activity, search subjects with dementia were placed into this category.

Dementia results in a wide range of changes in behavior and cognitive (thinking) skills. It ranges from mild, where the person is still able to perform all activities of daily living, to severe. The more severe the dementia, the more likely the subject is to wander and experience symptoms such as hallucinations and psychosis. Dementia is the loss of memory, reason, judgment, and language to such an extent that it interferes with daily living. Some of the earliest symptoms may be problems with short term memory. One or more cognitive areas are disturbed: (1) aphasia (problems with language, e.g., finding the right word); (2) apraxia (cannot move body correctly); (3) agnosia (cannot recognize common objects, especially faces); (4) decreased executive functions (planning, organizing, abstracting). Dementia often results in severe disturbances in how a person perceives and interprets events, sights, and sounds around him.

Furthermore, the visual field (peripheral vision) is narrowed, creating "tunnel vision." A reduction in peripheral vision results in poor navigators using only what they see in front of them versus excellent navigators who also use active scanning for landmarks they remember. This may account for dementia wanderers' trademark behavior of essentially moving straight ahead: They go until they get stuck. Direction of travel predicts a dementia subject's final location better than it does in most other subject categories.

Every subject is different, and determining the severity of an individual's dementia provides additional important insight. Mild to moderate severity is associated with more goal-directed wandering. Initially, the subject does in fact have a destination in mind. Distances traveled may be great. The subject is more likely to use public transportation.

In a short conversation with the subject one may not detect anything unusual. Dementia subjects are usually recognized by the public due to inappropriate dress, unsafe or inappropriate behavior, asking for assistance or an inappropriate response. If engaged in a conversation, then suspicion is usually raised by repetitive questions, phrases or words. Subjects with severe dementia tend to show random (i.e., no discernible goal) wandering, travel shorter distances, and may have profound sensory disturbances. Exit seeking behavior may be seen in both mild and severe dementia. One is more likely to see this behavior when a person is in a new location or has been taken out of a familiar environment.

Hallmark Behaviors of Dementia

According to research, dementia subjects may:

- go until they get "stuck."
- appear to lack the ability to turn around and may ping-pong off some barriers.
- will follow one primary direction of travel which is a good predictor of where they are found.

- will leave some sign so try to determine the exit door.
- are oriented to the past. The more severe the dementia, the further in the past they exist. Try to figure out where in the past the subject is currently "living" in order to determine possible destinations (e.g., a former residence, a work place). Investigative questions assist to better understand the subject's past (which, for them, may be the present).

Figure 47 Lake.

- attempt to travel to former residence, favorite place or what appears to be former place, or workplace.
- typically are found in structures or walking along roads in an urban environment. In both urban and wilderness environments, the subject is highly likely to cross or depart from a road (66%). If the subject leaves the road or travel feature, he does not travel far.
- often go unnoticed unless his dress is highly unusual. Track offset statistics for the dementia subjects are the shortest of all categories.
- typically walk or get stuck in brush/briars or drainages in wilderness environments.
- are found in structures.

- are attracted to water features and will walk into water (perhaps without even realizing it is water).
- generally are mobile for only a short period of time. In temperate domains, half of the subjects are mobile for less than an hour. In dry domains, subjects remain mobile longer.
- may not leave many verifiable clues.
- may not cry out for help or respond to shouts—only 1% are responsive.
- are viewed as "passive evasive." Since they do not perceive themselves as lost, they would not attempt to signal or even respond to shouts.

There is a 25% fatality rate if the subject is not found within the first 24 hours. Fatality rates are higher in hot climates and cold rainy climates. Many states are developing "Senior" or "Silver" alerts similar to AMBER alerts. Such programs are highly effective in alerting the general public.

When you find the subject, you should approach him from the front. Make eye-contact. Non-verbal body language is highly important with dementia subjects. After assessing safety, slowly move to the subject's side. Speak slowly and in simple, concrete terms. Break down commands, questions or directions into simple, easy-to-follow components. Touching, when appropriate, is helpful. Arguing with a person with dementia is pointless and may lead to a catastrophic reaction. Instead, redirect the person with a new line of reasoning. Telling the person that a favorite person or thing is waiting for him back at base may be acceptable. Keep in mind that other impairments associated with age, such as decreased vision, hearing, and walking ability, may also be present.

Summary

The following subject category algorithm provides us with a brief overview of a search:

1. Do any of the following external sources apply?
   abduction, air craft incident, natural disaster forces (such as wind, landslide, earthquake, flood water, etc.), urban entrapment, water
   If no, then…

2. Is the subject involved in an activity using wheels or tracks?
   ATV (QUAD), mountain bike, motorcycle, snow mobile, vehicle (if abandoned then apply cognitive rule.
   If no, then….

3. Does the subject have any cognitive disorders?
   Autism Spectrum Disorder, dementia (Alzheimer's), despondent, intellectual disability, mental Illness, brain injury
   If no, then….

4. Is the subject a child? (If a group, use the age of the oldest child in the group.)
   Ages 1-3
   Ages 4-6
   Ages 7-9
   Ages 10 – 12
   Ages 13-15 (also consider activity)
   If no, then…

5. Choose the activity that best matches the subject.
   anger, car camper, climber, gatherer, hiker, horseback, BASE Jumper, hunter, extreme sports, runner, skier, snowboarder, snowshoer, substance intoxication, worker.

Notes:

Figure 48 Track.

Chapter 7

Trackers

Objectives

- Recognize the need to develop clue awareness, track awareness and the higher tracking ability levels on your team.
- Understand that tracking abilities are needed by all searchers and comprehend how you can effectively use them on your search team's assignment.
- Appreciate and support the value of a successful tracker.

> *"Having a non-tracker decide whether tracking will work or not, is like having a painter decide whether or not surgery is required."*
>
> *Ab Taylor*

Wherever the subject has stepped, there *is* human sign. Each step taken by a person leaves some sign (footprint, crushed grass, etc.) and may leave thousands of clues. Tracking is therefore an important aspect of most searches.

When it comes to search and rescue missions we don't get to pick the route that our subject has traveled. The route has been chosen by our subject. If ever the analogy of following bread crumbs through the woods were truer, it is with tracking. We must understand and believe that wherever our subject has stepped; human sign has been left behind. There are *no exceptions* to this. Humans leave between 2000 – 3500 footfalls for every mile traveled. The individuals on your team may include a mixture of tracking skill levels. Each search team should have some level of tracking skill. The crew leader may find themselves with a team member that has higher skill ability in some aspects of tracking.

An effective Crew Leader will not need to be the "tracker" of the team but be able to take advantage of the team's collective tracking ability and will share the tracking tasks with the crew members that can best perform each task.

One of the leader's responsibilities will be doing a skill assessment of their team. This is easy if all of the team members are known to you. It is more difficult if the team is a mixture of personnel from different units. The presence of certifications or credentialing is a good place to start. A quick review of these and a glance at a *Tracking Log* should give a team leader a good handle on what to expect from their team when they offer their tracking skills.

Helpful Tracking Tips

- *Always* preserve your last good sign.

- Presume that there is a tracker with higher level of ability (or competent trailing K9) coming in behind you.

- Set your tracker egos aside – you are working on a team and working for the missing subject.

- Never allow your team to "jump track or soil the ground cover or environment until you (the tracker) think it is time.

- Know how to mark and in multiple ways protect the last known sign/step in mixed bare soil / ground cover environment.

- Become knowledgeable and plan a tactic to route trackers into a sign cutting task.

- When you have lost a track, re-acquire the line of sign without fouling the direction of travel.

Figure 49 Measuring a track.

The crew leader will have knowledge to direct or support (depending on crew leader's tracking skills) a tracking team in a proper tracking team formation. He/she will be able to detect the subject's sign, interpreting subject's sign, record pertinent sign information and think through proper tactics to trail this line of sign accurately and quickly.

Tracking Skill Sets

Breaking down SAR tracking we find it is made up of five distinctly different skill sets:

●**Detection** – the ability to perceive human sign (Clue and Track Awareness).

●**Interpretation** – the ability to make deductions about the human sign you see.

●**Recording** – the ability to record and communicate the pertinent information to other trackers and the CP.

●**Tactics** – the ability to read the terrain and come up with a plan to follow the subject using best practices that are accurate and quick. Sign cutting.

●**Trailing** – the ability to move forward on their subject's line of sign using best practices that are accurate and quick.

Each of these skill sets will develop at different rates within a novice tracker. Understanding where your tracker is in each set will guide you as to which tracking tasks to assign to which team member. An example would be to assign your tracker with the best ability to the sketch and measure task or recording the prime track. This may be your least experienced tracker – but one that is good at drawing.

Figure 50 Tracker.

Use Skills According to Ability

It is theorized that trackers need to spend at least 20 hours on each skill set to achieve a minimum proficiency. Five X 20 = 100 hours of honest "in the field" dirt time practice that may perhaps elevate the person and give them some credibility on a search. Ideally a member of your team that has achieved this training may make your team very effective on a search.
We find that a searcher possessing sufficient ability within any 1 of these 5 skill sets may start being called "the" tracker on a search team. Be cautious of bestowing this title too early on to someone in their search and rescue career. This title takes on a heavy burden because

the IC will count on their title to guide other search resources. Effective tracking of a subject can be achieved without the 'tracker' moniker. Do not bestow this title until you are sure that the person is ready to accept the additional responsibilities that will placed upon their shoulders.

Tracking Ability Levels

1. Clue Aware

In the beginning of our SAR ability path, we endeavor to have all our searchers become Clue Aware (CA). This is the first step towards becoming a searcher, as well as a tracker. This level can be achieved through constant training. This level can even be acquired through direct experience – time served on searches. Becoming Clue Aware is a development of mental focus and building perceptions of what object clues may "look like" in the field environments. Clue awareness *is knowing* what to look for and how best to "see" these items while on assignment. It is also knowing what factors may distract you from the focus while on assignment and dealing with these distractions immediately. CA is an ability that needs to be learned through experience and practice. You cannot learn it from a book or class room.

Figure 51 Shading a shoe track.

Figure 52 Are you clue aware? Can you spot the clue?

2. Track Aware

The second level for the tracking skills is Track Aware (TA). This is focusing the CA searcher more specifically towards human footfalls. TA level can usually be met after a searcher has taken the NASAR Fundamentals of Search and Rescue (FUNSAR) Course or a 4-8 hour tracking course that must include an element of Step-By-Step (S-B-S) practice. These experiences will lead to understanding thoroughly that "Wherever our subject has stepped, there *is* human sign," how to handle the footfall information, how to mark tracks and how to follow easy track-lines. The track awareness level can also be achieved through a mentoring process working with a tracker of reasonable skills and then followed by enough time practicing. Being *Track Aware* means that you can go from finding the clue, (CA) and then seeing, deducing, recording and following footfalls. In the beginning this will be for a short distance to re-establish the subject's direction of travel (DOT).

Figure 53 Tracker measuring with tracking stick.

3.

The next level of tracking is achieved through targeted independent study and experiential learning. This can be done through repeated 16-20 hour tracking courses such as the NASAR Fundamentals of Tracking (FUNTRACK), established tracking schools, state run courses, working with a mentor or even through individual practice. At this level, the basic tools, terminology and techniques that are needed by a tracker are learned. Developing this tracking core knowledge is important and your team members will need to hear and see a proper display of skills that will then need to be practiced to become proficient. Reading several of the available tracking books will be a good basis for this core knowledge.

All tracking training and search skills and performance should be well documented and logged in a *tracking log*. Documenting the practice through a tracker log allows the tracker to share the hours of practice with team leaders and SAR coordinators.

PLS/LKP Approach

Find prints/footfalls that could belong to our subject.

Deduct and isolate our subject's print.

Document subject print through sketching/picture/casting.

Determine direction of travel of subject.

Follow the subject's trail.

Assure contiguous line of sign from PLS/LKP.

Shorten time/distance factor utilizing sign cutting tactics.

SAR Tracking Tasks

Specific tasks the command staff may expect a tracker to perform include the following using the described techniques:

PLS Approach and Identifying Tracks

One of the first assignments on a search may be to identify a PLS/LKP/IPP approach. This assignment is crucial to a search mission and fraught with tons of expectations and responsibility. If you are the team with this assignment the IC/Search Manager is relying upon your team to offer up some direction of travel for the search and a specific track pattern that *all* of the other search teams need to be aware of and focused on while finding the lost person(s). You are identifying the type of bread (remember the breadcrumbs) that we will be following. If this is not done effectively the entire search becomes a big game of hide and seek, and we will need to be lucky instead of skilled.

Moving Forward on a Track Trail and Marking Found Tracks

Once you have a confirmed track at the PLS/LPK you will have a trail to follow. You must develop a tactic to best exploit this ultimate of search clues. Your tactic will vary based upon skill of your team, terrain, weather, time of day, age of track, soil conditions; the list is endless. The truth is you will need to make some judgment calls here. It is understandable that we need to speed up our travel to make up for the time lost during search set up. The subject (if still moving) can be counted on to add from ½ to 3 miles of distance for each passing hour.

Figure 54 Boot track.

Clearly seeing a single line of track off into the distance, barring your agency's protocol, you do not need to mark each track and you can advance to your farthest track seen. This changes rapidly if you are also clearly seeing cross traffic or even more importantly parallel traffic. Before you advance again, verify your prime track again.

Move fast and forward – *carefully*. Use 'out and around' sign cutting methods if terrain allows and it is safe to do so. Safe meaning that you reduce the risk of your team contaminating the line of sign.

Choices

If a higher skilled tracking team becomes available, suggest bringing them up to your position. Fall back to your agency's protocol or follow Step-By-Step (if this is not the case for your agency; it is strongly suggested to have this as your discipline) allowing other tracking teams to sign cut further ahead. S-B-S is the method of instruction used in many SAR tracking courses and remains as a valid tactic during a search, especially when terrain and soil conditions make it difficult to track. When the tracking is tough S-B-S is perhaps your only hope and it takes a skilled tracker to be able to achieve this persistently.

Figure 55 Grass Track.

What to Avoid

Avoid continuing up a trail (linear to your line of signs) hoping to "see" an easy "good" track. This is called "jump tracking" and should never be allowed on your team until you have allowed it. Mark your last good track and keep trying to continue S-B-S while trying to get a more skilled tracker to your location.

Avoid moving forward of the line of human signs that you have identified as belonging to your subject. You risk contamination of the trail of bread crumbs that are obviously tough to see.

Combining a K9 Asset with a Tracking Asset on your Team

Lost your track? Consider getting a trailing K9 to scent and run this track or, if they have a scent article, re-scent the dog and begin to follow via the K9's leadership. This tactic frees your trackers to perform a legitimate sign-cutting task; out around and far forward seeking out track traps and linear terrain features to use for guidance and documentation.

Summary

Obtain the training needed to perform tracking skills to the best of your ability or employ trackers whenever it is appropriate and they are available. They may be your best asset to determine a direction of travel or location of the missing person. As a method of review, find the sign on each of the pictures below?

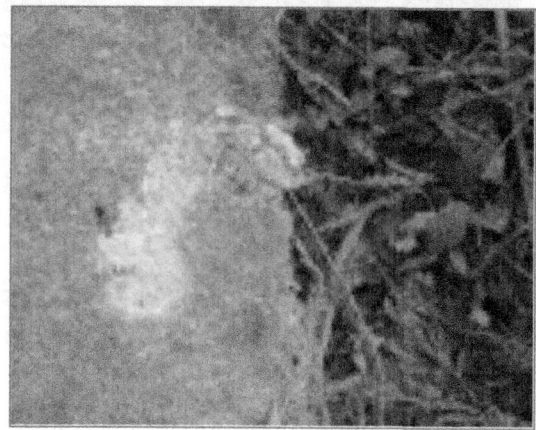

Signs & Clues.

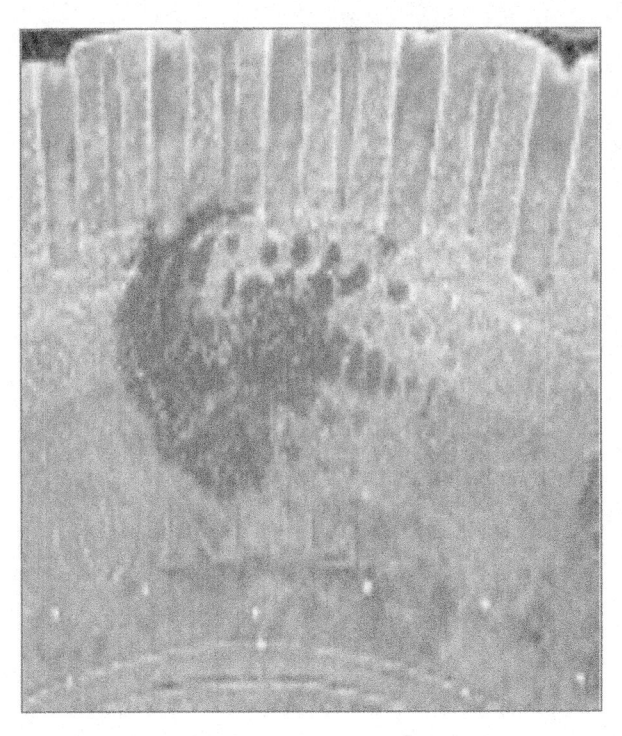

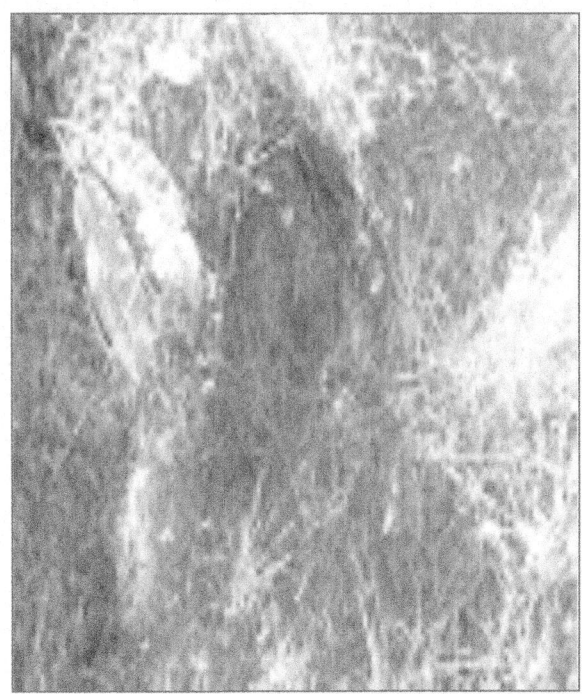

Figure 56 Sign and Clue Awareness.

Notes:

Figure 57 Canine.

Chapter 8

Canines & Equines

Objectives

- *Define each of the most common types of search and rescue dogs including Wilderness Air Scent, Trailing, Tracking, Human Remains Detection and Urban/Disaster search dogs.*
- *Understand the basics of scent theory as it relates to using a search and rescue dog and covering the assigned search segment in an effective manner.*
- *Understand the differences between a live find, cadaver and cross-trained dog as it relates to deploying each on a search.*
- *Define the FEMA concept of typing search dogs.*
- *List at least five best practices when working in the field with a search dog.*
- *Describe how to effectively collect a scent article for use by a search dog.*

To effectively deploy, lead, or search with a canine asset, one should have a working knowledge of search dogs. This section will provide an overview in order to allow the incident commander and his staff to order, deploy and utilize SAR dogs in an efficient manner, as well as, promote an effective working relationship with the Crew Leader in the field. Canine teams can help to locate the lost, day or night, and locate evidence in potential homicides such as clothing, weapons, or other items related to a crime.

Basically, all humans, alive or dead, give off microscopic particles containing the compounds in human scent. This scent changes shortly after death but can be preserved closer to a live scent for longer periods of time in cold conditions or drowning incidents. These scent clues help the dog to locate articles or the missing person.

In some circumstances it is not known whether the person is alive or deceased. In other situations, it is a known assumption that the person is no longer living (such as a witnessed drowning). A live find dog may be preferred on a disaster scene where live victims are the first priority to locate. A trailing dog may be the resource of choice if a positive *place last seen* is known. In other searches a human remains detection/cadaver dog may be deployed.

Some dogs are cross trained to identify both alive and deceased victims. The incident commander, planning and/or operations chief will normally determine what type of resource is needed and how to deploy the dog teams for the task at hand.

Figure 58 Trailing dog.

Types of Search and Rescue Dogs

Although many specialty SAR dogs are available (avalanche dogs, cave dogs, etc.) most search dogs are divided into three major categories...live find only, human remains detection only, and cross-trained dogs. (And yes, some dogs can and do switch from working a problem using an air scent technique to trailing technique...or vice versa, combining or switching from one discipline to another.) Generally, one can find the following types of trained search dogs available as resources:

Live Find Dogs – search for live persons.

•**Wilderness Air Scent Live Find Dogs – Non-Scent Discriminating:** are worked in primarily wooded environments, desserts, parks, etc.; dog is worked off lead. Will locate and alert on any human scent in the search segment. An Air Scent dog is defined by Scientific Working Group on Dogs and Orthogonal Detection Guidelines, SWGDOG, as "A dog using air scenting techniques to detect a trained odor."

•**Wilderness Air Scent Live Find Dogs – Scent Discriminating**: are able to differentiate between individuals when a properly collected scent article is preserved and available for the dog handler; primarily wooded environments, deserts, parks, etc.; dog is worked off lead.

Figure 59 Trailing Dog on lead.

- **Trailing Dogs** – work in any type of land environment. A place last seen must be identified and a properly collected scent article made available (if possible) to the dog handler. Often the dog handler prefers to collect their own scent article to avoid contamination by others. Trailing dogs may be worked on or off lead. The dog may actually trail parallel to the actual track of the person, sometimes as far as 50 feet from where the person actually walked; however, it will trail in the correct direct of travel.

At any given time the trailing dog may also track or air scent to the person using whatever method the dog chooses (trailing or air scenting) to locate the missing person at the end of the trail. A good trailing dog will always take the *freshest* scent - even if it is only fresher by 20 minutes. In the event of a lost person walking in circles and crossing the current trail the dog is on, the dog must be sure to turn in the correct direction on the freshest trail for that person. Trailing dogs have a greater window of deployment capable of locating the missing person's trail. They can even trail many hours or days after the subject has been reported missing.

- **Tracking Dogs** – work any type of land environment. A place last seen must be identified and a properly collected scent article made available (if at all possible) to the dog handler. This dog tracks foot-step by foot-step; the dog generally works on lead although a tracking dog may work off lead also.

Figure 60 Disaster Dog, FEMA certified.

- **Urban Search/Disaster Dogs** – USAR dogs work in an urban environment, including explosions, natural disasters, etc.; the dogs are trained to locate live victims only; these dogs have trained extensively on rubble and collapsed structures; the dogs are worked off lead and most often stay with the strongest source of scent digging and/or barking to indicate to the handler that they have located a strong source of live human scent. FEMA urban search and rescue dogs complete an intensive training regime and are assigned to one of the FEMA task forces throughout the nation. It often takes years of training for a search dog to reach that skill level. FEMA also certifies human remains detection dogs.

Figure 61 HRD Dog.

- **First Responder Dogs** – Usually involve using local search dogs that are deployed to disaster scenes immediately...usually within hours; they are available prior to the arrival of the FEMA dogs, if ordered. The first responder dogs respond and search natural disasters or explosions, etc.; these dogs have trained on rubble; may be live find only, human remains detection only, or cross-trained dogs; the dogs may be worked off or on lead but are usually worked "naked"... with no lead or collar to catch on the rubble.

●**Avalanche Dogs** – are trained to locate live or recently deceased persons under snow and/ or ice (usually cross trained dogs); they search on land; this is possible since the scent of the person rises to the surface of the snow through any air that may be trapped around the body. SWGDOG defines an avalanche dogs as, "A dog trained to search for, detect and/or locate people trapped in snow as a result of an avalanche."

●**Cave Dogs** – are trained to locate humans in a cave environment. This is a specialty area requiring extensive knowledge of caving and safety.

Figure 62 HRD dog indicates on bone.

Human Remains Detection Dogs

●**Human Remains Detection Dogs** – are usually worked off lead but may be worked on lead in certain situations. "These dogs are trained to find only human remains. Handlers should have training in crime scene preservation and burials, as well as scattered or disarticulated bones. They recognize all stages of human remains decomposition from dry bone to whole body. The searches might include remains like:

-Recent death to several weeks old.

-Older human remains with primarily or exclusively dry bones remaining.

-Burials – from recent to older burials of several years.

-Historic – 20 years to 250 years old and older; dry bone; however, a body on the surface of the ground can become skeletal in a matter of weeks or months depending upon the environmental and weather conditions. Dog teams primarily working older cases such as these will maintain their scenting threshold (ability to locate smaller amounts of HR scent such as dry bone) at these sensitive levels.

-Mass Fatalities – when dogs are able to indicate multiple victims where it is likely a mass burial/fatality; most often is the result of a disaster such as a hurricane, earthquake, or related event. In rare instances this will be a case involving historic remains such as victims buried many years ago.

-Water search – when dogs locate drowned victims in bodies of water; may include fresh and salt water; does not usually involve ocean recovery but may be used in the inland waterways for recovery of drowned victims; these dogs may be worked from the shore or from the deck of boats indicating to the handler when there is a human body under the water as the scent breaks the surface of the water.

Cross-Trained Dogs

Cross-trained dogs are those which alert on either live or deceased victims. The dogs may or may not have separate alerts depending upon the search situation and training. However, when the condition of the missing person is not known, the handler will determine which command (live or cadaver) seems most logical within the existing knowledge. Others are trained on the entire spectrum of human scent from live to deceased and given one command…just find the human. These dogs are usually worked off lead.

Figure 63 SAR Dog working in hazardous conditions.

Canine Typing according to the Department of Homeland Security

Canine teams and handlers are further "typed" according to the Department of Homeland Security into: Type I, II, III or IV based upon training, capabilities, available equipment, and certifications. The DHS currently recognizes the following disciplines:[9]

> **FEMA – DHS Dog Types**
>
> Avalanche Snow Air Scent
> Air Scent Dog
> Disaster Response Dog
> Land Cadaver Air Scent Dog
> Water Air Scent Dog
> Wilderness Air Scent Dog
> Wilderness Tracking/Trailing

K9 Performance Variations

Some dogs will range away from the handler to find the missing person; some on lead and some off lead. In other cases the dog will not return to the hander once he has located the missing subject. Instead he may be trained to stay with the missing person or strongest odor and bark or perform another trained behavior. In other training styles the dog is taught to return to the handler, perform his trained alert/indication behavior, and upon command by the handler, take the handler back to the missing person. Once the handler has recognized and identified the dog's alert and/or indication, he/she will inform the Team Leader and crew members. At this time, the Team Leader and navigator on the crew should note the location, perhaps flag the area quickly, and either wait until the handler returns to this area to resume searching or follow the handler as he/she responds to the dog information/scent information. If the Team Leader decides to remain at the said location, a crew member will be assigned to accompany the handler to the area the dog is indicating. Never allow the handler to move too far from the rest of the team without a fellow team member for safety reasons.

Often the entire crew will proceed in the direction indicated by the dog and handler. They may decide to return to this original location if the missing person is not located or stop to evaluate the terrain and environmental conditions which may be affecting the dog and his behavior. In any case, the Team Leader should consult with the dog handler to determine an appropriate course of action based upon recommendations by the dog handler.

---

[9] Refer to FEMA typing and descriptions for more information on each type and capability. www.fema.gov

A variety of training techniques are employed to train dogs. There is no one right or wrong way to train or work a search dog and it behooves a Team Leader to be aware of the types of SAR dogs and common working patterns through observation and training with dog handlers. The appropriate technique is the one which can be demonstrated to be reliable and accurate through certification processes and documented in training logs.

When to Request and Deploy a Search Dog

Search commanders are encouraged to order and deploy SAR dogs as early in the search as possible, especially before the search areas are heavily contaminated by other volunteers or family. This provides a more pristine environment for the scent conditions. However, search efforts should not be stopped while waiting on canine response since, depending on their location; it may take several hours to arrive on the scene. Consider requesting search dogs immediately upon notification that there is a search. It is better to have search dogs and handlers in route and turn them around if the missing person is found in short order than to waste valuable time trying to decide *if* a search dog is needed. They are almost always needed in a search for a missing person unless there is not a search area to be searched such as a "drive away" situation or missing from school (leaving school but not arriving home), or other similar case. In these scenarios, the search area is ROW (the rest of the world).

If a search area has been identified, a search dog is needed. Deploy search dogs as soon as it is determined that a person is indeed missing and there is a likelihood that the missing person may be in the identified area. You may also deploy search dogs even if it is yet undetermined that the missing person is in the immediate area.

Search dog handlers may arrive on scene with team mates who are comfortable flanking the dog handler and provide needed support services for the handler. The search commander will assign flankers for the handler and these folks are a good choice. Assign resources rapidly and also consider using law enforcement canine officers to flank SAR dog handlers when available. A team chief may provide information for the incident commander to facilitate the best assignment for each dog handler.

Search dogs can work during the day or night in most all types of environments, most types of weather and in all kinds of debris including woods, brush, natural and man-made disasters; and even water environments. They work in conjunction with multiple agencies and for all ages and types of missing persons.

Working with a Search Dog

In all cases, the Team Leader assigned to work with a handler and dog will need to have open and frequent communication with the dog handler throughout the mission. A thorough knowledge of the way each dog works, the environmental conditions, terrain, and search criteria will guide the handler as he/she suggests the most opportune way to search the assigned search segment.

If no PLS (place last seen) is known, or at the same time that the trailing dog is attempting to obtain a direction of travel from the PLS, command personnel can deploy an air scent dog team into an identified high probability of area (POA). This will likely be an area away from the PLS or adjacent to the known PLS but out of the area the trailing dog is presently working. The search area should be noted on a map with a copy given to the handler and have recognizable terrain borders such as roads, trails, hills, rivers, electric poles, ditches, etc.

Figure 64 Air Scent dog/handler working off lead.

The Team Leader will assign a crew member to navigate and keep the air scent team within the search segment unless the air scent dog has picked up the scent of the missing and needs to leave the search area to locate the missing person. Depending upon the terrain and the location of the neighboring dog teams or crews, the Team Leader will need to determine whether to call into the base to report a change of location, change of direction, change of search segment or request permission to do so. In some cases, operations and planning may wish to deploy additional teams in the direction that the dog is indicating scent if that is out of the currently assigned search segment. The correct action is never clear without many additional details which may be known collectively by the Team Leader, search managers and dog handler; another reason for open and frequent communication.

The air scent dog will work in whatever direction the handler indicates, often based upon wind direction and terrain features, effectively quartering the search area. Team members with the dog handler should always proceed about the same pace as the handler, if possible, always staying at least 10 to 20 feet behind the dog handler. The dog position will always (most often) be in front of the handler and in front of the other crew members. The dog may take a few minutes to sniff each person on his/her crew and quite instinctively know these are not the missing persons. This is sometimes done while still in base camp or at the beginning of the search mission. Once the dog begins to search, he normally would not spend much time checking back in with his fellow search crew members. If the dog does return to a search crew member, the member should simply ignore the dog and continue searching, looking for clues, or navigating just as he would with or without a dog on the search crew.

Once the dog has completed searching the assigned search segment, the handler will advise the Team Leader that the dog has completed his mission and make a recommendation as to whether it might be wise to cover the same area from another direction, recommend another crew search the same segment, or that the segment has been adequately covered by the crew.

Due to the working nature of the trailing dog they are not assigned a search segment because it is not possible to know where the scent trail will lead. If no tracks are evident/known and a direction of travel is not known for the missing person, but a place last scene is known, search managers can deploy a trailing dog team to the PLS providing a properly collected scent article for the trailing dog team. Handlers often prefer to collect their own scent article; this ensures a properly collected and uncontaminated scent article. Continue to preserve this scent article for other dog handlers who may be participating at a later time or during the next operational period.

Remember that a properly collected scent article is an appropriate article that has not been touched by any other person. It is collected using surgical gloves and stored in a paper bag away from other articles. Examples of good scent articles include pillow cases, shoes, dirty laundry (if not stored with other family member clothes), linens, clothes, or other items touched only by the missing person. Beware of items collected by family members as they will inadvertently touch the items before placing in bags...and never admit to touching the item. No one likes to admit they were the one who contaminated the scent article...it is best to let the handler collect it himself.

On lead trailing dogs will begin their search at the place last seen or last known point, with or without a scent article, and proceed in the direction of the scent...not having an assigned search segment. In those cases, the crew will follow the handler and dog at the pace set by the dog handler. In this search, the crew also stays 10 to 20 feet behind the dog and handler, slowing the pace as the dog handler slows the pace and stopping when the handler/dog stops. At the same time that the dog is moving / searching /trailing, the crew will be navigating, mapping, tracking, sign-cutting, and looking for clues as the pace permits. The dog handler should keep the Team Leader advised as to the dog effectiveness throughout the trail. These teams may cross in and out of areas that are being searched by an air scent team. The trailing team's movements and locations should be communicated to the air scent team in the corresponding area since the air scent dog may alert on them.

A trailing dog may be able to follow the trail all the way to the missing person or may "lose" the trail at some point due to a myriad of poor environmental conditions. If a trailing dog identifies a direction of travel but is unable to follow the trail to the missing person, air scent dogs can be deployed to this location.

If a trailing dog has identified a direction of travel, air scent dogs can be deployed ahead of the trailing team to help bring a quicker resolution to the search. The scent from the forward deployed air scent teams will not interfere with the trailing team because their scent is not the scent of the missing person.

If the dog is unable to pick up a direction of travel, the dog is usually returned to another point last seen or last known place to try to determine if "that" is the last point. These will usually be identified by planning and operations chiefs or other search managers. If no direction of travel is identified, the dog may be returned to the staging area and the crew reassigned to another search area, with or without a dog. Remember, no direction of travel may also indicate that the person has not entered this area or is no longer in this area. This may be important information for the search operations to determine future search segments and missions.

If tracks or the footsteps of the missing person are identified, man trackers can be deployed to follow the tracks. Dog teams can be assigned just ahead of the trackers to determine if there is a direction of travel or air scent available. If the dog handlers identify tracks ahead of the man trackers, search commanders can leap frog the trackers to the dog team location and place dogs ahead of the trackers once again. Regardless of the technique used, the tracks should always be identified so easily spotted and flankers and dog handler/dog team avoid destroying them or the immediate area where additional tracks may be located as much as possible.

General K9 Do's and Don'ts

1. When there is evidence that the missing subject may likely be in a given area or search segment, try to *keep others out of this area* until a scenting dog has been deployed and had the opportunity to work the area, if a dog team is available in a timely manner.

2. In a building *shut the door of the missing subject's room*. This both protects any evidence in the room but also lessens cross-contamination by the family until the dog handler can secure their scent articles. (Note: Normally one of the first things

the missing person's family may do is clean the room which can cause problems down the road for law enforcement and the K9 teams.)

3. When *collecting scent articles, follow appropriate protocol* by using surgical gloves and protecting the scent article from further contamination. Allow the dog handler to collect his/her own scent article if at all possible and they request such. Use paper bags to store scent articles and preserve them for future dog handlers who may come to the scene at a later time or operational period.

4. Provide a well-ventilated area for search dogs to stage in base camp *away from gasoline, motor oils and vehicle exhaust.* Store search scent articles away from these fumes.

5. *Call in the search dogs immediately* during a search mission. *Consult with team leaders/ Chief to determine the best use of each dog/ handler* of that team or a recommendation to another team member who knows the capabilities and training of that dog/handler when available. Ask if they have a preference on flankers and assign navigation savvy individuals as flankers for each dog/handler team. Police or law enforcement dog handlers are often happy to work with volunteer SAR dog handlers in the field.

6. Dog teams are *most effective during temperatures between 40 degrees and 80 degrees.* Consider deploying dog teams during these optimal temperatures and allowing them to rest during extreme temperature times, if possible. However, dogs can and do work in temperatures above and below these levels quite effectively.

7. *Provide a decontamination area for the dog* and handler to decontaminate the dog if needed. This might include a water supply (hose), oil cutting detergent such as DAWN, and towels, as well as, assistants to aid in the cleaning process.

8. *Provide a water supply for dogs* to be cooled down in extreme heat conditions. This might involve a small child swimming pool filled with cool water or ice misting machines.

9. *Ask the handler for his/her recommendations* on future searching of the search segment when they have completed their search area. Determine hazards and the need to research the area based upon, handler recommendations. If the handler recommends, deploy another dog crew to search the same area if available resources permit. Otherwise deploy a ground team to research the area if resources are available to do so.

10. The direction of air movement is important to the efficiency of the dog/handler team; therefore *allow the dog handler to determine the appropriate direction to search the segment* based upon temperatures, air movement, and terrain features. When in doubt, ask the handler.

Scent Articles

When collecting a scent article always use sterile gloves to collect a scent article. Never touch the scent article with your hands or other part of your body. Never trust that someone else has not touched the scent article. If you have the option of collecting a new article or make scent pads preserving the original scent source using the technique below:

1. Place sterile gauze deep down into the toe of a shoe or the inside sleeve of a coat. These two items are most likely not contaminated and will provide the best source of scent for a scent specific dog like a trailing, tracking or air scent – scent discrimination dog.

2. Allow the gauze or scent pad to rest for 15 to 30 minutes. Remove with gloved hands and place inside a zip lock bag to protect it from contamination by any other scent.

Other sources would include anything which might contain the DNA of the person such as cigarette butts, chewing gum, etc. Make sure the collector asks if anyone else has worn or used the item. Children, of a similar size, will wear each other's clothing or coats. The same holds true for some adults. Tooth brushes are good, also jewelry worn by the subject on a regular basis such as a wrist watch or necklace. Other sources which may be used are Kleenex, underwear, or clothing. We are not 100% sure what the dogs are capable of scenting but experienced trailing handlers have long used these types of items with success.

With proper training, the trailing dog can use these types of articles. Ask the handler for suggestions on scent sources or allow the handler to collect their own article. Place article or sterile gauze in a paper bag. Roll down bag to close it tightly. Place in an unused/low to no traffic area to avoid contamination. If not wet or damp, items can be stored in a zip-lock bag. If wet or moist, use a paper bag. *Do not use plastic trash bags.* Store it in an unused/low traffic area.

Multiple gauze pads can be made in order to be able to provide a scent article to each dog handler and not be concerned that it is returned. Individual scent pads can be placed in zip lock bags and taken with the handler into the field.

Figure 65 K9 Training with a mannequin.

Trained, Reliable and Certified Dog Handler Teams

All dog teams requested and used on a search should be trained, reliable and certified. In addition they should show the agility, dependence, endurance and ability to provide search services. They must be able to perform in all types of safe weather conditions and be able to respond to emergencies. Most often the SAR dog handler is a member of a recognized and reputable unit where they train regularly and document their training activities. Training regularly usually means an industry standard of at least 16 hours per month. Documenting their training activities usually involves keeping a log of training activities and results. Certification can be within a team unit that has documented standards in place or other reputable agency or organization. These standards should be in line with nationally recognized standards for organizations such as NASAR (National Association of Search and Rescue), IPWDA (International Police Work Dog Association), NAPWDA (North America Police Work Dog Association), or other state organizations supporting SAR.

Training Standards

Handlers should be proficient in land navigation, map and compass, radio communications, wilderness survival and first aid for humans and the dog. They should carry minimum equipment into the field for the conditions. Many handlers choose to earn NASAR technician certifications demonstrating their field skills. NASAR field certifications include the SAR Tech I (highest level), SAR Tech II, and SAR Tech III.

Most resources are placed in the area of highest probability as determined by the command planning and operations personnel. However, it is the dog handler and Team Leaders who make recommendations during debriefing which can greatly influence these decisions. The assigned search segment is the area where it makes the most sense that the person may be located based upon lost person behavior, characteristics of the lost person, terrain, past experiences, dog reactions, handler recommendations and other factors.

How to Find and Request SAR Dog

SAR dogs can be any breed but are primarily the working, herding and sporting breeds. Under no condition should the dog be aggressive toward humans or other dogs. Most often the dog has reached at least one year of age, has documented extensive training, and passed some type of certification test for the discipline to be deployed.

Ideally, local search resources should be identified prior to the need. However, search dog teams are located across the nation and most often known by the state agencies, especially the departments of emergency management and police agencies. Often, a call to the 9-1-1 communication center will provide available resources and if not, a call to the state emergency management offices will lead to viable and reliable resources.

Under no circumstances should an IC deploy a dog handler team which just "shows up" on scene, looks like a searcher, has a dog, and offers his services. These would be considered self-deployed individuals who may or may not possess the skills needed to provide services. If in doubt about the credibility of the individual, ask for training records, logs, and certifications as well as references (and check those references before deploying.) The last thing an IC wants is an unaccounted for resource who also gets lost. Make sure you are using reliable, trained and certified resources.

Most SAR dog handlers do not charge for their services; however, if at all possible, consider assisting the handler with food provisions, lodging (which may be a bunk house in a fire department), and some gas for the return trip home. These are always much appreciated and help the handler to defer the expense of responding to a search, often taking time off from work and family. However, be wary of SAR dog handlers who charge huge upfront fees and guarantee results. Charlatans abound in every arena and search is no exemption. Anyone can buy a SAR dog vest…make sure your resource is credible.

Figure 66 Water Search.

Canine Summary

Debrief the dog handler thoroughly after completing the search segment to obtain information which is valuable for future operations and planning. Assist with obtaining veterinary services, in consultation with the handler, if needed. Take care of your canines (shelter, lodging, water, medical services, rest, etc.) just as you would your searchers … they are a valued part of the team.

Team Leaders are ultimately responsible for the safety and return of all crew members and dogs. If it is necessary, because of environmental or physical conditions, the Team Leader should terminate the search, returning all personnel back to base. This may be due to injury, weather, performance, or other issues.

Dog teams are a resource that can search a large area more effectively and more efficiently than ten times the number of ground pounders. Remember that the canine team is but one resource used during a search but if used safely and properly can provide important information including direction of travel; and, quite possibly find the missing person in an efficient and timely manner.

The Mounted Unit – Using Equines in SAR

"Horses speak to us every day. Their voice cannot be heard, but their communications are strong."[10]

Objectives

- *Gain an understanding of the preparation of the Mounted Unit and necessary gear.*
- *List at least three ways to effectively use a Mounted Unit during a search.*
- *Understand how the rider can interpret the communication from the horse in locating persons or scent.*
- *Recognize safety concerns when using equines in SAR.*

The Mounted Unit is designed to support and supplement search resources to the ground pounder and K9 units of the search. This unit is often a component of the SAR team and the riders are often expected to train and certify in the same fashion as the K9 handlers in that they are "searchers first" and riders second. In other areas, the Mounted Unit operates as an independent SAR team…composed of primarily horses and riders. "By taking advantage of the keen senses that horses possess, we add an important tool in the SAR toolbox. As a prey animal, they have a great understanding of their environment and are constantly in tune with their surroundings. These qualities in the horse combined with a trained rider provide a tremendous advantage on a SAR mission."[11]

"Due to the exceptional hearing of the horse, they are able to detect sounds that a human might miss. From a rustle in the bush, a kitten's meow or a muffled cry for help, most horses will hone in on that sound. It is up to the trained rider to notice the change in the horse's behavior."

"Horses' ears can move 180 degrees using 10 different muscles (compared to three muscles for the human ear). This enables the horse to single out a specific area to focus their attention. This unique anatomical feature allows horses to focus on the direction from which the sound is coming, isolate it, and alert his rider. It becomes a valuable tool in the SAR world."[12]

---

[10] North Georgia Mounted Search and Rescue Team. Capabilities of Mounted Search and Rescue Powerpoint. May 16, 2013.
[11] IBID.
[12] IBID.

Equine Certification and Readiness

Horses selected for the mounted unit should be expected to pass a Mounted SAR Horse Certification Test prior to being used or deployed as a search and rider unit. Ideally, all riders should have completed their Search and Rescue Technician III certification prior to requesting testing/evaluation as a mounted resource. These testing standards will vary with region and type of searching primarily done but will help to verify the rider knowledge and readiness for search in conjunction with other SAR assets.

Equine Safety and Liability

The ultimate responsibility for the care, behavior, and safety of the horse is that of the rider. All members should be watchful for possible injury to equines or damage caused by the horse. The Mounted Unit director should maintain a file on each horse to include:

- Copy of current Coggins Test.[13]

    The Coggins Test is for a virus called "Equine Infectious anemia – EIA. There is no vaccine or cure and it is more common in warm, wet regions of the United States. There are three stages and the horse may take over a month to test positive where between 30 to 50% of horses infected will die within two to four weeks of showing initial symptoms. The results of the Coggins Test should be with the horse trailer at all times.

    In addition, it is recommended that the horse be vaccinated for rabies in addition to regular immunizations and be in good apparent health.

- Documentation of birth date, rider's name, owner's name and horse's name.

- Certification Records.

- All horses should be compatible with people, dogs, and other horses.

- All horses must be transported humanely.

- Riders should also maintain a training log.

---

[13] Petracek, Ron. What is the Coggins Test? http://ezinearticles.com/?What-Is-the-Coggins-Test?&id=509657

Training Sessions

All riders should be responsible for participating in training sessions on a regular basis and maintaining logs of training, missions and certification. It is recognized and accepted that a rider/mounted unit is a very specialized search function and requires specialized training and practice to maintain certification status and readiness level. Therefore, riders should be required to participate in a minimum number of mounted/team training sessions per quarter/year.

Figure 67 Horse relaxed.

Responding to a Search

When responding to a search, the horse shall remain in the horse trailer until such time as the rider has logged into the staging/command post area and determined whether the mounted unit is needed in this location or would best serve a search function to be transported to another nearby area. Horses shall remain under the control of the rider at all times.

Required Equipment

The rider shall provide for the needs and care of the horse to include:

-Horse feed and water for a minimum of 24 hours.
-Necessary medications.
-Equine first aid kit.
-Appropriate Tack.
-Extra halter and lead rope.
-SAR Gear: day pack and equipment as required by the Search Commander or other authority having jurisdiction during the search, and modified for the riders and environment.

The North Georgia Mounted Search and Rescue Team compiled the following information which may be helpful in the deployment of Mounted Units:

1) Mounted searchers are trained to "Look Where the Horse Looks." Horses will exhibit behavior to indicate "*something*" is different. With practice, the rider can determine if the horse has sensed the presence of a person, an animal, a sound, sees something at a distance or senses danger.

Example: Beyond the trees, almost ¼ mile away, a car begins to move in a small parking lot. One quarter mile (¼ mile) is equivalent to four football fields. Did he see it....hear it....or both?

Horses have a number of adaptations that allow them to visually outperform humans in dim light. They are able to function under a greater range of lighting conditions which gives them a more panoramic view of the search area. With their acute ability to detect movement, they can instantly change their focus from near to far objects. A horse alerted to sound or movement will automatically indicate to the rider the exact direction of that sound or sight based on their body language.

Figure 68 Horse detecting change. Sees or hears something?

2. "Equine Scent Training" is gaining interest in several MSAR units. Working along with K-9 units, the horse and dog can detect an array of smells. Since a horse cannot bark or alert like a canine, it is up to the trained rider to recognize the signs and behavior of his horse.

Not all MSAR horses are formally scent-trained. Many riders depend solely on their horse's acute sense of smell to pickup anything out of the ordinary, not necessarily pick out a specific scent.

Figure 69 Horse heads toward smell then finds bucket with source material.

A trained SAR horse can pick their way through rough terrain, brush and tall grass. They can search on known trails, ridges, drainages and also locate unmapped trails. Horses are often able to go into areas that are inaccessible to ATV's and vehicles.

3. SAR horses are also very agile and have the ability to cross creeks and traverse to high elevations easier than vehicles or ATV's.

Mounted SAR teams have several capabilities but are not deployed as a single rider/horse team. They are always deployed in a strike team, often with three horses/riders working together. Some of the advantages to a Mounted crew are that they:

-Have an elevated view with a broader view and able to see farther than on land. (I.e. sweep width for a rider is larger than a ground searcher.)

-Have the ability to cover a larger area in a shorter amount of time, conserving energy of the K9 units and ground searcher.

-Are able to conduct grid/line searches either on horseback or with ground searchers providing another viewpoint from horseback.

Figure 70 Horses in Line Search...close together for training purposes.

-Can do containment, perimeter searches, establish trail and road blocks, or a hasty search of a designated area or grid in a quick time frame. When working along perimeters and other containment assignments, teams can create 360 degree coverage by stationing themselves head-to-tail. This creates 4 sets of eyes looking in all directions.

Mounted Units can:

- act as an attraction and be comforting to the lost person,
- act as a relay,
- provide unique self defense capabilities providing the rider with a quick escape in a dangerous situation, and
- provide transportation if the person is not afraid or allergic. (They can be transported via horse back to base or the closest extraction point for motorized transport.)

Several safety precautions are taken into account when transporting another person including: ensuring the person is secure in the saddle, ensuring the person does not have a traumatic injury, using a safety helmet, and the handler is in control of the horse at all times.

Figure 71 Horse hearing from the distance...sight or sound?

Safety Considerations when Using a Mounted Unit[14]

When operating with mounted teams, there are several things to consider:

- Never touch one of the horses without permission of the rider.
- When approaching, be sure to announce your presence and have the rider acknowledge.
- Never approach too close to the rear of a horse. Leave a distance of at least 10 feet between you and the back of a horse. *While SAR horses are well trained, there is no guarantee that the horse will not kick.*
- Remember the two blind spots of the horse-behind the tail and the forehead.

Other considerations:

- Each truck/trailer takes up a significant footprint.
- Relatively flat areas are important for parking the rigs.
- Ideal would be to have an area where a small pen can be put up.
  However, it is not absolutely necessary. Horses can be tied to the trailers or cobbled.

Summary

In summary, with a trained horse and rider, you gain:

- a second set of eyes and ears that are more sensitive than humans,
- an elevated view,
- an extended search range in shorter time periods, and
- a mobility in rough terrain.
- The horses keen sense of hearing, vision and smell,
- an ideal hasty team,
- a team able to conduct guide/line searches with fewer searchers,
- additional containment/road block capabilities,
- a vehicle for transportation of lost persons in rough terrain,
- an attraction object.

---

[14] IBID.

Figure 72 Mounted and Ground Searcher

Figure 73 Hazardous Terrain.

Chapter 9

Hazardous Terrain Safety

Objectives

- *Be able to explain the differences between low-angle operations and high-angle operations in hazardous terrain.*
- *In a low angle environment, demonstrate the safe movement of a crew member over hazardous terrain using a rope system.*
- *Understand and direct a team in proper litter movement over hazardous terrain.*

When it comes to search and rescue missions we don't get to pick the terrain. In practice the more inhospitable the terrain the more likely we are to have a mission there. As a crew leader you must move yourself, your crew and your patients safely through this terrain.

There is a difference between high angle terrain and simply a hazardous terrain. High angle terrain is defined as a very steep environment in which a person is primarily supported by the rope system. One or more ropes are *necessary* to prevent the involved persons from falling.[15] Low angle terrain is defined as a flat or mildly sloping area, in which a person is primarily supported by the surface and not the rope system. One or more ropes *may* be used for safety or lowering. Imagine a staircase, with many steps and a handrail on one side. If we use ropes to construct a "handrail" to keep us from slipping it is a *low angle* system. If we must use ropes to construct the "stairs" it is a *high angle* system. When we ascend or descend stairs we hold onto the handrail but our weight is on the actual stairs since we merely use the handrail to keep from slipping. Any terrain beyond *low angle* or *simply hazardous* is beyond the scope and practice of this material and should not be attempted without additional training, equipment and preparation.

---

[15] Hudson & Vines. <u>High Angle Rescue</u>. P 2. C. 2004.

So, what are we talking about? We are addressing the efficient movement of people and patients across, up or down terrain that could be crossed without a rope system but having the rope system provides a backup in case of a slip or stumble. It allows us to move quickly and efficiently without having to take extra precautions to prevent any slip or fall. In a low angle environment the rope keeps you from rolling down the slope if you lose your footing. You simply land on your rear, get up and move on. When moving a patient in a litter the rope system prevents the litter from becoming a run-away roller coaster down the slope, if some mishap were to occur.

The low angle rope system is a system somewhat like a chain. The strength of the entire system rests on the weakest link. The links are the anchor, the hardware, the rope, and the operator. If one fails; they all fail.

The Anchor[16]

The crew leader must construct a suitable anchor for the system. The simplest solution is to rig to a nearby well-placed tree. Wrap the rope three turns around the tree and connect the end. This is a tensionless hitch anchor and results in the highest strength available.

There are some cautions: First make sure the tree is alive and has suitable root strength to hold the load. *Trees growing at the tops of cliffs are trying to survive in very shallow soils and often tenuous conditions.* The forces in a wrapped tree can 'unscrew' a poorly rooted tree from the ground. This tensionless rig is suitable if all you need is a fixed line.

If we need to do something more we must rig a separate anchor. Using your 20 foot long, one-inch tubular webbing piece, wrap the tree loosely three times and tie the ends using a water knot with overhand backup safety knots. Place the knot against the tree trunk and pull the other two loops outward. Clip the carabiner into these two strands of webbing. This anchor rig is called a wrap three pull two system. This type of rigging can be used on large rocks or object. If additional webbing is needed add length by tying an additional 20 foot webbing piece together. Always tie your webbing with a water knot and an overhand back up knot.

The Hardware

Carabiners are used to connect things together. In these rescue systems, only locking carabiners should be used. Carabiners have a strong and a weak axis. They can hold a tremendous load pulled end-to-end with the gates secured. They can be extremely weak if loaded sideways or if the gate is accidentally opened. Always load carabiners lengthwise and check the locking gate.

If you are simply rigging a fixed low angle anchor, any locking carabiner will do. However, if you are going to utilize a Munter hitch to manage the load on a rope, then you

---

[16] See Anchor figures in Appendix H.

need to use a properly shaped carabiner to facilitate this process. A pear-shaped carabiner, or technically called an HMS carabiner, is best suited for Munter hitch operations.

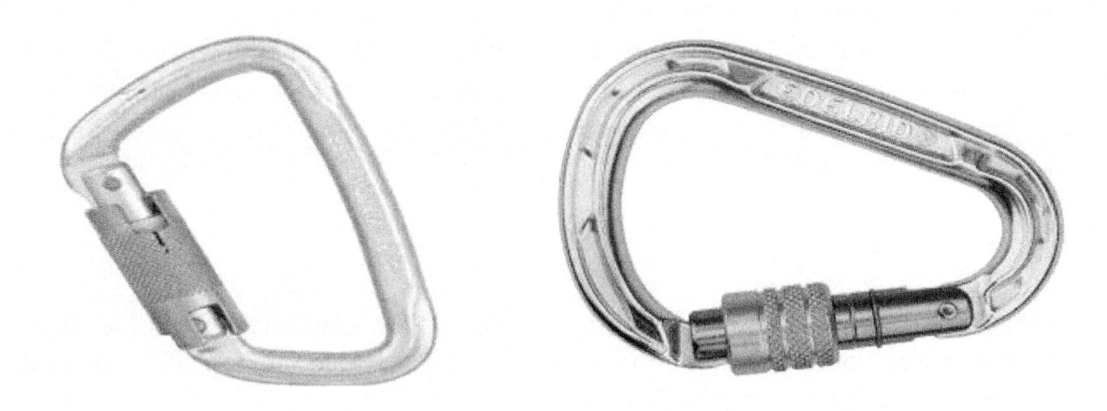

Figure 74 D-shape and pear-shape carabiner.

In addition, never load a carabiner over the edge of a drop off, timber or other potentially abrasive item/object.

The Rope

For low angle rigging, as described here, only a single person load is acceptable. Larger loads go beyond this scope and fall into the realm of high angle rigging. Suitable rope for a single person rescue load is 11mm (7/16 inch) or 10 mm static kernmantle nylon rope. An 11mm rope means the breaking strength (MBS) is 30kN/6744 lb. A 10mm rope MBS is 27 kN/6070 lb. Both fall within the limits for a light use rescue rope as set forth in NFPA[17] standard 1983-2001 of 20kN/4496. It should be noted however that NFPA 1983-2001 states in paragraph 1.1.2: "This standard shall not apply to rope and equipment used for special rescue operations including but not limited to mountain rescue, cave rescue, lead climbing operations, or where

---

[17] NFPA. National Fire Protection Association. http://www.nfpa.org/

specific rescue situations dictate other performance requirements."[18] Suitable lengths for hazardous terrain are 75 feet if using 11mm (7/16 inch) or 100 foot rope using a 10mm rope. Both would weigh the same and would be manageable lengths for low angle evolutions.

The Operator

Different hazardous terrain operations call for different skills. People or loads can go down, up, or traverse sideways so the operator must possess several different skills. Rappelling is a high angle skill and beyond the scope of this program. As a crew leader you may be called upon to move either a load or personnel down a slope. This operation is called a top brake lower. Gravity is often your friend.

To Move a Crew *Down*

Select and rig a suitable anchor, rig your pear-shaped carabiner into the anchor sling. Make absolutely sure your rope is long enough to reach a stable landing spot out of harm's way. If *any* doubt exists, the operation becomes a high angle exercise and suitable training experience and equipment are required to proceed.

Each crew member should don their tied field expedient harness, finished off with their locking carabiner. The crew leader should inspect each crew members rig prior to descent.

A figure eight on a bight with an overhand backup should be tied in each end of the rope. The knot should be constructed with a small loop suitable for clipping in a carabiner. Overall knot length should be kept short.

The main line should be attached to the anchor rigging with a Munter hitch using the pear-shaped carabiner. The operator must wear leather palm gloves suitable to manage the rope and impart additional friction, if needed. The main line should be clipped into the crew members' carabiner on their harness.

Communicate intentions (high angle belay commands are appropriate) and begin the operation. The crew member should lean back into the rope but keep sufficient weight on their feet to maintain footing. Feet should be placed as widely apart as is comfortable to prevent tipping over. The crew member should move down the slope at a steady brisk pace.

Upon reaching the safe landing the crew member will communicate, unclip from the carabiner, and then untie the terminal knot leaving the mainline end free to travel back up the slope. The crew member moves out of the way and communicates, ready for the next person.

The crew leader attaches the other figure eight knot to the second crew member reverses the Munter hitch and repeats the operation. This speeds up the operation as the rope need not be hauled back up the slope to reset the operation. When the free end reaches the top they need only to re-tie the figure eight and attach the third crew member.

---

[18] NFPA 1983-2001 states in paragraph 1.1.2

Upon completed movement of the crew the crew leader has several options to de-rig the equipment by:

1. doning the equipment and then carefully descend the slope, minimizing fall exposure,
2. using the line doubled around a tree and proceed using both ends of the rope as a hand line, or

3. if another trained person is present and rope length is sufficient, lower from the bottom and either sacrifice the top rigging or utilize a tree to pass the rope around. When the crew leader reaches the bottom, simply untie knots and pull one end of the rope.

To lower a litter over this same slope can present enormous problems. If we put the patient in a litter and have six people attach themselves to that litter, then, using a single rope attempt to lower this load we can create a worst case scenario for a rope evolution. For the sake of calculations let's assume everyone weighs 200 pounds. The patient plus six handlers equals a total weight of 1400 pounds. While negotiating the slope, if they slip off a three foot high ledge and shock load the system, this could easily double the load that all the components must handle. Now our total load is 2800 pounds. Over a ton! This is a serious high angle rope rigging problem and it is on a slope we can almost walk up or down. How do we deal with this in our low angle/hazardous terrain context?

First, we make sure the load stays at one person (200 pounds) then we place crew members on the slope situated where they are stable and able to handle a litter without slipping or having to move. Remember crew members *can* negotiate this slope without a rope. If a rope is required to support them, the evolution becomes a high angle problem. Crew members can even sit and pass the litter over their laps. The rope is rigged to the head of the litter. A Munter hitch is used to control the progress of the litter down the slope. The litter can be stopped mid-slope, crew members then move safely down the route and repeat the passing until the bottom is reached. The rope, with its Munter hitch belay, is a 'safety device' so in the event someone loses their grip or their footing gives way, the patient in the litter stays put on the slope. They may bump or jostle but they don't make a wild ride onto the rocks below in their litter (now a sled). Simply reverse the operation to move a patient litter up a slope. (See belay commands in Appendix H.)

To Move a Crew *Up*

As a crew leader you need to get the rope to the top of the slope. The easiest way is to carefully scramble up the slope trailing the rope behind you. Upon reaching the top rig the rope to a fixed anchor point. Crew members should don their field expedient harness and affix a Prusik[19] rope to the main line; then attach it to the harness carabiner.

The crew member should then communicate and move up the slope following the main line. Care should be taken not to grasp the main part of the Prusik knot. The proper method is to grasp the 'handle' of the knot, push in to loosen the coils slightly and move it up the rope. If a climber grasps the knot directly, then falls, the basic instinct is to grasp the knot preventing it from engaging. When all crew members are safely up, simply pull the rope up and move on.

To move a litter up we see the same issues as in lowering. A *Munter Hitch Belay* can keep the litter from becoming a run-away sled if someone slips or loses grip.

To Move a Crew *Across* a Slope

Brief the crew and have them don their field expedient harness and have their Prusik knot sling at the ready stage. Don your field expedient harness. In one end of the rope, tie a figure eight on a bight with an overhand back up and rig a tensionless hitch to a suitable anchor using a locking carabiner to finish the hitch. In the other end, tie a figure eight stopper knot. Instruct the designated last crew member to cross, how to de-rig the tensionless hitch, and attach it to their harness when directed to do so.

As crew leader attach your Prusik knot to the line and climb across the slope diagonally and carefully, playing out the rope as you go, moving the Prusik knot along. If the slope is such that if in moving across to set the far anchor point, a slip would cause you to tumble down the slope until caught by the rope, then crossing this slope becomes a high angle evolution which requires additional training, equipment and practice and is beyond the scope of this procedure.

Upon reaching the far side and stable ground, disconnect your Prusik knot and field expedient harness. Locate a suitable anchor, construct a webbing anchor (W3P2) attach your pear-shaped carabiner and tie a Munter hitch. Pull slack from the main line but *do not* pull tension or make it tight. Maintain the Munter hitch.

Points to Ponder

- Can we wait for a litter/medical team to arrive?

- Do we have enough help to safely move the patient?

- Will patient comfort and safety be enhanced by waiting?

- Will the crew safety be enhanced by waiting or moving immediately?

- Do we need to begin movement NOW to keep our patient alive?

- Are there hazards we need to cross in daylight?

---

[19] Prusik. The knot is named after Dr. Karl Prusik who described it in 1931 in an Austrian mountaineering journal. Correct style is to spell with a capital "P;" correct is: Prusik knot.

Communicate to the far side and have team members attach their Prusik knot to the line and move carefully across one at a time. When all are across except the designated last member, communicate and have them de-rig and stow the tensionless hitch and then attach the line directly to their harness using a figure 8 on a bight with an overhand back up knot. When ready they move across the slope as you belay with the Munter hitch already rigged in the rope. Upon the last crew member safely reaching your side, de-rig the anchor and stow the main line. Have them de-rig the tensionless hitch and stow the gear. Then tie a figure eight on a bight in the rope, back this knot up with a safety knot and attach it to their harness.

To move a patient in a litter across a slope, affix a loop with a carabiner which can be affixed to each end of the litter. The crew can position themselves in stable positions and pass the litter across. The rope system acts as a backup safety just in case someone slips or loses their grip. If the litter is supported by the main line, not the crew members, the evolution becomes a high angle exercise and additional training, practice, and equipment is necessary and is beyond the scope of this procedure.

Patient Transport

Hazardous terrain may be a hindrance to rescuers but to an injured or exhausted patient it is an absolute barrier. Patient condition and terrain conditions dictate the choices we have in moving our patient towards help. A patient with a broken arm can walk slowly toward civilization. A more seriously injured patient must be packaged for transport and carried. Even if a helicopter evacuation is to be used, the patient must be packaged and moved to the LZ or pick up point.

Patient condition and the risk/benefits of various strategies weigh in during the decision process of how and when to move the patient. Above all we must do no harm to our patient. Because of the distances, terrain and time delays in a wilderness setting, for the most part, patients are stable or dead. Time to a hospital is not measured in minutes but hours or even days so take time to make a wise decision.

If the decision is made to begin movement immediately, the first and foremost concern should be: is the medical condition of our patient such that, with our improvised patient care and litter, we can safely move toward help? With the gear we have, can we fashion a suitable patient litter? We have nylon webbing, shelter tarps, jackets, tracking poles, and the always useful duct tape. Nearby small green trees can be sacrificed and a litter fashioned. Wilderness medical courses cover litter construction and the NASAR SAR Tech I and II equipment recommendations provide a wonderful assortment of useful materials to assemble a litter.

If we wait for a litter we can use many of the items we have to protect the patient and begin to prepare for transport. We are going to build a giant patient burrito. When the litter arrives we must prepare it before we place the patient on board. The patient package consists of several parts, in addition to the actual litter.

Near the patient, preferably in a flat open place, position the litter with the head slightly uphill. First position: Use one or two shelter tarps to act as the outside cover when everything is closed up. It is usually best to offset the tarps to one side so the final opening is on one side of the litter.

Next build the insulation layer, a sleeping bag or blankets with a foam pad underneath, if possible. Now is time to add the patient. Remember the patient is going to be in this contraption for quite some time. Remove bulky items from back pockets, loosen boot laces, empty the bladder if possible or add an adult diaper. Do not package with a helmet as the increased height of the head can severely occlude the patients airway. Place a pair of goggles on the patient. As we package and then carry this package all manner of debris, sweat and trash are going to fall upon our patient. They cannot protect their eyes while strapped on their back so we must do it. If in the patient extrication, there would be the occasion to lift the litter by rope, add a field expedient harness to the patient now and have a loop exit the package near the patients head. Place padding underneath the knees, between the legs, small of the back, under the neck and behind the head. [20] Remember our patient is going to spend a lot of time in this litter; they are already injured so do not add to their suffering. Now close the burrito, fold the tarps carefully to seal the package, and, using webbing, lash the patient onto the litter.

Figure 75 Litter Handling.

---

[20] High Angle Rescue Techniques, Hudson & Vines, MosbyJems, St.Louis MO, 2004.
Fire Service Life Safety Rope and System Components, National Fire protection Association, Quincy MA, Standard NFPA 1983-2001 edition.
On Rope, revised edition, Padgett & Smith, National Speleological Society, Huntsville AL, 1996.

If the terrain is steep, fashion foot loops to hold the patient's feet in place. Use caution around the patient's neck so that if they were to slip downward in the litter the straps would not strangle them.

One useful tip is for long term evacuations with lots of individuals helping to pass the patient along. Use a sharpie and a piece of medical tape to print the patient's first name and place it on the chest area of the package. This labeling will allow everyone along the way to speak to the patient by name.

Patient packaging is an art form and for long term wilderness evacuations it a necessary part of patient care. Litter handling is a team effort. As crew leader you direct that effort.

The litter crew consists of several parts:

Crew leader,   Route finder,
Obstacle removal team,   Carry crew,
Patient medic,   Gear Sherpa's

As crew leader you monitor the entire effort. You brief on lifting safety, call for breaks when necessary, and pick the best route for the evacuation. One of the critical jobs of the crew leader is to prevent the litter crew from moving too fast. This is especially true at the beginning of the carry or whenever any fresh crew is added. A slow steady pace is best for the patient and crew members do not get hurt in their haste. The obstacle removal crew works ahead of the litter removing fallen sticks, tree limbs, rocks and other obstacles as you traverse the route. The carry crew (typically six) should talk to each other with the front telling the others about path conditions such as announcing: *step up now, rock on the left, slow because the folks in the rear cannot see their feet.* Behind the litter, near the patients head, is the medic. The medic's job is to care for the patient, monitor their condition and protect and comfort them. The medic can also advise the patient as to what is happening around them. Following up the procession are the gear Sherpa's. They carry all the extra medical kit, extra gear, water, and the patients' belongings. Occasionally the crew leader swaps personnel around (except the medic) to give folks a rest or a chance to ease up a bit. [21]

Litter Wheel in Use - Litter Carry Methods[22]

---

[21] High Angle Rescue Techniques, Hudson & Vines, MosbyJems, St.Louis MO, 2004.
Fire Service Life Safety Rope and system Components, National Fire protection Association, Quincy MA, Standard NFPA 1983-2001 edition. On Rope, revised edition, Padgett & Smith, National Speleological Society, Huntsville AL, 1996.

[22] IBID.

For many wilderness evacuations the best thing since sliced bread is a litter wheel. Even if it must be removed to traverse hazardous terrain it will pay off in reduced crew fatigue during the carry. If a litter wheel is not available, creating webbing carry loops works well. For each of the litter crew members, a piece of webbing is girth hitched to the litter rail, and then it is passed up over the shoulders and neck of the crew member, then down to their off hand.

An overhand knot is tied there and by pushing down with the offhand the load is carried on their shoulders and grip strength is not necessary to hold the litter. When the terrain gets difficult the best method for litter movement is the *caterpillar method*. The litter assumes a thousand legs for stability. Litter handlers stand in one place and pass the litter forward. When the litter clears their location they scramble forward and get in a new position to receive the litter. Crew members can be in place standing or sitting. A *lap pass* is the most stable method of moving the litter across tough terrain. The technique is simply: set, pass, peel, move, reset.

Summary

The Crew Leader, when working in difficult terrain, must use their training, experience and equipment to protect their crew and the patient from harm while accomplishing their assigned task. Judgment is essential. Is this the best route? Is there another way that is easier? Do we need a rope here? Is this low angle or do we need to call for a high angle crew? Refer to Chapter 13 for additional information on Rescue operations in the Hazardous Terrain narrative.

Notes:

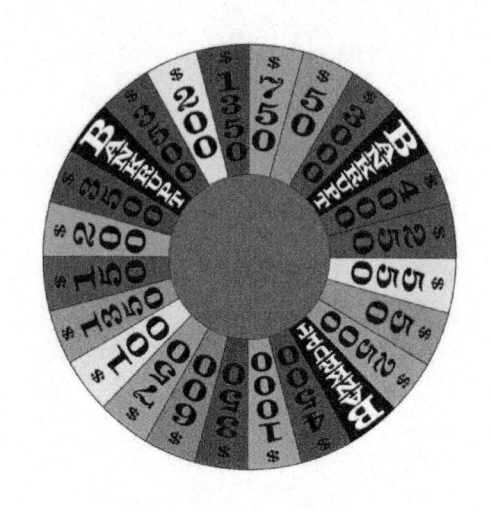

Probability...

What are my chances?

Chapter 10

Applying Probability and Critical Spacing

Objectives

- *Describe the probability theory and how it affects search planning.*
- *Describe the differences between LKP, POS, POA and POD.*
- *Describe critical spacing during a search mission.*

In this chapter we will discuss Probability Theory, how it is used to determine your search area assignment, and how you should apply probability and critical spacing while searching. What we will *not* do is to press complex mathematics and the theory used in developing such probabilities. We will focus on the "hands on" field application to produce an *effective* and *efficient* search.

Often an analogy is useful to illustrate the gist of what we will be doing, so here it is: Three people are walking down one side of the street. Across the street are three dogs: a Poodle, a Labrador retriever and a Malinois. The individuals could discuss (argue) as to which is the best dog for many hours citing many points of view. It is highly unlikely that they could reach a consensus with nine possibilities (3 persons times 3 types of dogs). However, if each person assigns a number (normally between 1 and 10, with 10 being best) they can then total each dogs "score" and it becomes the consensus of the group. This simple example illustrates how probability can be applied to achieve the "best guess" as to where to look in a SAR operation. We can now discuss probability in a search.

Search Probability

The total essence of search probability is found in the formula: POS = POA X POD whereby:

POS = probability of success (our goal).
POA = probability of area (where to look).
POD = probability of detection (of the lost person(s) or missing evidence.

143

This chapter will provide a brief description of how the ICS Planning Section determines each factor. The goal is to help you understand the *how* and the *why* of such planning *and* to evaluate, *in the field,* any factor that would affect those calculations.

Critical spacing (CS) will be discussed later in this chapter. CS may well be the most important field factor to understand, appreciate and adjust in the field while actively searching.

Last, but not least, the *method* of attaining the data needed to apply the above formula is explained. We have categorized the related sources of information into the following five categories:

1. **Missing Person Report (MPR)**

   The MPR is the first and most important source of information–a myriad of data which applies to all aspects of the probability formula. For instance, obtaining LKP and intent of the missing person(s) are obviously key factors in getting a valid consensus on POA. Knowing the description of the person(s) and what they are wearing will help determine critical spacing and POD. The MPR should be an on-going process – we often get "misinformation".... but we can never have too much valid information. Effective interviewing and careful analysis of all information received will separate misinformation from the valid information needed to increase probabilities. We mention it here so that everyone can be "clue oriented" at all times. Sometimes a casual observation can be the key to success.

2. **Theory**

   Theory is discussed in some detail in Chapter 6. This theory is based on considerable experience and historical data–both empirical and anecdotal. It is not an absolute indicator, but it does raise the probability in determining the parameters of a search.

3. **Statistical**

   As mentioned above, *this* information is important. There are two (2) main sources of lost person behavior. The first is books like *Lost Person Behavior* by Koester (see bibliography). Second are "local sources." This may be anything from the local search team to state-level data based on locally attained historical data or experience. It should be noted that the most important statistic may be the "distance travelled."

4. **Subjective Reasoning**

   This is done by using a map of the search area to determine barriers, attractions, routes of least resistance, etc. This same reasoning is applied to the assigned search area.

5. Deductive Reasoning

This type of reasoning is a bit more elusive. It requires one to place himself in the mind of the missing person and develop scenarios such as "If I was a lost six year old child, or 40 year old hunter, what would I do?"

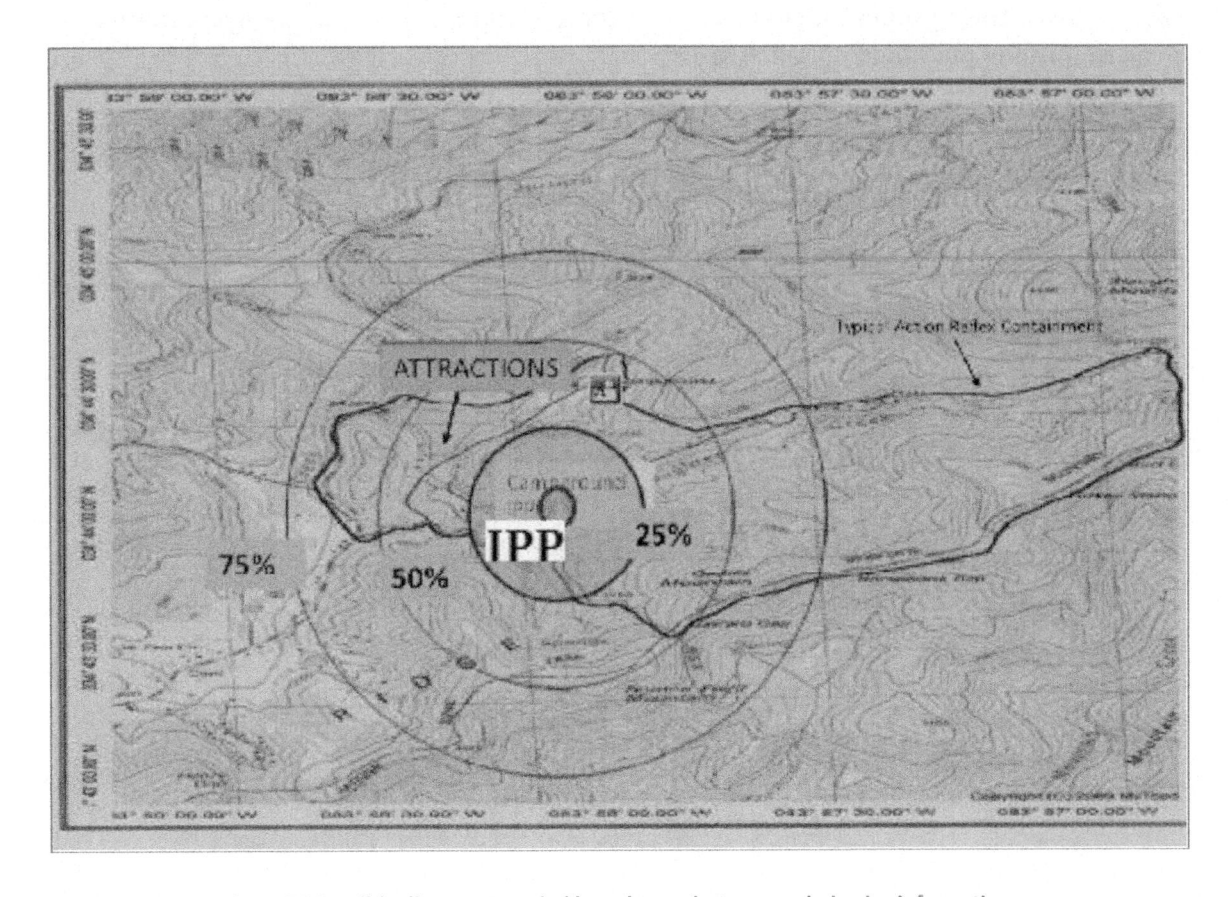

Figure 76 Possible distance traveled based upon lost person behavior information.

Now apply all of this information to the figure above to illustrate how this works. Note that, based on the MPR we have established an *Initial Planning Point (IPP)*. This is normally the LKP (last known place) or PLS (Place last seen). It *will not* change as a search progresses (if we start with a LKP and a PLS develops, the IPP remains the same. Note the barriers, attractions and likely routes indicated. These are all used in determining several (normally three) scenarios. Now consider the first element of probability theory. Remember the three dogs? Here we will use our three most experienced searchers. They will look at the three most likely scenarios and assign each a probability value from 1 to 10. This is applied to a simple chart to determine the POA.

There are many factors that can and will affect the POA. Detailed discussion of these may be found in the Search Management manuals and courses.

Probability of Area (POA)

The five sources are now used to determine the POA. Starting with the LKP/PLS and applying the probable distance travelled (by the type of missing person (see the "Lost Person Behavior" text), this produces a circular area (items 2 and 3). Now, by applying item 4 and 5 one can determine probability of each area.

Probability of Area Chart (POA)

Name	Area 1	Area 2	Area 3	TOTALS
Smith	9	9	4	
Jones	7	8	5	
Johnson	5	7	8	
SUBTOTALS	21	24	17	62
	21/62	24/62	17/62	62/62
Consensus Weight	34%	39%	27%	100%

Figure 77 POA Chart.

Probability of Detection (POD)

The Probability of Detection (POD) is based on the concept that if the subject(s) is/are in the assigned search area (based on the POA), what are the chances that you will detect the subject(s) of your search? First, can you see (detect) them within the assigned spacing?

With SAR training and experience, you will tend to focus on a search subject. For additional information see Chapter 7.

There is a large body of material on *how to detect*. Tracking manuals (see Chapter 7) have excellent instruction on how to detect. These discussions are beyond the scope of this manual but any serious searcher should *read and train on detection*.

Average Probabilities of Detection (POD) over an area for visual searches using parallel sweeps. Probability of detection show in percentages on the left side of the chart.

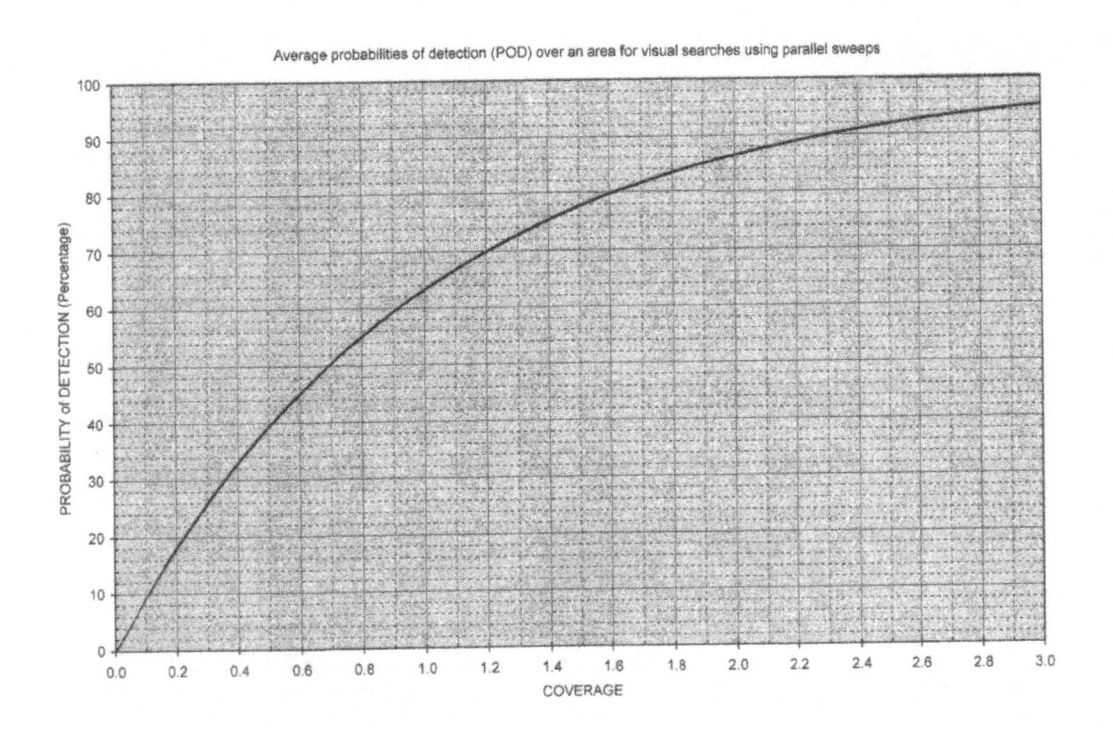

Critical Separation *(CS)*, Average Maximum Detection Range (AMDR) and Sweep Width (SW)

CS, AMDR and SW are interrelated terms used by search planners to determine POD. Their calculations are based on estimates derived from local experience, empirical data and/or local experimentation. We will briefly discuss CS/AMDR so you can understand how the Planner came up with a sweep width assigned to your search. In the field we often use the "Northumberland Rain Dance" to determine critical separation. An object similar to that being searched for (I.e.: Using a backpack of similar color) to represent a person that is down in the search area. One searcher, starting some distance away, can start going around the search sample in concentric circles reducing the distance with every revolution until the item is detected the object (hence "Northumberland Rain Dance). This is the least accurate but most expedient approach.

Searcher	Detection	Extinguishment
1	17	30
2	14	23
3	15	27
4	15	26
5	20	38
6	30	53
7	28	53
8	28	45
TOTAL	167	295
AVERAGE	20.875	36.875
AMDR	**28.875** meters	

Figure 78 Calculating AMDR.

AMDR Chart

1 — 30m
2 — 23m, 17m, 14m, 28m, 45m
8 — 45m
7 — 53m, 28m
3 — 27m, 15m
4 — 26m, 20m, 15m
5 — 38m
6 — 53m, 30m

(Values shown around the diagram: 30m, 23m, 17m, 14m, 15m, 27m, 28m, 45m, 53m, 28m, 15m, 26m, 20m, 30m, 53m, 38m)

....

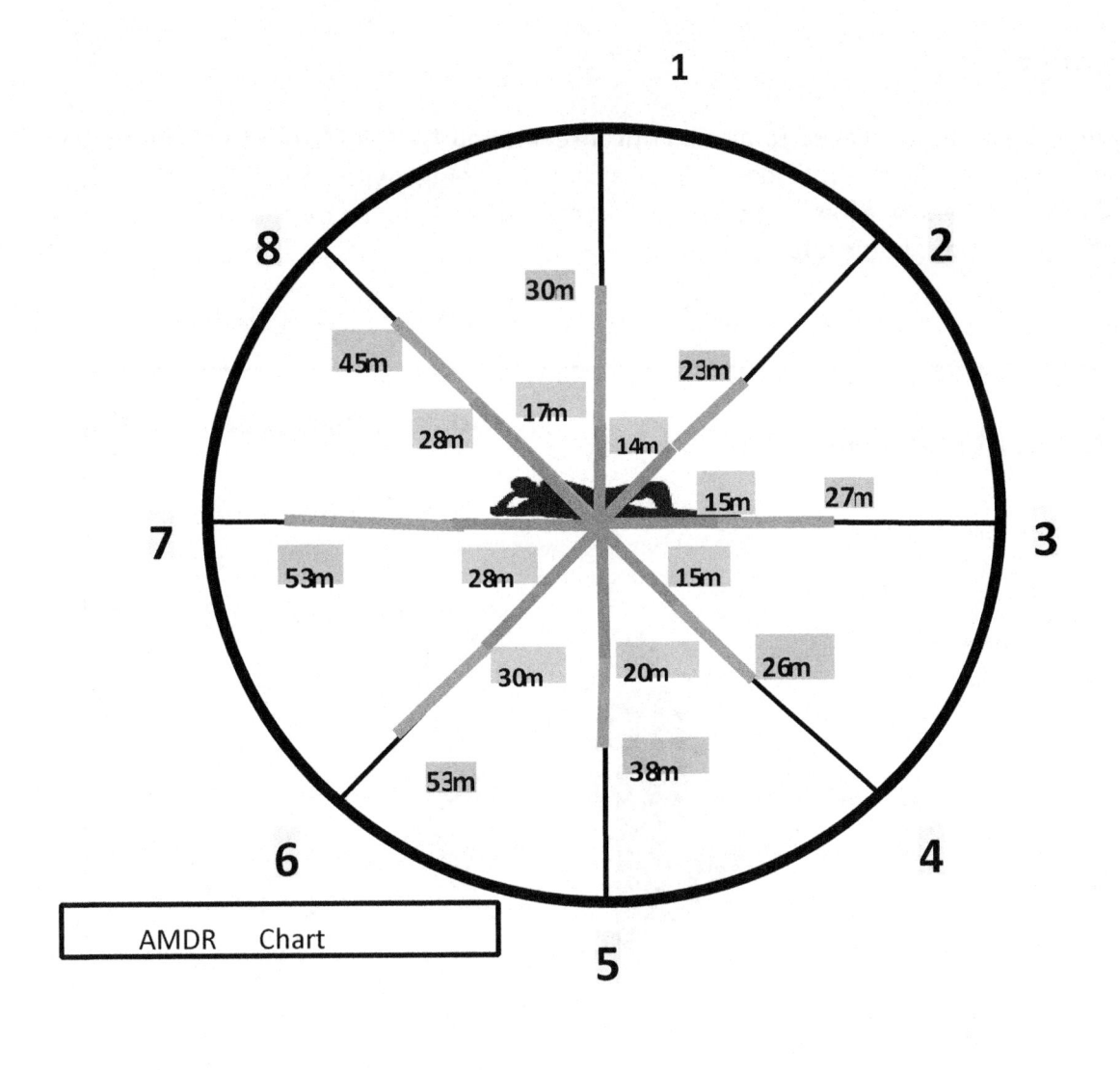

A more thorough approach to CS is the Average Maximum Detection Range (AMDR). It factors in vertical obstructions such as trees, horizontal obstructions such as ground cover and terrain. Here the test personnel move forward until they detect the search object (detection range) which they record then they move away from the object until they can no longer see the object (extinguishment range). The averages for *detection* and extinguishment are averaged to attain the AMDR Calculation of AMDR and are shown on the chart earlier in this section.

Critical Spacing

The AMDR is now *doubled* to attain critical separation (see the figure to illustrate why we double the distance). This provides a theoretical full coverage with no overlap. For larger areas and few searchers on a low to moderate risk search the CS can be extended leaving space between CS's and using "purposeful wandering."

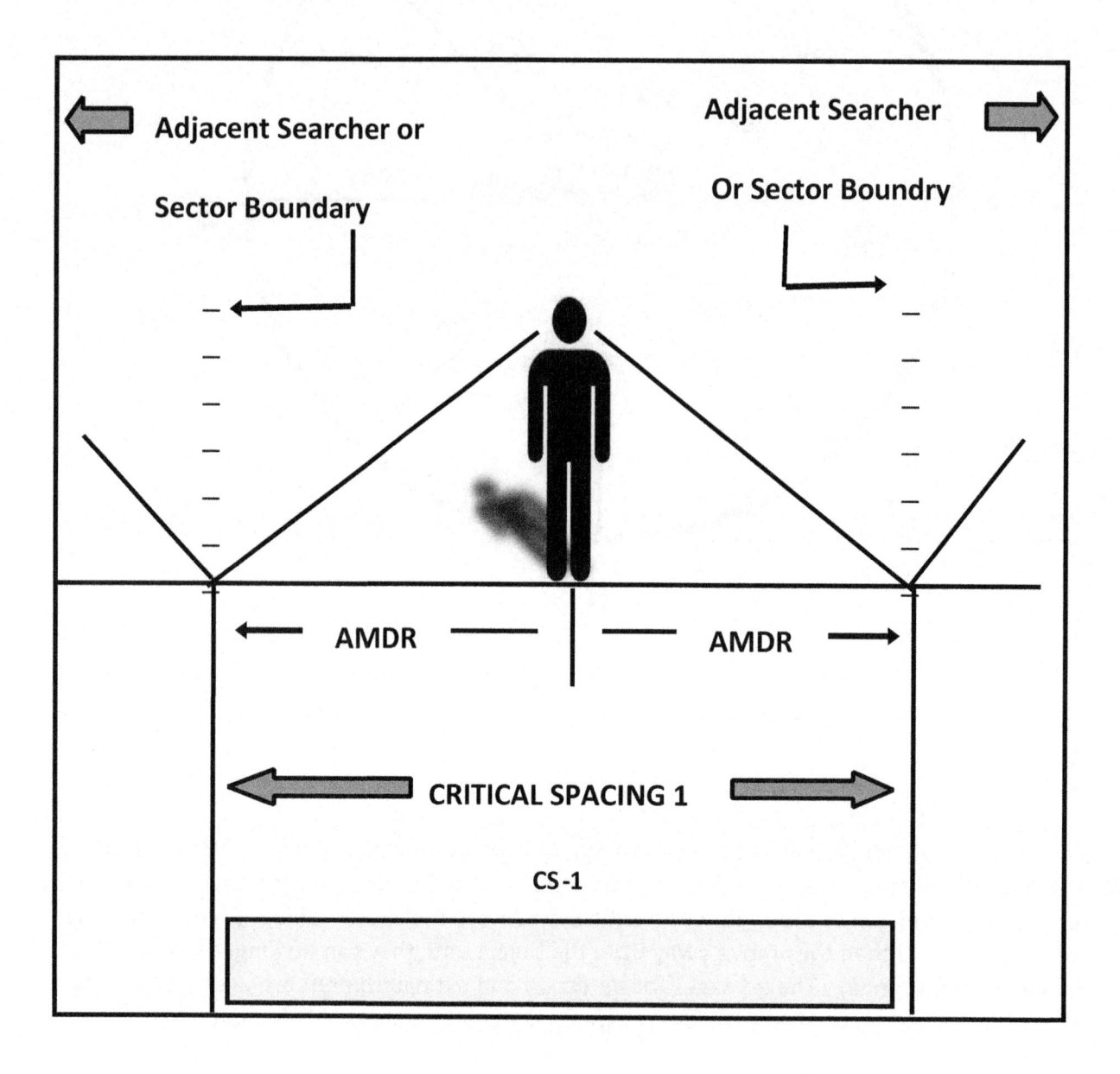

Figure 79 Critical Spacing Chart.

This provides a more accurate figure for determining *critical separation*. At the Planner (macro) level this will work but at the searcher (micro) level it will require constant leadership and well-trained searchers to maintain critical separation while moving along the environmentally changing track line. In a worst case scenario planned track line time and/or critical spacing may have to be adjusted to maintain a planned POD.

In such a case you should consult the ICS command post. Such conditions will reduce your area of coverage within a given time frame. The IC may want to provide more assets (searchers) to counter this, a common impediment.

Notes:

1. CS-1 = 50% POD
2. CS-1 with purposeful wandering = 80%

Calculating POD

To complete a POD calculation one must first decide how many searchers are available to cover a high POA scenario/search area, how fast can they move effectively, and the allotted time based on the CS established above, and how much ground width can be covered. This is how your mission should be determined and executed.

What if the subject is not found? The *planners* must look at all other POA. Will a new POA provide the highest POS or will a second search of a high POA produce the highest POS? Remember, the highest POS will determine the priority of assignments. The Planning Section can calculate revised POS's for a second or even third search of a sector.

As you can see, knowing the input parameters will help you understand what is expected and to keep the IC updated on the inevitable variances (i.e.: If your travel speed is *not* what was estimated, your performance will vary accordingly.)

POD Calculations

Let's take an example:

You have five (5) searchers plus yourself.

You estimate that you can move at 1.5 Km/Hr.

Your CS is determined to be 10 meters.

Your search time is 6 hours.

First, calculate the area expected to be covered
6 searchers X 10m= 60 meters total sweep width

1.5Km/Hr X 6 Hrs = 9 Km track line Length (TLL)
9Km = 9,000m X 60m =540,000 sq/m

540,000/1,000,000 = .54 sq Km

Assigned Search Area 1.08 Sq Km

Coverage equals area covered/area assigned or
= .54/1.08 = .50

The POD chart can then be used to determine that POD of .50 = 40%.

We have provided you some questions to ask at the briefing and relevant information to for your ICS Form 214. Remember, each search will have a myriad of factors that can change the POS. Ask; there are no stupid questions!

Calculating POS

$$POS = POA \times POD$$
$$POS = 0.39 \times .40$$
$$POS (area2) = .39 \times .40$$

$$POS = 156$$

Note: Remember this is a relative figure. It is compared to other Sector POS's to determine assignment priorities.

Summary

This short course on Probability Theory was designed to give you a better understanding of how probability is calculated and used, what goes into the calculations, and how these calculations affect you, the Strike Team Leader in the field while searching.

In conclusion, always remember that we are dealing in *probabilities,* not absolutes. We want to provide the highest (best) probability attainable with finite resources. We must always remember that the missing person may well need the best possible scenario to survive.

Figure 80 Assessing terrain.

Notes:

Figure 81 K9 Air Transport.

Chapter 11

Aviation

Objectives

- Describe a suitable landing zone.
- Understand the importance of prior planning when using aircraft.
- Describe conditions to consider when planning a hoist.
- List several obstacles which might impair a landing by an aircraft.
- Describe whiteout and brownout.

Crew leaders and SAR managers can ease operations with aviation by having some preplanning done before their arrival. Not everything in this section will be applicable to every SAR operation and the more complex the incident the more detailed planning needs to take place as the staff fills out the Incident Command System plan.

Figure 82 Landing Zones.

Task Lists

First and foremost, develop a plan for the use of the aircraft. Based upon the employment techniques, develop a plan for how you would like to use this asset. A good method is to develop a task list which will include operations such as the terrain you would like for them to search, loads, and the locations for the loads to be delivered. This will be followed by tasks you would like to be completed if time permits. Preparing a task list will help you avoid the "what will we do next" dilemma while you are burning fuel.

Design a task list to plan your loads from the pick-up zone (PZ) to the landing zone (LZ) so you will not waste valuable fuel while you gather your resources. Identify the type aircraft available and their capabilities. Do not worry if you do not immediately complete your task list.

Air Communication Plan

A communication plan should be developed at the SAR management level for the crew leader and aircraft personnel. Determine what frequency you will use to communicate with the aircraft. If there is more than one aircraft in the air, there should also be an Aircraft to Aircraft frequency for them to communicate with each other. The land crews will operate on a different frequency to avoid overlapping channels.

Air Space Plan

There should also be airspace *Deconfliction Plans*. This can be as simple as letting the pilots work this out between themselves or placing two air assets in two different search areas.

Figure 83 Pilot.

Mapping the Air Space

You will need to determine what GPS format you will be using for land and airspace. This can be most frustrating for pilots working search missions. It is important to know what format of latitude and longitude you will be using during the search in order to establish common terminology. Discrepancies are often not noticed until target information is relayed over the radio. Most of the time the aircraft GPS can be configured to meet whatever format you are working from for land operations (for example UTM/degrees/minutes/ or degrees/minutes/seconds). It is also important to work from the same data reference such as NAD 83 or NAD 27.)

What to Look For

Any information that you can provide to the air crews in order to focus their efforts is valuable. Information such as a possible color of equipment, what equipment the person has with them, possible place last seen or last known point, and what the intentions of the lost person was if known, are helpful.

Aircrews will talk in the air, the same as you do on the ground, trying to piece the puzzle together. Even if their task is to simply insert ground teams, it can be valuable to provide any known information to the pilots in the event they may have a sighting to and from the landing zone.

Landing Zone Selection

As a Crew Leader, one task you should be able to accomplish is to select a suitable Landing Zone. Pilots are often asked "what do you need for a place to land?" There is no hard and fast answer to that question. Many factors, including the skill of the pilots, the type of aircraft, the type of load, the slope of the terrain, and the winds all play a part of what may be suitable. This section is meant to provide some general guidelines to selecting your LZ but always allow the pilot to take a look at the location and decide if it is suitable.

Generally speaking, a good landing zone is about the size of a football field; 100 meters/yards wide by 300 meters/yards long. Some air operations dictate exactly how far from the rotor system obstacles must be in order to land. Typically you will be able to get an aircraft in and out of smaller locations but always allow the pilot to make that decision. It is always beneficial to have this football field *oriented into the wind from one goal post to the other*. It is not always possible but it does allow the pilot a straight forward landing and take-off which is preferred.

The current wind information is important information to provide to the pilots. Many Crew Leaders will tie a high visibility streamer to a ski pole or some vegetation to provide the pilot with a wind reference. Helicopter pilots are good at figuring out the wind conditions but they can vary with what they are on the ground. If known, give a wind direction and estimated velocity. Wind direction is reported in the cardinal direction they are blowing *from in knots.* For example: winds are estimated at 245 degrees at 15 knots meaning winds are blowing from 245 degrees at 15 knots. (A Knot equals 1.15 miles per hour. However, ground searchers can also just use miles per hour as the pilots can do these conversions easily.) Do not worry about conversion of miles per hour to knots. Estimated direction and velocity is helpful.

If communications are poor, another way to convey wind direction is to use a ground guide sometimes referred to as a parking tender. If a Crew Leader is familiar with hand and arm signals, he can guide the aircraft to landing. It will be understood to the pilot that you are standing with the back to the wind. The pilot may not land exactly where you are indicating but will understand the wind orientation.

Obstacles

It is critical to consider obstacles in your landing zone. The pilot can usually see trees but may not be able to see wires or small poles or other obstacles obstructing the landing. It is important to point out any wires around the LZ since it may impact the approach even though it may not impact the landing. It is always better to be safe than sorry in regards to wires so point them out every time.

Figure 84 Providing the pilot with a reference point.

Figure 85 Hazards...power lines which may not be visible to the pilot.

Marking a Landing Zone

There are multiple ways to mark a landing zone. The pilot may not be able to see you so some type of marking should be done. Every field can look very similar from the air. Anything of high visibility such as equipment or a tarp can be laid out to mark the LZ. If a tarp is used, once the pilot has visibility, the tarp can be removed if it is not weighted so it does not get picked up by the rotor wash. Remember that it must contrast with the ground. A space blanket will not be appropriate for a ground covered with snow but may be fine for a grassy field. Snow markings are easier since your tracks are typically a good contrast. Walk around in the snow area with skis to tap the snow down. This helps with white-out mitigation also.

Whiteout and brownout are beyond your control but you can assist the pilot during these times. A brownout occurs when a helicopter lands in a sandy and dusty environment and the ensuring cloud created by the rotor wash engulfs the aircraft and obscures the vision of the pilot. A whiteout occurs when this same phenomenon occurs with snow.

You can help the pilot by providing them a reference point within the landing zone or creating one of your own. A contrasting reference point inside the rotor diameter within the landing zone where you want them to land can be seen by the pilot and help prevent them from drifting and perhaps coming in contact with an obstacle. In a snowy field, a backpack placed in the landing zone can assist the pilot as an excellent reference point. Make sure that your chosen reference point is not going to be blown around by the rotor wash. Pine boughs would be blown around and may lead the pilot right into a tree.

Figure 86 Brownout conditions.

Figure 87 Smoke bomb showing wind direction.

Additional Air Operations Considerations

In the event that you have found your missing person, keep in mind that most likely they will have had no experience with helicopters. It is important to share with them the dangers of the pick-up and prepare them for the noise and wind they are about to experience. Your crew has worked hard to get to this point; be sure to finish the job.

Always approach a helicopter from the front after ensuring that the pilot is aware of your presence. STAY AWAY FROM THE TAIL ROTATOR!

Hoist

Conducting a hoist mission is one of the highest risks in working with a helicopter and should not be taken lightly. The potential exists to take a subject with life threatening injuries to either injure them further or worse yet kill them. Every alternative should be explored prior to a hoist to include moving the victim to a suitable landing zone. Landing pickup should be considered *first* before any hoist mission.

There are occasions when the victim cannot be moved or accessed by ground teams. Sometimes the hoist is your only option. If you have never trained in hoist operations, an actual rescue is not the place to try it. The tactics of conducting hoist operations vary from team to team and unit to unit but the basics are generally the same. Due to these variations and the complex nature of the operation, only the basics will be covered in this text. If the potential exists for your unit to conduct hoist operations, seek out that potential asset and coordinate training with them prior to needing them. In any case, face to face coordination is preferred prior to executing a hoist. Ask the aircraft to shut down and talk about the event beforehand if at all possible. We refer to this as slowing the operational tempo down in an effort to not push a bad situation. The emergency procedures and contingencies should always be thoroughly discussed. Take the time to do it right as the helicopter hoist will save considerable time.

Communications is difficult during hoist operations. Rotor wash and antenna proximity usually impede radio communications during the hoist but radio communication is the preferred method and should always be attempted first. Sometimes teams/units prefer radio silence during the execution of the hoist. You should consider this in the planning stages. Hand and arm signals are the backup methods of communication. Of course, these need to be coordinated in advance and practiced before the hoist.

Figure 88 Helicopter Operations.

Patient packaging should be trained prior to attempting a hoist. Securing the patient inside a stokes basket, Bauman bag, and/ or SKED is somewhat of an art form. Securing a patient vertically and laterally is only part of the task. With a hoist you must also secure the head and feet in case the patient starts to spin or they may be flung out of the system. Prepare the patient by explaining what is about to happen, what to expect, and how much noise will occur to encourage the patient to remain calm.

Helicopter Hand Signals

Clear to Start — Make circular motion above head w/arm

Hold on Ground — Extend arms at 45 thumbs down

Move Upward — Arms extended sweeping up

Move Downward — Arms extended sweeping down

Hold Hover — Arms extended w/clenched fists

Clear to Take-Off — Arms extended in take-off direction

Land Here — Extend arms w/wind at back

Move Forward — Arms extended & wave copter toward you

Move Rearward — Arms downward using shoving motion

Move Left — Right arm extended left arm sweeps overhead

Move Right — Opposite of move left

Move Tail Rotor — Rotate body w/one arm extended

Shut Off Engine — Cross neck w/hand palm down

Fixed Tank Doors — Open arms outward Close arms inward

Release Sling Load — Contact forearm w/other hand

Wave Off Don't Land — Wave arms & cross overhead

Figure 89 Air Operations hand signals.[23]

Tag lines should be used if at all possible. A tag line is a line attached to the system as it comes down (this procedure is unit dependent). It is attached to the system and a breakaway

---
[23] Helicopter Hand signals. wikirfm.cyclicandcollective.net

163

as the system is hoisted. The line is used to keep the patient from spinning during the lift. Be sure to check the line before the lift to be sure it is not wrapped around the leg of a rescuer or other obstacle.

Forward Looking Infrared Imaging (FLIR)

Forward Looking Infrared Imaging (FLIR) became a practical means of ground surveillance from helicopters during the Vietnam War. Those FLIR systems were used to detect movement of personnel and equipment along the Ho Chi Minh Trail. Since then considerable improvements have been developed in both detection and imaging. Today's thermal imaging capabilities are standard equipment for both the military and law enforcement. Normally, larger law enforcement agencies can be called upon to provide FLIR support. FLIR works best in cool weather and in cleared areas. It is also quite efficient in hardwood areas when foliage is off the trees.

Search Managers usually call in FLIR support early in the search to "clear" large areas based on time-distance projections thus increasing the POA for the remaining areas. FLIR becomes a real "asset multiplier." FLIR does have some limitations that must be considered. First, it works best detecting a warm object against a cool/cold background. Therefore, it does not work well in searching for the well-dressed hunter! It also cannot penetrate through dense evergreen forest. In conclusion, keep this asset in mind when called upon to set up reflex actions.

Unmanned Aircraft

Unmanned Aircraft or "drones" have been developed for efficient military surveillance and offensive actions. The surveillance success has been transferred to civilian SAR applications. These drones have been used to perform hasty searches of trails, especially in open and mountainous areas. Like FLIR, they can be considered an "asset multiplier" if properly used. Remember, however, that it is most imperative that the pilot of any manned aircraft must be forewarned of their presence in the search area. In addition, drones (with their camera capabilities) may have a limited distance capability from the controller and limited flight time due to battery reserves. However, as this asset improves, it will surely be proven valuable in the SAR world. Stay in tune with legal ramifications and local regulations for using drones as this is a new venture for most SAR personnel.

Summary

Working with Aviation in SAR can be high risk but can also be high payoff. The mobility capability alone can be invaluable in SAR work, especially in rugged country. These machines come with a cost so prior planning and training are a must to ensure you receive the asset again in the future.

Notes:

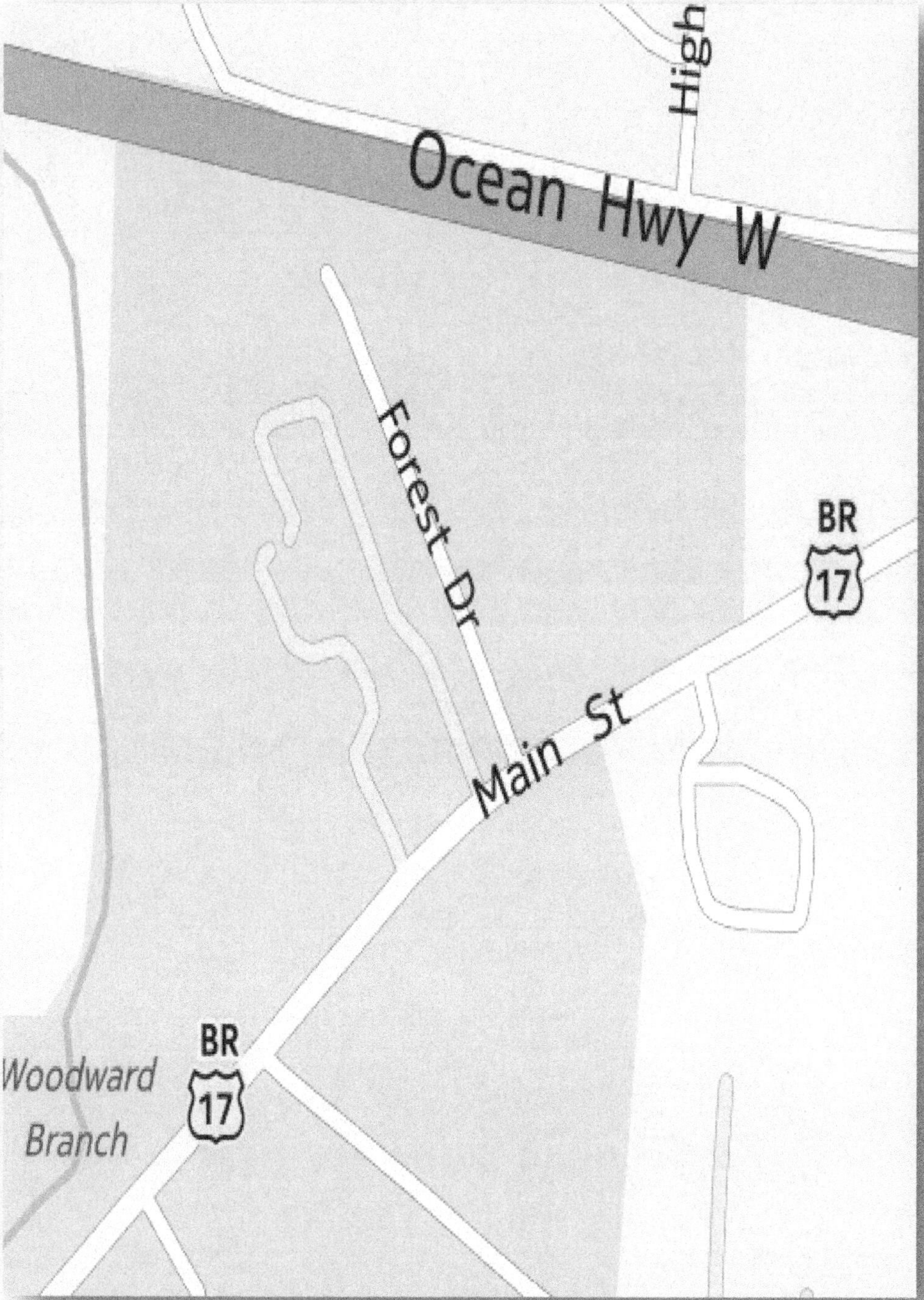
High
Ocean Hwy W
Forest Dr
BR
17
Main St
BR
17
Woodward
Branch

Chapter 12

Urban Searches

Objectives

- *Describe the difference between a wilderness and an urban environment.*
- *Understand the differences between urban tactics and search strategies.*
- *Describe the techniques of door-to-door canvassing.*
- *Describe the techniques of interviewing.*
- *Describe the techniques involved in building searches.*
- *List various SAR resources that can be useful in the urban environment.*

With the increased urbanization throughout the world we live in, search and rescue personnel are now being called upon to provide services in metropolitan setting. The search scene becomes the canyon of downtown office buildings, the suburban residential streets, the open space, the city parks, back alleys, easements and industrial sites. Search and rescue teams, known for their resources and training are now requested to apply their skills in what can be a very complicated and intimidating environment. The information in this chapter will provide the necessary skills to function safely and effectively as field teams and team leaders.

The Environment, Common Types of Searches, and Vulnerability Assessment

As searchers we are faced with the new challenge of searching in an environment that may be common in our everyday life, yet foreign to our field skills. We may live near or even in the big cities but our entire search experiences may be limited to the wilderness areas. What will it take to search a suburban housing tract or a canyon of high rise buildings? You are dealing with hard surfaces, which do not yield many clues. As with any search, we need to start pre-planning and specifically study the vulnerability assessment. In assessing our vulnerability, we need to look at the most common types of searches found in an urban environment.

In the urban environment we find some of the same types of searches common to those seen in the wilderness setting. These include the lost hiker or fisherman that is now supplemented with the occasional lost jogger or mountain biker. Other types may be seen less in the wilderness but they are not unique to the urban setting. These include the Alzheimer patient or the developmentally disabled walk-away from a care facility or family caregiver's control, or the despondent/suicidal individual. There are also others that seem to be unique to the urban environment such as criminal/evidence investigations, child abductions, runaways, and the occasional "CYA" (cover your assets) type of searches. These are the requests by Law Enforcement agencies to prove the missing subject is "not in my city." To compound the issues, all of these types of searches can be made increasingly more difficult when you add the variable of public transportation. With access to public transportation the missing subject may be out of the immediate search area.

Vulnerability Assessment

With an understanding of the types of search missions that may be encountered, it is incumbent on all searchers to become aware of the local environment where you will be searching.   These may include, but are not limited to:

- city open spaces and parks,
- city walking trails,
- skilled nursing homes,
- assisted living, board and care facilities,
- day care centers (both child and adult),
- local transit locations and routes, and
- high crime areas (and potential safety concerns).

Planning and Strategies

It is prudent to preplan in order to prepare for urban searches. In urban environments it is often difficult to find appropriate working maps of the area. In the wilderness search, the use of USGS maps is fundamental. However, when working in the city, USGS maps are not detailed enough nor are they kept current.   Automobile Association maps work better.   In many locations, guides map books are available.   Other sources of detailed maps include fire department run maps, county assessors' maps and utility company infrastructure plans, all of which show specific lots and house numbers. Segmentation of search areas are broken down into blocks, one or both sides of the street, alleys or easements, depending on the denseness of the buildings.   Streets can run in grid patterns, meander, or dead-end into a cul-de-sac.

Boundaries are difficult and may have to be arbitrarily based on the area to be covered by the resources available. This will become clearer under the discussion of door-to-door canvassing searches.

Investigation

The largest generator of clues in the urban search comes from heavy emphasis on investigation and interviewing. Management will start immediately building a profile based on interviews with people who have firsthand knowledge of the missing subject. In many cases we find that the initial call for a missing child as a possible abduction is determined later through investigation to be a run away or a case of the child forgetting to call home.

For searchers to be effective and better prepared to search, SAR management should pass on as much subject profile information as possible. This will allow the searcher to better sort through the massive amount of field information and clues encountered "in the field." Some of the investigative information we are looking for will include, but not limited to:

- Their mobility and ability to travel. Can they walk, ride, hitchhike or drive? Do they have access to a vehicle, horse, boat, plane, or knowledge and use of public transportation, rapid transit, trains, buses, and taxis?

- Their ability to survive. Do they have any money with them; do they have a cell phone or tracking device; do they know how to call home; are they familiar with their surroundings (do they live in the area)?

- Their intent. Was it to go for a walk; find something or someone; did they leave a note; do they have a diary? Do they use social networks?

- Their ability to respond. Will they avoid responding because they are afraid of punishment; is there a family "safe" or "pass" word established; is there a physical or language problem?

- What attracts their attention? Video games, crowds, or do they prefer solitude?

- Is there something that recently occurred or in the past that might affect their mindset?

Possible Scenarios

The question is: how do you deal with the thousands of potential clues? The answer is that the investigation, which is under the *Plans function,* may be made at a separate General Staff Section Chief level. The function needs to be expanded with enough resources to manage and sort through the information and clues as they are discovered. This is an operation that continues until the missing person is found or the search is terminated.

Field Operations

The field operations from the initial call out for hasty assignments will consist of a saturation search in a ¼ mile (300 meter) radius around the Point Last Seen (PLS) or Last Known Point (LKP). This is based on statistical and historical information that most missing subjects in an urban environment are located within this radius.

The Initial Call-Out

The key to successful searching in metropolitan environments is *containment* coupled with rapid response. Time is our worst enemy. Having your team attached to a public agency will give you a better head start. Public agencies such as Offices of Emergency Services (OES), sheriff departments, park and recreational authorities, or local police jurisdictions are already plugged into dealing with emergencies. They have means of rapid communication and dissemination of information already in place.

The Hasty Search

In the metropolitan area, getting to a search site is as close as the highway. Dispatching a contingency of key personnel and multiple resources will provide the best means for rapid containment and gathering of what clues are available before they are distorted or lost. The resources should include overhead managers, investigation and interviewing personnel, a public information officer, trailing and air scent dogs, and vehicles. After establishing the overhead command structure, the first assignments will need to be focused on investigation and *containment*.

Attractive Nuisances

Some possible sites of attractive nuisances are those things that likely attract children or the Alzheimer walk away such as malls, stores, churches, and community centers. Each area has its own special "hang-out." It may be the local convenience store with its video games, or other places like culverts, ditches, canals, creeks, and utility easements. Review hiding places like backyards, abandoned cars and old refrigerators, out buildings, sheds, and woodpiles. Investigators will help establish the high probability areas based on the lost subject's profile and behavior pattern. It should be noted that when dealing with an Alzheimer subject it is important to remember that they are living their life in reverse. Alzheimer patients cannot remember the recent past. They think they are somewhere long ago. Knowing this history can help plan what would attract them. As an example, if it was found that the subject grew-up on a farm and was accustomed to taking naps outside or in the barn, then, a review of likely outbuildings or comfortable sleeping areas may be required.

Institution Check

A system to check area hospitals needs to be established. A John or Jane Doe admitted with injuries or a mental problem may be the missing subject. A check also should be made of local jails, shelters, and alcohol or drug detoxification and rehabilitation centers. Someone who is disoriented may be construed to have a mental or other problem.

Containment

The longer it takes for a loved one to report a subject missing and the longer the requesting agency waits to call the search and rescue team, the harder it will be to set up containment. If they wait too long the missing subject could be miles away, past several jurisdictions or even in the next county. There are no natural boundaries for containment. Streets and roadways make the use of private transportation (cars, motorcycles, bicycles, etc.) easier for the subject. The same holds true with public transportation. Busy streets are not boundaries, even for small children.

Confinement and containment in any search operation are set up to limit the search area size. Many subjects are found just walking down the street or in an open area. Therefore look in that critical ¼ mile radius. Most containment in the hasty search mode can be handled by road patrols with trained observers. The observers will require good briefings and information about who they are looking for with accurate descriptions and a good profile. Here again the investigation information is critical.

There are a lot of people out there that might look like the missing subject. The more accurate the subject's information is the greater the chances of success. Updated information needs to be given out, as it becomes apparent through the investigation.

Field Team Tasking – Door-to-Door Canvassing and Interviews

The Incident Management Team relies on field teams to generate clues and one of the largest generators of clues is the door-to-door canvass and interview of the general public on the street. Door-to-door interviews answer the question "did the subject pass by this way." The task is simple. Two-to-three person teams go down both sides of a street, stopping at each house and asking questions. However, the amount of effort to cover that ¼ mile radius can be very labor intensive taking as much as 15 minutes per house adding up to many hours.

To differentiate between wilderness "Type 1, 2 or 3" search operations and prevent confusion, we categorized neighborhood canvassing into "levels." The search teams will be asked to do the following:

- Level I: Searchers will interview everyone in the household and follow up with a property/yard search and request an interior search by residents.

- Level II: Searchers will interview everyone in the household and request the resident to search their property/yard.

- Level III: Searchers put a flyer on each door with a description of the missing person and a request to the resident to search their yard. This is also used when no one is home.

Some words of caution: Door-to-door canvassing should be mostly limited to daylight hours. That is not to say you cannot knock on doors at 2 o'clock in the morning but you may not get much cooperation from the residents. Also, searches will need to know basic interpersonal and interview skills.

As with any operation or assignment everything should be pre-planned. Each team should have an assignment and be briefed on which *level* to work towards. Ideally there should be a three person team. Two that will go to the door and one will remain at the sidewalk and act as communications as well as the Safety Officer. The two person team will need to decide who will be asking the questions and who is filling out the paper work as well as rehearse the questions. The Safety Officer is responsible for the welfare of the other members of the team. If he sees a dog coming around corner and not barking he can warn his team members. A working knowledge of the neighborhoods to be searched may prevent someone from getting hurt, like someone inadvertently walking up and knocking on the door of a "crack house." The Safety Officer may have to be from the local law enforcement jurisdiction. Find out what authority team members have to enter private property to check out back yards or out buildings.

Upon approaching the house look around to be aware of your surroundings for any dangers and make mental plans for an escape route if necessary. This would include leaving any gates open. Also, what do you see in the yard. Are there cars up on blocks, kid's toys strewn around? This will give you an idea of whom you might meet behind the door. Before you knock on the door and announce your presence, first listen. What do you hear? Is the TV blaring, kid's playful screaming or a vacuum cleaner running? These are all signs that someone is home but they may not be able to hear you knocking at the door. You may need to wait for things inside to quiet down.

For searcher safety, you should never stand in front of a door before knocking. If the person behind the door does not like cops or people that look like cops and thinks you are one, some might shoot through the door. This is not to make searchers paranoid but to be cognizant about their own safety. A better position is to stand to the side of the door, then knock hard and announce your presence loudly "Search and Rescue." Ringing the doorbell may not convey a sense of urgency and should be avoided.

When the resident comes to the door, state that you are ____ from the ____ search and rescue team and let them know the reason you are there. Stand far enough away from the door to invite the resident to come outside. As noted earlier, one person should be asking the questions and the other should be filling out the responses on paper. One can also look beyond the resident to see into the house. Are there other residents to talk to? Is there a big dog to be concerned about? Review the missing person flyer with the resident. Have extra copies available to "leave behind."

If it is not part of your assignment to request permission to search the house and yard, then for your safety do not enter even if asked.

Before leaving make sure that you've spoken to all residents. When leaving thank them for their time and back away while still facing the resident, until they enter the house and close the door. Then turn and walk to the next house. This is for searcher safety in case the resident opens the door and the family's aggressive dog comes up behind you.

If the team encounters someone who is belligerent or non-cooperate, just thank them for their time and leave. Make a note of the encounter for possible follow up by sworn law enforcement to return to see it he really has some information.

Carry minimal equipment. Maps of the area, note pad and pencil, some form of identification beyond a uniform, flash light for viewing dark areas and a camera to record any findings or anything suspicious that may need follow up. The majority of the team members 24 hour equipment pack can be placed in a vehicle close by if needed.

The Urban Interview Log developed by the Bay Area Search and Rescue Council (BASARC) (BASARC Form SAR 132) is used to keep track of where the team went, who they talked to and who was not home. The form is self-explanatory and easy to fill out. In the columns with Y it means yes, N means no. The last column suggests a follow up visit. This is where you would check yes for the person we did not want to deal with earlier. (Forms are available on the internet and in the Appendix.)

Additional forms include a Clue Log (BASARC SAR 134) and Clue Report (BASARC SAR 135). Any time someone obtains some information from a door-to-door interview it is radioed in and logged on the Clue Log. When the team returns from the field they complete the Clue Report which gives the details about what they found, as well as any suggestions for follow up later.

The interview questions for the resident needs to be scripted and planned out. Always give the minimum amount information and have a prepared "lie test" question ready. A "lie test" question is one that solicits information that only an eye witness might have seen. For example the missing subject is known to be wearing a hat with the word "Teamster" written on it but this information is not mentioned on any flyer or description. If the question is asked was the person you saw wearing any head wear? If they say yes, but got the color wrong or say it had "49er" written on it, then it might be assumed that the sighting is not of the missing subject. If they fail the test then thank them for their time and move along. Also, be suspicious of people who seem overly anxious to give you information. It has been documented that some of these people are actually the perpetrator of a crime related to the missing person incident. If information appears accurate make sure you document how to contact them at a later date.

Besides a standard question such as "Did you know the missing subject and have you seen them recently," consider other questions that are oriented to determining what is normal for the neighborhood. We are looking for the *unknown witness*. For example: the subject went missing around 0400. Who is up in the neighborhood at 0400? The answer might be newspaper delivery, garbage pickup, bus drivers, early risers for work, those coming home from work, folks walking their dog or joggers. Could any one of these see the subject but did not think much of it. During the day who is in the neighborhood? Consider the following: Mail delivery; public transportation and the guy across the street that runs a business out of his home and has UPS and FedEx coming in and out all day. How do you get in touch with these "unknown" witnesses? You may consider calling their dispatchers; they may still be working. Contact them at work or whatever it takes to reach them.

Flyers

Have a flyer prepared to leave behind. Important things to keep in mind when preparing a flyer:
- Use a good (and recent) picture.
- Include a good description of the subject.
- Leave out some information for the "lie test" questions.
- Make sure the phone number posted at the bottom is manned 24/7 and those answering the phone are prepared for receiving the inevitable influx of calls.

Training

Because these skills may be new to search teams, practice is essential. Setting up a door-to-door practice can be done very simply. Set up in a building that has long corridors with lots of doors. If you are really ambitious, make arrangements to practice in a real neighborhood. Place someone behind each door with a different personality (i.e. impatient, eager to help, very busy watching the ballgame, etc.) and have the searchers go from door-to-door asking questions. Behind one of the doors will be someone that has good information if the searchers ask the right questions. Once they have practiced the exercise bring everyone back and discuss what they learned, what they would add, and what would they have done differently?

Building Searches

There may be times during a search when it is necessary or wise to search a building systematically. The decision to search a building depends on the circumstances surrounding the subject and the incident. For example, a task during the initial investigation is to search around the PLS, and if it is a residence, to make sure the missing person is not hiding or asleep there. Reporting parties sometimes overlook children and people with dementia, even if they say they have searched the house.

There are legal considerations to searching buildings which depend on applicable laws. Searchers should be made aware of these laws, either during the assignment briefing or when advised by the local authority while the search is in progress. In general, teams can search private residential property when granted permission by the owner, manager, or authorized agent. Usually, a cooperative resident or business manager grants permission, but if there is hesitation or refusal, search personnel should try persuasion. Where the grantor imposes restrictions, it should be reported to command for further instructions. If all else fails, authorities can get a court order to search the property. Furthermore, if the authorized agency determines this *is a life or death emergency*, and it falls under the definition of "exigent circumstances," it can order the search to extend into closed areas. It is important to understand the use of exigent circumstance, and in the preplan to spell out who has the power to authorize warrantless entry into a building.

Public and commercial properties, which are normally open to the public, are also open to searchers during operating hours. Vacant and open buildings that may be an attraction to the missing person can usually be searched without permission. Remember to search outbuildings, such as sheds and garages. In any situation where the search extends to private, occupied property, permission must be obtained first. All of these scenarios should be considered during urban search training, and applicable guidelines should be established by the authorized agency.

Firefighters and police SWAT teams have long used special tactics for searching buildings, from single-story houses to high-rise offices. They operate under emergency provisions of the law, however, which allow them to use dynamic (forced) or covert (secret) entry, tactics that consider the probability of high risk and possible hostile subjects.

The urban searcher does not typically face such scenarios, thus they are not considered here; however, the method of searching once the team has gained entry may apply to non-threat searching.

The procedure for searching the interior of a building is simply a systematic, careful room by room sweep. The search plan depends on the urgency of the situation, the probability of finding the subject in the building, and the resources (I.e., people) available for the search. For example, if a child is reported missing from his home by his parents, and there is no indication of foul play, the initial investigation team (usually two searchers) could conduct the search accompanied by one of the parents. Other residents should be kept in a central room to avoid contaminating the scene and possible evidence, such as scent articles for trailing dogs.

If it is suspected that the missing person is avoiding searchers or abduction has occurred, the search plan should incorporate more safeguards, one of which is *perimeter containment*. Perimeter containment would hopefully prevent the subject from leaving the building unnoticed and would keep track of other people going in. This is accomplished by positioning observers at diagonal corners of the building where each can watch at least two sides of the building. Obviously, if the base of the building is multi-faceted, or there is a basement, additional personnel are needed. Exit corridors, such as elevator lobbies or stairwells, also need to be watched. All personnel should have radios.

Next, search teams sweep each floor systematically, starting at the upper-most level (or roof), checking each room behind every door. By following a set pattern, searchers can avoid missing areas or not finding a subject who is well-hidden. The search should run from the floor to the ceiling and should be conducted either in a clockwise or counterclockwise direction. This includes rest rooms, janitor closets, mechanical rooms, electrical rooms, storage cabinets, and lockers, under and around furniture, and through all of the assorted clutter that is usually underfoot. Make sure all of the lights are on for maximum detection. If feasible and plausible, it may be necessary to search above dropped-ceiling spaces or crawl spaces.

Although this description assumes a minimum two-person foot team, another technique is to use dogs to clear rooms. Air-scent dogs work well for this task.

If it is an office or commercial building, a building manager who knows the layout of the building and has a master key should accompany the team. As each room is checked, the doors should be relocked or sealed. If a building floor plan is available, it can provide a good map and means of recording which rooms have been searched. In a multi-story building, as each floor is secured, the teams can then move down to the next level. The process is repeated until the entire building is swept and secured. Exterior perimeter containment should continue until the entire building is secured to prevent any unauthorized entry into the building.

The most common mistake made by building searchers is that of speed. Methodical searches are done at the rate at which the room or structure can be controlled and thoroughly searched. There is no need to go faster than that. This can take a long time with extensive resources and should probably be limited to thorough searches conducted after less intensive searching has turned up nothing. Finally, please note that building search is an extremely perishable skill that should be practiced during annual maintenance training.

Other Field Operations

Yard searches can take a long time depending on the size, the number of out buildings and possible hiding places. Make sure to check abandon cars. There are lots of documented cases where kids have accidently locked themselves in the trunks and died. Even the elderly can be found in someone else's car and no one noticed until the owner goes to use it.

Briefing and Debriefing

Briefing of teams in the metropolitan environment needs to be more detailed. The more information provided the better. Detailed description of clothing will help the teams weed out potential subjects from the crowd. Personality information also is helpful to give team members an insight as to what the subject might do in a particular situation. Anything that is unusual about the subject should be mentioned. The test/lie question should be discussed and agreed upon. Safety issues about the neighborhood will need to be emphasized and understood prior to leaving for the assignment.

Debriefing teams is equally important. It is critical to clearly note what areas were covered as well as those which were not and must be checked later. In some instances if an urban door-to-door interview is taking place simultaneously with a search of an adjacent open space, separate debriefs may be required to prevent confusion or missed information.

Documentation

Detailed and thorough door-to-door interview logs as well as other investigation interview reports are important. As stated earlier, these are the largest clue generators. They may produce more pieces to the puzzle and may lead the search in a totally different direction. As with wilderness searching, the most important thing about documentation is to back up your decision to drop to a limited search condition. What we call a limited search in this setting is that all avenues have been exhausted and there are no clues. If search coverage is good, it may be acceptable to say the subject is out of the area. The search is then turned back over to the agency with jurisdiction.

Documentation is kept together in the event that something breaks and the search resumes. If the subject is eventually found deceased under questionable circumstance, the documentation may help clear up the case.

Applying Other SAR Resources

Trailing Dogs and Air Scent Dogs

Trailing dogs are a very effective resource, especially if there are no footprints going off into the sunset. They may be the only source for finding a direction of travel, and they may help narrow down the search area. These types of dogs follow a specific scent trail. They can also be trained to indicate if the missing subject got in a vehicle and left the area. Trailing dogs can be combined with air sent dogs to form a task force. The trailing dog can trail to a garage or outbuilding that can be quickly cleared with the air scent dog.

A word of caution, if the point last seen was a residence or a place where the lost subject frequents, it may be difficult for a trailing dog to find their way out of the scent pool. This means it is important in the investigation to find out where a child may play or where the elderly travel on a regular basis. Knowing this information will be helpful to the dog handler to interpret the dog's trail and may prevent misleading the search effort.

In a metropolitan environment, safety of the dog and handler is paramount. The handler has to pay close attention to the dog in order to "read" what the dog is doing. Since the handler's focus is on the dog, others need to be on the alert for dangers. The others should consist of two runners that stay to the side and just behind the dog. One runner has a radio and reports in to the command post their location, direction of travel and any pertinent indications by the dog. Trails usually run along roadways heavy with vehicle traffic. The runners are responsible for alerting or stopping vehicle traffic if the scent trail leads across the roadway. A marked vehicle with overhead lights also should follow behind the dog team and assist in traffic control, as required and appropriate.

Other Considerations

Many law enforcement agencies are not trained and may lack the resources and skills to manage a search effectively. When asked to assist in a search, the search manager needs to be aware that these agencies sometimes have a tough time understanding what search management is all about. Therefore, it is incumbent on the leaders of the team to approach these agencies and educate them as to the teams' abilities and resources. For teams made up primarily of volunteers, this task is difficult. Training and formal presentations to these agencies, with an emphasis on "we are here to help" and the hat-in-hand are good approaches. Encouraging the agency to call the team when they first get the call of a report of a missing subject greatly increases the chance of success. In some cases, the agencies will recognize the advantages of a trained search team, and will bend over backwards and allow the team to manage the search directly.

Remember...

- Understand your environment and develop the preplan accordingly.

- Be extremely thorough in the investigation and interviewing.

- Develop an accurate profile of the missing subject.

- Consider public transportation and realize that the missing subject may be out of the area.

- Trailing dogs are a very effective resource.

- Considerations must be made to train personnel to implement the labor intensive and time consuming tasks of investigation and door-to-door interviewing.

Professionalism in how you present yourself is important. A uniform will help to maintain this image. If team members are going to be doing door-to-door interviews and walking the streets then they will need to present themselves with some authority. The general public may not seriously respect the searchers presenting in the wilderness work attire such as a "T" shirt, baggy pants, and hiking boots. Having picture identification issued by an agency and/or a badge also will help with the persona of professional authority.

Summary

The management of the suburban search process is not complicated, but it does require some innovated thinking and an understanding of the environment. Some modification of the basic search management skills will be required. The success of searches in the metropolitan environment relies on several factors.

Figure 90 Waiting for an assignment.

Chapter 13

SAR Rescue

Objectives

- *Understand how to pre-plan, size up, gain access, assess the patient, stabilize, package, and extract the subject in search scenarios.*
- *List the five steps of an initial patient assessment.*
- *List the five priority assessment patient categories.*

The following scenario is provided as a representation of a few common problems that are faced by many SAR professionals and team leaders. It will be referenced several times in this chapter.

"You are called to a well-traveled hiking trail in your area for a person who is reported four hours overdue for the scheduled pick up. The trail runs through fields and wilderness involving some small mountains with caves and cliffs. You arrive at the command post and receive a briefing. Your team is given an assignment from command to search an area of the trail about four miles long which involves the mountain area. By the time you assemble your team, brief them, and get ready to move; It is 16:00 hours on a Sunday afternoon in late Fall.

After searching for two hours the person is located on a ledge about 30-40 feet off a cliff and appears to be injured. Upon safely gaining access to the person, you do a quick assessment to find that the person has an open fracture to the left ankle and a palm size contusion to the right upper abdomen. The person complains of thirst, weakness, and dizziness. Heart rate and respirations are elevated. The cliff is only accessible from below. You notify command of the situation and request more resources. You also notice the sun edging behind the small mountains and feel the chill in the air."

The term "Search and Rescue" is used to describe the operations of finding a lost person and getting them to safety. The words "search" and "rescue" are used together but each word describes a different operation. Search involves various techniques to locate the lost person. Rescue is the stabilization and extraction of the found person to safety.

According to the NASAR FUNSAR manual, Rescue is defined as "An operation to retrieve persons in distress, provide for their initial medical or other needs, and deliver them to a place of safety" (FUNSAR 7). Rescue is a very broad subject and there are many resources that address the various areas involved in rescue. A team leader must be familiar with the various types of rescue. However, reviewing each type is beyond the scope of this book.

Figure 91 Handling a litter.

SAR responders and team leaders study the various aspects of searching. They range from search techniques to search theory however once the person is found, the mission changes from search to rescue or recovery. From an overall command perspective, the mission evolves from a broad spectrum of searching for clues and/or the lost person to a focused mission of getting the patient to safety. The team leader's mission also changes from searching an area to a more focused rescue effort. Wilderness rescue involves risk versus benefit. The team leader is the person on the scene. He/she must assess the situation, relay information to command, help formulate a plan, call for resources, and manage the team to successfully rescue the person. Being a leader can be very demanding and requires more than management skills. A leader should address the following considerations:

Pre-planning
Size Up
Gaining Access
Patient Assessment
Stabilization
Packaging
Extraction

Pre-planning

Pre-planning is essential to any skill or operation. It can start before a leader is called to an incident. A leader can pre-plan for certain common responses in his/her area. Rescue missions that have been conducted in the past can provide clues as to what response to plan for and what rescue resources may be needed for future rescues. Research the response area characteristics such as the seasons, weather, terrain, and activities of people in the area that may require search and rescue.

Once the incident has begun, the leader can pre-plan the possible rescue response based on the incident briefing. A leader must gain as much information as possible to prepare the crew for the possible rescue response.

Figure 92 Patient Packaging.

Size up

Sizing up the situation and the scene can be vital to the entire rescue operation. Size up begins from the initial dispatch and briefing. Factors such as time of day, weather, terrain, victim experience, team abilities, etc. can provide information as to what may be needed. Size up is an ongoing process. The team leader must be observant to the situation and the scene for possible hazards and needs to conduct the rescue. He/she must perform a mental checklist to size up the scene, determine the urgency, and to develop a plan to rescue the person.

The following are considerations that the team leader should address in *size up*:

- **Determine if the mission is a rescue or recovery.** The entire operation can change on this answer. If the scene is a recovery, the scene must be secured and the effort can take a slower pace. If the scene is a rescue, the time factors are determined by the condition of the person found and the situation.

- **Maintain scene safety and observe for the possibility of hazards.** The safety of the team is first priority. Team members are on the scene to rescue the person and not become victims themselves. The team leader must constantly make observations as to the safety of the team.

- **Gain access and perform an assessment.** The assessment of the person found will determine a great deal about the urgency, the time factors, the rescue effort, the needed resources, and the extraction. The person should be assessed and placed into one of the six categories discussed in the assessment section of this chapter.

- **External factors should be considered during size up.** The time of day, weather, exposure to the elements and patient stability can effect rescue efforts and determine how much time the rescue will take.

- **Determine needed resources for the rescue.** A search team does not have the capability to carry the vast amounts of equipment that may be needed for every rescue scenario. The team leader must determine what is needed to perform the rescue and evaluate what resources he/she has on hand. A rescue may be as simple as helping the person to find his/her way out of the situation to safety or it can be as complicated as a high angle rope rescue. Another consideration is the number, ability, and strength of the team. If the team has been searching for several hours, they may be too tired to complete a complicated rescue. The team leader should use the scene size up to evaluate the team as well as the situation. Time is always a factor so needed resources should be called early.

●**Size up also involves finding the fastest and easiest way out with the person.** The team leader should take a few minutes to look at the surroundings and a map to evaluate the fastest and easiest way to get the person to a safe place. Command may be working on an extraction plan but the team leader is in the field and should provide input to that plan.

Gaining Access

Gaining access to the lost person may be as simple as walking up to them or is can be very complicated. The person may be down a cliff, up a mountain, miles away, etc. There may also be obstacles to gaining access such as terrain and natural barriers.

Scene size up can determine what is needed to gain access to the patient. Do not rush in. Safety is always a consideration. Like many aspects of rescue, gaining access involves risk versus the benefit. Do not work above your or the team's capabilities. If other resources or specialty trained personnel are needed, call them early.

Patient Assessment

Command and a team leader should always consider having a medically trained person on a field crew. The medical person should be trained to the level of at least the Emergency Medical Responder and have the capabilities of treating team members as well as to evaluate the person once found.

Medical evaluation of the person found can be critical to determining the rescue mission and the time factors. An *Initial Assessment* should be performed involving the five steps of:

  A – Airway management and cervical spine stabilization (if needed),
  B – Breathing and ventilation,
  C - Circulation and bleeding,
  D – Disability, and
  E - Environmental factors (Exposure).

Every team should have a "medical person" that is responsible for team health and for the patients once on a scene. Paramedics would be preferred.

The initial assessment is used to search for possible life threatening injuries. Abnormal findings in one or more of these assessment steps may indicate a life threat. The patient should be considered a priority patient. Treatment to correct the life threat should be initiated immediately and command notified of injuries/illnesses.

Once the initial patient assessment is completed and all injuries and illnesses are found, the patient is placed in one of five priorities:

Priority 1 – Severe to Moderate/major injuries, needs significant field treatment, extraction by a rescue team, possible air evacuation,

Priority 2 - Moderate/major injuries, needs significant field treatment and assistance with extraction,

Priority 3 - Minor injury or illness, needs field treatment/support/assistance, able to walk out,

Priority 4 - No injury or illness and able to walk on their own, or

Priority 5 – Deceased.

These categories determines the resources needed, rescue speed, and the treatment given to the patient. The priority classification also can assist with triage on rescue scene with multiple lost persons.

Patient assessment is an ongoing process and should be repeated throughout the mission. Patient priority and injuries will determine how often secondary assessments should be performed. Patients should also be reassessed after treatment and any major mission activities such as difficult movements, high angle rescues, air rescue, weather changes, etc. At any time the patient condition deteriorates, the team leader should notify command that the patient priority has changed.

Stabilization

Prior to extraction, the patient must be stabilized. Stabilization essentially is providing treatment to the patient which enables the patient to survive extraction to safety. Stabilization of the patient involves treatment of the life threatening injuries and illnesses found in the initial assessment. Most education on EMS field treatment is based on a patient contact time factor of approximately 10 to 30 minutes; however rescue operations may last for hours. To add a challenge to stabilization and treatment, the patient will be moving, either on a vehicle or a stretcher. Field stabilization should be completed quickly and while the patient is being packaged for extraction.

Stabilization needs of the patient are determined by the injuries/illnesses of the patient and the priority category. *At this point the need for a trained emergency responder should be obvious. Do not provide care for which you are not qualified but seek the nearest qualified individual to provide care beyond the scope of your training and understanding.*

Priority 1 –

Persons in the category of moderate/major injuries, needs significant field treatment, extraction by rescue team, possible air evacuation present a difficult treatment scenario and the extraction mission will become a major difference in life or death. These cases present with life threats found in the initial assess and severe injuries/illness. The treatment can range from airway maintenance, ventilation, bleeding control, treatment of major wounds, priority splinting, spinal immobilization, oxygen administration, intravenous fluids and emergency drug administration. Higher trained medical personnel such as paramedics are needed in these situations.

Air transport is needed in priority patients. Command should be notified immediately of high priority patients and arrangements for extraction should be made.

Priority 2 –

Persons in the category of moderate/major injuries, needs significant field treatment and assistance with extraction present with a treatment and an extraction mission. These cases can be as simple as an injured ankle rendering the person immobile to more severe injuries. The treatment can range from bleeding control, treatment of wounds, splinting, spinal immobilization, oxygen administration, intravenous fluids and emergency drug administration. Higher trained medical personnel such as paramedics are needed in these situations.

Priority 3 –

Persons in the category of minor injury or illness need field treatment/support/ assistance are patients who may be lost, tired or have minor injuries. These cases usually involve persons who have been lost or missing for more than 24-48 hours or who were not properly prepared for the conditions. They are able to walk on their own but need support from the team such as treatment of minor wounds; assistance with carrying equipment or pack; rehydration; food; warmth or cooling; or simple encouragement.

Priority 4 –

Persons in the category of no injury or illness and able to walk will be assisted to safety. These cases are usually a lost or misplaced person who has lost their way. They only need assistance to a place of safety.

Priority 5 –

Deceased persons are discussed in the recovery section.

Packaging

Packaging is an important part of the stabilization, treatment and extraction of a patient. Often it is not considered until on the scene and the patient is in need of rescue. Search and rescue members should review equipment and the technique of packaging a patient. These techniques should be taught in initial training and practiced on a regular basis. Persons needing packaging are often higher priority patients.

On a rescue scene, team leaders should develop a plan to package a patient based on extraction plan, terrain, weather, medical needs, team members and patient comfort. As with most rescue situations, packaging can vary due to the many factors to consider.

The first rule is *"do no harm."* Placing a patient on a litter and extracting them to a safe location is difficult. Safety of the crew and the patient should be considered at all times. The patient should be properly placed in the litter and secured. Safety equipment such as helmet and harness for the patient may also be considered. Terrain may dictate the need for additional packaging and securing of the patient. The last thing a team leader would want is a patient to fall out of the litter or be injured due to lack of packaging.

Weather is always a consideration for many aspects of rescue. Package the patient accordingly. Cold weather requires multiple layers to conserve body heat. Hot packs may also be used to maintain heat. In warm weather, keeping the patient cool is also a consideration. Rain, snow, wind and other elements should be considered in the packaging plan. Sunscreen and insect repellant may also be needed. Patients can inform members of conditions and needs. Team leaders must maintain a situational awareness with patients who are not able to relay comfort to the team and reassess needs of the patient. If the team member needs something, it is very likely that the patient may have the same need.

Spinal immobilization may also be required. Injuries to head, neck, or back suggest spinal immobilization. Local protocols should determine the need for full spinal immobilization based on injury, deficits, and risk versus benefits of immobilization. Patients who require full spinal immobilization should have rigid cervical collar in place and be placed on a long back board, secured with straps and head immobilization devise. Liberal use of padding will make the patient more comfortable during a long extraction. The board and the patient should also be secured to the litter for extraction. Full body vacuum splints are very useful to immobilize and secure patients.

Patients with significant injuries may require access by the medical personnel and treatment as the patient is being moved. Packaging should not be so cumbersome and complex that medical personnel do not have access to the patient. Periodically, the patient may need "repackaging" due to the movement of extraction. Packaging should be assessed during rest stops and after major rescue movements such as high angle extraction.

Extraction

At the beginning of the chapter, search and rescue was described as one team covering two separate operations. Extraction of a person is part of rescue but it can be considered a third operation due to the planning, resources involved, and the extensive labor needed for some missions.

Extraction of the patient is the main goal of rescue and may be the most demanding of the rescue mission. The steadfast rule for extraction is finding the fastest, safest, easiest way to get the person to safety. As the team leader on the scene, the factors previously discussed such as size up, gaining access, patient assessment/priority, stabilization needs, and packaging should help determine a plan for extraction. Other considerations are time of day, weather, terrain, on hand resources, and resource needs. The team leaders should be involved in the plan to extract the patient. He/she needs to relay vital information to command to help formulate the plan.

Figure 93 Preparing safety lines.

The located person's ability to walk on their own or with assistance can be very valuable to the team leader. Every effort should be placed on assisting the patient in walking to safety. If the person does walk, do not exhaust the person, or injure them, place them in unsafe area, or make injuries worse. Let them move at their own pace with the support of the team.

Persons who are unable to move on their own must be transported out by the rescue team. Priority 3 and 4 persons may need assistance and treatment in order to prepare them for movement. Moving a person in a rescue situation can be dangerous, exhausting, and time consuming. The team leader should call for more teams and resources if the patient must be carried to safety.

The workload should be rotated between qualified team members so members can rest. Fresh members working the rescue operations and stretcher will promote safety. Safety cannot be over emphasized. The team leader should promote safety in every aspect of the mission and encourage the team to point out safety concerns.

The route that the team took to locate the patient may not be the best for extraction. Team leaders should be familiar with the area and possible extraction routes. Map and compass skills are essential to the team leader due to the possible need to extract the patient to another location or possible landing zone for air evacuation. The team leader may be called to direct the extraction to the other location.

Equipment used to extract the patient varies from organization to organization. The team leader should be familiar with all equipment used to extract the patient and know how to troubleshoot any problems that may be encountered during the extraction.

Recovery

Unfortunately there are times when the person is found but they are deceased. The mission is then classified as a recovery. Recovery operations have similar considerations as rescue operations with the addition of assisting with investigation and security. Law enforcement or coroner should be involved in any recovery situation. A leader should address the following considerations of recovery:

Figure 94 Securing a scene.

Preplanning

Preplanning for a recovery is similar to the preplanning of a rescue. The team leader should be familiar with the standing orders or protocols for a recovery. Organizations should have protocols in place for the handling of a recovery incident. The team leader should be familiar with his/her role involving investigation and recovery of a lost or deceased person prior to the incident.

The briefing from command and the conditions of the mission can help the team leader preplan for the incident. When briefing the team for a mission, the team leader should prepare the team for the possibility of a recovery. The team leader should also request a code word to be transmitted to command if the team discovers the person and it is a recovery.

Size up/Gaining Access and Patient Assessment

Size up, gaining access and patient assessments are the same for recovery as with rescue. The team leader and/or medical person should insure that the person is deceased and not recoverable. Special cases such as hypothermia may present challenges to determining the cause of death of a person. The team leader should follow established protocols and consult medical control or command for questionable situations.

The most pressing issue encounter is that the scene could be a crime scene. Gaining access and performing a patient assessment should be completed while preserving the scene and possible evidence. The team leader should limit the number of personnel in the area. Any clue located by the team that may be evidence should be treated as such. Do not remove, handle or tamper with any clues, evidence including firearms and weapons, or the body. The team leader should be aware of the scene and make observations. These clues and the scene should be recorded by the team leader. GPS location of evidence and clues should be recorded.

Investigation and Security

Once the scene is determined to be a recovery, command should be notified and the team leader should prepare the team for the recovery operation. There are several factors that change when involved in a recovery. Scene security is very important when involving a recovery. The team may be involved in securing the scene from bystanders, family members, or other persons in the area. Marking tape should be placed around the scene to prevent any unauthorized persons from entering.

Law enforcement and coroners may be involved in the investigation and evidence collection. Team leaders should follow organizational protocols involving the role and the amount of assistance the SAR teams are involved in these activities.

Documentation is paramount for the team leader. Start early and document all aspects and events on the scene. This information can be shared with law enforcement and provided to command. The team leader may also be called to provide a statement or testify in court. A case may not be brought to court for years. The team leader's documentation can provide forgotten details that can be used in court and in testimony.

Packaging and Extraction

The team may be involved in the removal of the body to another location. Safety is always the first priority. The team leader should evaluate the risk versus benefit. The life and safety of a rescuer should not be risked for the recovery of a body. The urgency is reduced and the team can take more time and can call more resources to recover the body.

Packaging and extraction should involve securing the body in a disaster bag, securing to stretcher and removing to another location. The extraction should be coordinated with command to avoid possible media or family members in route or at the end point. An extraction plan should be completed with a recovery as it would with a rescue. Team members should never take pictures of the deceased or of the scene! Law Enforcement officers and the Coroner will take any required photos.

Other Considerations

The team leader should be aware of how well the team is handling a recovery. There may be situations that can be very stressful for team members. Scenes that are very graphic or traumatic or involve children may be more than a rescuer is able to deal with at that time. Other factors such as situation, length of the search, the mental state of the member or the fatigue of the team will affect the way in which the team member will respond. The team leader should recognize signs of stress and assist the team member.

Summary

Rescue and recovery are very important aspects of the Search and Rescue operations. The team leader must be knowledgeable and prepared for the rescue or recovery operation. He/she must also be aware of the changes involved in going from a broad search mission to a narrower rescue or recovery mission.

The team leader must address the considerations of rescue and recovery operations. The team leader should always consider pre-planning, scene size-up, gaining access, patient assessment, prioritizing patients, stabilization, packaging, and extraction. In recovery operations, security and investigation assistance may also be considered by the team leader. In all scenes, stress recognition and management should be on the team leader's mind. Take care of your team.

Notes:

STRESS: What is on the outside may not always be what is on the inside…..

Chapter 14

Stress Management

Objectives

- *Define the term stress.*
- *Define and explain the role of stressors.*
- *Identify three types of stressors.*
- *Identify and describe the four categories of symptoms relating to adverse stress reactions.*
- *Explain the four ways adverse stress reactions can be prevented.*
- *Describe when Critical Incident Stress Debriefing (CISD) may be needed.*

Stress is a part of life. A moderate amount of stress is essential if an optimal level of alertness and performance are going to be maintained. Too little or too much stress generally has a negative impact on one's alertness and productivity. Every person involved in a search and rescue incident will experience stress. *Stress is not something to be avoided. It is something to be managed.* But, it must be managed properly in order to be dealt with effectively. If it is ignored or emotionally denied it may lead to an adverse stress reaction, diminished effectiveness during an operation and, possibly, "burn-out."

The stress experienced during a search and rescue incident is not the only stress experienced by the SAR personnel. The stress experienced during an incident is in addition to the stress brought to the SAR operation. Difficulties in interpersonal relationships, vocational tensions, environmental factors, fatigue, etc. all contribute to one's stress level. The amount of stress one experiences can heighten or hinder performance. *The effects of stress on one's performance are unique to each individual.*

This chapter will assist the SAR leader in understanding the nature of stress and its impact on the individual. The leader must be able to appropriately manage stress and help others in their management of stress in order to ensure and maintain safety standards and optimal performance during an operation. Topics covered in this chapter include understanding stress.

Stress-free living is impossible. Stress, in moderate levels, can enhance one's life and performance. The term stress is defined by the Federal Emergency Management Agency

(FEMA) as "a physical response of the body that occurs whenever we must adapt to changing conditions."[24]

Those things which affect an individual are known as stressors. There are four basic types of stressors.

Stress is a part of the search and rescue operation. Stress impacts one's performance during an operation. It is important that the SAR leader be acutely aware of his personnel and the types of stress brought to, and being experienced during an operation.

> **Types of Stressors**
>
> 1. **Environmental Stressors** *are those created by the incident context, i.e., terrain, weather, etc.*
>
> 2. **Incident command system Stressors** *are issues and problems, decision making, involved with being in charge, etc.*
>
> 3. **Psychosocial Stressors** *are those which come through interaction with others-communication problems, crew conflicts, interpersonal problems, etc.*
>
> 4. **Personality Stressors** *are those which one creates for him/herself reaction to criticism, inability to say "no", inability to set personal limits, self-imposed guilt for not handling a situation beyond one's control.*

Symptoms of Adverse Stress Reactions

The leader must be aware of the symptoms produced by an adverse stress reaction. It should be noted that "Emergency responders tend to suppress their fear, ignore clues of danger and press on with a belief they cannot be harmed." This ability, which can be a major asset during a critical operation, is also the emergency personnel's greatest liability.

The health and safety of operational personnel is of the highest priority. Therefore, it is essential that the four categories of adverse symptoms of stress be known, recognized, and addressed with utmost urgency before, during and after an operation.

●Category I: Cognitive Symptoms are a person's ability to think clearly. This may be evidenced by an inability to make judgments and decisions, lack of ability to conceptualize alternatives or prioritize tasks, confusion, inability to evaluate one's own functioning, etc.

●Category II: Psychological Symptoms are a person's psychological demeanor. This may be evidenced by emotional mood swings irritability, depression, apathy, anger, hyper-excitability, lack of patience, etc.

---

[24] *Stress Management: Model Program for Maintaining Firefighter Well Being.* FEMA/USFA, Feb. 1991, p.19.

- Category III: Physical Symptoms or physical characteristics. This may be evidenced by hypochondria, loss of energy, loss of sleep, appetite irregularities, gastrointestinal distress, chills, sweats, etc.

- Category IV: Behavioral Symptoms. This may be evidenced by excessive fatigue, hyperactivity, inability to express one's self verbally or in writing, etc.

It is essential that the leader be able to identify and assess the stress level of crew members in order to ensure their health and safety. Remember that each crew member is already experiencing stress prior to the incident and that this stress is compounded by the incident. This is especially true when it is an extended operation, involves children, taking place in adverse weather and terrain, when foul play is suspected or involved, etc. The key to preventing an adverse stress reaction is to *proactively* manage stress during the operation.

Managing Stress during an Operation

Stress management must be taken seriously during an operation. The SAR leader must be able to identify symptoms of stress in one's self and others. There are four ways that one can assist in preventing an adverse stress reaction.

1. Establish appropriates ground rules for personnel during the search.
2. Make sure each member's level of training and skill are ascertained and appropriate responsibilities assigned.
3. Inexperienced SAR personnel can receive valuable "on the job training," but be sure that they are being properly supervised.
4. Recognize that all people have limits. These limits must be acknowledged and respected.
5. Be alert to mental, emotional and physical fatigue.
6. Make sure that appropriate rest is provided and that each member's intake of calories and liquids is adequate.
7. If you are working with volunteers remember that they may have to work their regular job the next day.
8. Maintain realistic expectations. SAR personnel are human. Do not expect yourself or others to act in superhuman ways.
9. Recognize stress, allow individuals to discuss frustrations, express limitations and respond in an affirming and encouraging manner.

Preventing problems in the field requires that the leader be an astute observer of the crew members.

- Take breaks, discuss matters other than the operation,
- make sure assignments are appropriates to a person's technical skill and training,
- provide oversight,
- teach and instruct rather than criticize and reprimand,
- ensure that each member takes time off from the operation,
- and be willing to remove SAR personnel from the operation rather than compromise the health and safety of the individual and crew.

Should I Request Critical Incident Stress Debriefing (CISD)

Critical Incident Stress Debriefing is a valuable response and is appropriate when an acute or unusual emotional reaction to stress is experienced which interferes with one's ability to function at the scene or later. CISD may be appropriates when a disaster is involved, a young child is involved or other extreme situations. CISD is a tool which aids the SAR personnel in dealing with the emotional stresses resulting from an incident. It encourages personnel to:

→ Share their feelings about an incident and allow a facilitator to assess them.

→ Discuss the signs and symptoms of stress with a trained facilitator.

→ Develop a plan of action with a facilitator, including the need for further debriefing or counseling if appropriate.

Figure 95 SAR dog.

Summary

SAR personnel must fulfill a variety of roles and have a myriad of responsibilities as well as the stress brought about by the incident which sometimes overloads the capability to cope. The leader must be able to effectively identify symptoms of stress in order to ensure the health and safety of each crew member. The SAR leader who *proactively* manages stress will be able to perform optimally during an operation and make a significant contribution to its overall effectiveness.

As a footnote....do not forget to de-stress your dog also! A nice bath and a massage can work wonders.

References and Recommended Reading

Donald D., Ed. <u>Fundamentals of Search and Rescue.</u> National Association for Search and Rescue. Cooper. Sudbury, Massachusetts: Jones and Bartlett, C. 2005. Print.

Freeman, David. <u>Maintaining Our Resources.</u> (n.p. Critical Incident Stress Debriefs of Florida, n.d.).

Hudson., Steve & Vines, Tom. <u>High Angle Rope Rescue Techniques</u>. Mosby Jems, St. Louis MO, p. 2, C. 2004. Print.

Judah, Christy. <u>Building a Basic Foundation for Search and Rescue Dog Training</u>. Coastal Books. C. 2007. Print.

Judah, Christy. <u>Training a Search and Rescue Dog for Wilderness Air Scent</u>. Coastal Books. C. 2014. Print.

Judah, Christy. <u>Water Search: Search and Rescue Dogs Finding Drowned Persons</u>. Coastal Books. C. 2011. Print.

Judah, Christy and Sargent, Trace. <u>Training a Human Remains Detection Dog</u>. Coastal Books. C. 2015. Print.

Judah, J. C. <u>Buzzards and Butterflies: Human Remains Detection Dogs</u>. Coastal Books. C. 2008. Print.

Koester, Robert. <u>Lost Person Behavior</u>. dbS Productions LLC; 1st edition. C. August 31, 2008. Print.

Koester, Robert. <u>Lost Person Behavior: Practical Map Exercise</u>. dbS Productions LLC; 1st edition, C. January 12, 2014. Print.

Koester, Robert and Koester, Emily. <u>Incident Command System Field Operations Guide for Search and Rescue.</u> dbS Productions; 2nd edition, C. May 1, 2014. Spiral Bound.

Mitchell, Jeffrey T. and Brady, Grady. <u>Emergency Services Stress: Guidelines for Preserving the Health and Careers of Emergency Services Personnel</u>. Englewood Cliffs, Brady, 1990.

National Association of Emergency Medical Technicians. *PHTLS Prehospital Trauma Life Support. 7th ed.* St. Louis, Missouri, C. 2011. Print.

National Fire Protection Association. Fire Service Life Safety Rope and System Components, Quincy MA, Standard NFPA. 1983-2001 edition.

O'Conner, Daniel. Managing the Lost Person Incident. National Association for Search & Rescue, The; 2nd edition, January 3, 2011. Print.

Padgett, Allen & Smith, Bruce. On Rope; North American Vertical Rope Techniques; For Caving....Rapellers. Revised edition, National Speleological Society, Huntsville AL, 1996. Print.

SAR Fundamentals, p. 202, 204. Print.

Stoffel, Robert. The Handbook for Managing Land Search Operations. Cashmere, Washington: Emergency Response International, C. 2001. Print.

Vis, Greg. Ed. Paramedic Care: Principles and Practice. Special Considerations/Operations. Upper Saddle River, New Jersey: Prentice-Hall, C. 2001. Print

Young, Christopher S. Urban Search: Managing Missing Person Searches in the Urban Environment. dbS Productions LLC; 1st edition, C. October 1, 2007. Print.

About the Authors

Anne Brandt

Anne Brandt is the current Vice President\Command for NGMSAR (North Georgia Mounted Search and Rescue).

Anne comes to Georgia from one generation off a South Carolina Farm. She grew up playing with the horses and spending her days in the woods. The woods are still her favorite place to spend time and she has no hesitation in getting out there wherever she is needed.

As a member of NGMSAR for the past 5 years, Anne is SAR TECH II certified until 2019, a First Responder and currently the Training Director for Dawson County C.E.R.T. Anne runs Incident Command as the only non-horse owner in the organization; yet loves to ride.

Anne is also working to obtain her SAR TECH I and continues to grow with another keen interest in Tracking and Wilderness Survival.

Anne is married with one son, four grandchildren, and two German Shepherds.

Her personal objective: *To continue learning in order to grow and know what to do when helping others in need.*

Shirley Cox

Shirley is the Secretary/Records Maintenance Manager for NGMSAR (North Georgia Mounted Search and Rescue). She is Cobb County C.E.R.T. trained whose certifications include Level 1 First Responder and Rescue Specialist. Although always loving horses, Shirley didn't begin riding until her mid 40's and has enjoyed every minute since.

Typical of Shirley is her favorite quote: *"I have a lot to be grateful for in my life, and volunteering for the community is a small thank you for that gift."*

George Dresnek

George Dresnek grew up on a family farm in eastern Ohio. After college he worked for several oil companies including Sunoco, Kitt Energy and Sohio Alaska. While in Alaska he demonstrated his hiking and wilderness skills in the Chugach Mountains.

When George moved to California he went to work for Sonoma County as a probation officer for the supervised adult crews and then held various positions with the Sonoma County Sheriff's office including serving with the Sheriff's Search and Rescue Team for ten years. His primary focus was as a Tracking Crew Chief and was a search manager for eight years. During this period George had the opportunity to enhance his tracking skills through his association with Ab Taylor, Del Morris, and many other pioneers in developing the art and science of tracking. He continues to work with Del Morris in the development of NASAR instruction and evaluation procedures.

George is currently a NASAR Instructor for FUNSAR, Tracking, Advanced Search and Rescue, Urban Search, and Managing the Lost Person Incident. He is also a Lead Evaluator for SAR Tech I and SAR Tech II. George is also a member of the Board of Directors for NASAR.

R. David Dyer, Jr.

R. David Dyer Jr., B.A., is trained as a NREMT-Paramedic and is the Deputy Emergency Management Director Union County Emergency Management, Blairsville Georgia; Fire Chief, Union County Fire Department, Blairsville, Georgia; SAR Tech II; Level II EMS Instructor; NPQ Fire Instructor; BLS, ACLS, PALS, and PHTLS Instructor.

He previously served with the Union General Hospital EMS program for 24 years. He has served in the levels of EMT, Paramedic, EMS Captain and EMS Director. He was an instructor for BLS, ACLS, PALS, PHTLS, and BTLS for Union General and North Georgia Technical College. He was also a flight medic for Rescue Air and Omni Flight for five years.

David served the Union County Fire Department for 25 years as a Firefighter, Lieutenant, Captain, Battalion Chief, and Fire Chief. He is currently serving as a Fire Chief. He has taken Search and Rescue courses through West Georgia Technical College and obtained SAR Tech level II. He has served as the Lieutenant in command of the search and rescue team of Union County and the lead instructor for the team. David has an AAS degree from West Georgia Tech in Fire Science and a BA degree in Business Management from Truett-McConnell College.

Bernard Fontaine

Brigadier General (Retired) Bernie Fontaine, a member of NASAR's Board of Directors at the time of this writing, came to Search and Rescue from a military and firefighter background. He volunteered for the draft in October 1960. After graduating at the top of his class at the NCO Academy, he was selected for the OCS program. Over the years he went up through the Officer ranks. He served in the Infantry, Armor, Engineer and Signal Corps. As an Infantry Officer he completed Airborne and Ranger Schools where he picked up some navigational skills before serving in Vietnam. At Fort Leavenworth, KS he completed the Command and General Staff College. Then while serving with the Georgia National Guard he completed his PhD coursework in Political Science.

After retirement he became quite active in Firefighting and attained National Professional Qualification as a Level 2 Firefighter. Since firefighters in Georgia also perform Search and Rescue missions, this interest led to his certification as a SARTECH I and II Evaluator, and a FUNSAR, ADSAR, MLPI, Tracking and Urban Search Instructor.

Christy Judah

Christy Judah earned a Masters degree in Counseling from Campbell University and a Bachelors Degree in Education from the University of North Carolina at Pembroke. She is retired from her primary career as a school counselor completing 30 years in the NC Public School System. She is a Search and Rescue Technician I and has actively participated in search and rescue for twenty years. She has responded to over 300 callouts and has multiple finds working her 4th certified SAR dog. She continues to respond to callouts with her team, Brunswick Search and Rescue, in North Carolina.

Judah has written extensively on the topics of search and rescue and canine training, publishing multiple books. Some of the SAR books include Building a Basic Foundation for Search and Rescue Dog Training, Buzzards and Butterflies: Human Remains Detection, Training a Search and Rescue Dog for Wilderness Air Scent, How to Train a Human Remains Detection Dog (co-authored with Tracy Sargent), How to Build a SAR Team From the Ground Up, Water Search: Finding Drowned Victims, A Tribute to Search and Rescue Dogs, and Meet the SAR Dogs. In addition, she has written several books documenting the history of southeastern North Carolina, as well as life during the slave period from the early 1700s through the War Between the States. She is also published in multiple magazines, featured in several national articles, television programs, and is the Chief and lead trainer for her SAR team.

Robert Koester

Robert J. Koester is the founder and CEO of dbS Productions LLC. He first joined the Appalachian Search & Rescue Conference in 1981 and since then has participated in hundreds of searches, including over a hundred as Incident Commander. He holds a MS from the University of Virginia in biology (neurobiology) and is currently a Fellow at Kingston University in London. His contributions to search and rescue include seminal research on lost person behavior (with an early emphasis on dementia). A Search and Rescue Mission Coordinator, instructor for the Virginia Department of Emergency Management and past-president (15 years) of the Virginia Search and Rescue Council, Robert has also worked for the United States Coast Guard (conducting visual sweep width experiments), and the Federal Emergency Management Agency (as an instructor).

Robert provides research, publications, software, and training services for search and rescue (SAR). Currently, he has a Phase II SBIR contract with the US Department of Homeland Security Science & Technology Directorate to develop initial response software and tools for first responders. With funding from a USDA SBIR, he created the International Search and Rescue Incident Database (ISRID). This database allowed the creation of spatial models that help predict the location of lost persons such as children, those with dementia, autistic spectrum disorders, hikers, hunters, or missing aircraft. Over 40 different subject categories have been developed. Robert has done research for National Aeronautics and Space Administration (conducting missing aircraft radar research), National Park Service (responding to major searches and writing the draft NPS SAR Field Manual), SAR Institute of New Zealand (conducting sound and light sweep width experiments), and Justice Institute of British Columbia (reviewing management texts). He also coordinates over 200 instructors worldwide who teach the Lost Person Behavior training class. Robert has authored numerous books and research articles on search and rescue, including *Lost Person Behavior*. He has presented in Aruba, Australia, Iceland, Ireland, Norway, Poland, United Kingdom, and throughout Canada, New Zealand, and the United States.

Del Morris

Del Morris has over 30 years in search and rescue participating in both tracking and search management. He was on Sonoma County Search and Rescue Team for over 25 years and currently is on the Amador County SAR team in California.

Del was one of the founding members of the Bay Area Search and Rescue Council in California and helped develop the original Section Chief Class (which was the forerunner to Managing the Lost Person Incident course).

He was a friend and student of Ab Taylor. He is currently the head of the NASAR Tracking Committee and developed the NASAR tracking class in 2011. In 2014 he developed the NASAR tracker evaluation, the first of its type in the country for trackers.

Allen Padgett

Allen Padgett has a Bachelors degree in Public Administration from Brenau College of Gainesville GA. He is retired from 34 years service as a wildlife officer in Georgia and 10 years as an Emergency Medical Technician with a local service provider. He is a Fellow and Merit Award recipient from the National Speleological Society and is currently a cave rescue instructor. In 1989 he co-authored the technical best seller "On Rope" for the caving society.

Padgett has been involved in search and rescue for over 40 years and is currently a NASAR SAR Tech II evaluator. He authored a rescue curriculum for the Georgia Emergency Management Agency and is currently a Rescue Specialist instructor. Padgett has been the chairman of Search and Rescue Dogs of Georgia since 1988 and is still currently active with many aspects of the SAR community. In partnership with another retired officer, he teaches and consults on land search skills in the Southeastern part of the United States. He currently resides near Lafayette Georgia with his wife Karen and her fourth search dog, Tybee.

Anthony Somogyi

Lieutenant Colonel Tony Somogyi is the Commander of the High-altitude Army Aviation Training Site (HAATS) located in Gypsum, CO. He holds a B.S. in Aeronautical Studies from the University of North Dakota where he also earned his Rotorcraft Commercial and Instrument Licenses. After spending eight years on Active Duty, he has been stationed at HAATS for the last nine years where he is also instructs in the OH-58A, CH-47D, and UH-72A helicopters. HAATS is primarily responsible for teaching pilots the art and science of Power Management and Environmental Flight Techniques in a mountainous environment.

In addition to student training, the HAATS conducts Search and Rescue missions fairly regularly as part of their state mission as National Guardsmen. LTC Somogyi has conducted numerous SAR missions in the mountainous regions of Colorado. He is a graduate of the Colorado Search and Rescue Board's Search Management Course and has dedicated a great deal of time in integration efforts between National Guard and Civilian SAR agencies. HAATS currently has a partnership with both Vail Mountain Rescue Group and Mountain Rescue Aspen wherein they train and execute missions in a virtually seamless fashion. HAATS has been recognized with awards from NASAR and the American Helicopter Society for their efforts and successes on Search and Rescue missions.

Chris Young

Christopher (Chris) S. Young has been active in Search and Rescue since 1981, managed searches since 1986, is the past reserve Captain for the Contra Costa County Sheriff's Search and Rescue Team and serves as chairman of the Bay Area Search and Rescue Council, Inc. (BASARC). Chris is a retired Instructor for the POST Direction and Control of the Search Function Course for the State of California Office of Emergency Service for the past 25 years, is currently an Instructor/Trainer for the Managing the Lost Person Incident and Urban Search Management (developed by Chris) courses sponsored by the National Association for Search and Rescue (NASAR).

He is an Instructor/Trainer in Emergency Medical Response and first aid for the American Red Cross since 1973, as well as specialized topics in Search Management, including Search Management in the Urban Environment, and Investigation and Interviewing in SAR. Chris has also written, published and presented search management papers at the National Association for Search and Rescue conferences, the Canadian National Search and Rescue Secretariat SARSCENE conferences, the William Syrotuck Symposiums on Search Theory and Practice, the Canadian Coast Guard College, the Provincial S'ret' Du Quebec Police and several State Search and Rescue conferences on the subject of Search Management in the Urban Environment. He is also co-author of the book Urban Search: Managing Missing Person Searches in the Urban Environment, published 2007 by dbS Publications as well as a contributing author on several other books for search and rescue. Additionally, Chris is a Level 1 law enforcement reserve with the Sheriffs Dept and the City of Danville and an EMT 1 Instructor.

APPENDIX A

TEAM BRIEFING OUTLINE

MISSION

What is the specific objective? Apply the SMART criteria (Specific, Measurable, Achievable, Relevant, Time related):

S:
_____

M:
_____

A:
_____

R:
_____

T:
_____

EXECUTION

Specific area of search, Critical Spacing (CS), Track length, etc. (use map and map overlay whenever possible):

Assign Responsibilities:

Navigation _____

Tally _____

Documentation_____

Specialized tasks _____

Expected POD based on CS, Track Length, Speed and time allotted: _____%.

Time In: _____ Time Out: _____.

Location (UTM): _____

Drop Off Time: _____   Pick UP Time: _____

Clue awareness, Clue Handling/Protection:
_____
_____

Scene Protection:
_____

_____

Other Pertinent Information:

ADMINISTRATION and LOGISTICS

Food and Water Requirements:
_____

_____

Special Equipment, PPE, etc.:
_____
_____

Medical Support:
_____
_____

COMMAND and COMMUNICATIONS

Chain of command:
_____
_____

Communications:

_____
_____
_____
_____
_____

Radio Nets/Frequencies:
_____
_____

Cell Number:

_____
_____

Other:

_____
_____
_____
_____
_____
_____
_____
_____

APPENDIX B – Selected ICS Forms

ICS Forms
    ICS 202 Incident Objective
    ICS 203 Organization Assignment List
    ICS 204 Assignment List
    ICS 205A Communications Unit Leader
    ICS 206 Medical Plan
    ICS 214 Activities Log

Other Forms, as required

NOTE: All ICS Forms, in Word fillable, are available on line under FEMA ICS Forms. They are also available for you to print in booklet format.

INCIDENT OBJECTIVES **ICS-202**	1. INCIDENT NAME	2. DATE PREPARED	3. TIME PREPARED

4. OPERATIONAL PERIOD (DATE/TIME)

5. GENERAL CONTROL OBJECTIVES FOR THE INCIDENT (INCLUDE ALTERNATIVE

6. WEATHER FORECAST FOR OPERATIONAL PERIOD

7. GENERAL/SAFETY MESSAGE

8. ATTACHMENTS (CHECK IF ATTACHED)

　__ ORGANIZATION LIST (ICS 203)　　　　　　　__ TRAFFIC PLAN
　__ DIVISION ASSIGNMENT LISTS (ICS 204)　　　__ FIRE BEHAVIOR FORECAST
　__ COMMUNICATIONS PLAN (ICS 205)　　　　　__ WEATHER FORECAST
　__ MEDICAL PLAN (ICS 206)　　　　　　　　　__ OTHER
　__ INCIDENT MAP

9. PREPARED BY (PLANNING SECTION CHIEF)

ORGANIZATION ASSIGNMENT LIST
ICS-203

1. INCIDENT NAME	2. DATE PREPARED
3. TIME PREPARED	4. OPERATIONAL PERIOD DATE: TIME:

5. INCIDENT COMMANDER AND STAFF

- INCIDENT COMMANDER
- PNF MANAGER
- DEPUTY
- SAFETY OFFICER
- INFORMATION OFFICER
- LIAISON OFFICER

6. AGENCY REPRESENTATIVES

AGENCY	NAME

7. PLANNING SECTION

- CHIEF
- DEPUTY
- RESOURCES UNIT LEADER
- SITUATION UNIT LEADER
- DOCUMENTATION UNIT
- DEMOBILIZATION UNIT
- PRES. FIRE BEHAVIOR ANALYST
- FIRE BEHAVIOR ANALYST
- TECHNICAL SPECIALISTS

8. LOGISTICS SECTION

- CHIEF
- DEPUTY

a. SUPPORT BRANCH

- DIRECTOR
- SUPPLY UNIT
- FACILITIES UNIT
- GROUND SUPPORT UNIT

9. OPERATIONS SECTION

- CHIEF
- CHIEF
- DEPUTY
- CHIEF

a. BRANCH I - DIVISIONS/GROUPS

- BRANCH DIRECTOR
- DEPUTY
- DIVISION/GROUP
- DIVISION/GROUP
- DIVISION/GROUP
- DIVISION/GROUP
- DIVISION/GROUP

b. BRANCH II - DIVISIONS/GROUPS

- BRANCH DIRECTOR
- DEPUTY
- DIVISION/GROUP
- DIVISION/GROUP
- DIVISION/GROUP
- DIVISION/GROUP
- DIVISION/GROUP

c. BRANCH III - DIVISIONS/GROUPS

- BRANCH DIRECTOR
- DEPUTY
- DIVISION/GROUP
- DIVISION/GROUP
- DIVISION/GROUP
- DIVISION/GROUP
- DIVISION/GROUP

d. AIR OPERATIONS BRANCH

- AIR OPERATIONS BRANCH DIR.
- AIR TACTICAL GROUP SUPER.
- AIR SUPPORT SUPERVISOR
- HELICOPTER COORDINATOR
- AIR TANKER COORDINATOR

10. FINANCE SECTION

- CHIEF

	b. **SERVICE BRANCH**		DEPUTY TIME UNIT PROCUREMENT UNIT	
DIRECTOR COMMUNICATIONS UNIT MEDICAL UNIT FOOD UNIT			COMPENSATION/CLAIMS UNIT COST UNIT	

PREPARED BY (RESOURCES UNIT)

1. BRANCH	2. DIVISION/GROUP	**DIVISION ASSIGNMENT LIST**
		ICS-204
3. INCIDENT NAME	4. OPERATIONAL PERIOD DATE: TIME:	

5. OPERATIONS PERSONNEL

OPERATIONS SECTION CHIEF: DIVISION/GROUP SUPERVISOR :	BRANCH DIRECTOR: AIR TACTICAL GROUP SUPV:

6. RESOURCES ASSIGNED THIS PERIOD

STRIKE TEAM/TASK FORCE/RESOURCE DESIGNATOR	LEADER	NUMBER PERSONS	TRANS. NEEDED	DROP OFF POINT/TIME	PICK UP POINT/TIME

7. OPERATIONS

8. SPECIAL INSTRUCTIONS

9. DIVISION/GROUP COMMUNICATIONS SUMMARY

FUNCTION		FREQUENCY	SYSTEM	CHAN.	FUNCTION		FREQUENCY	SYSTEM	CHAN.
COMMAND	LOCAL				STATUS/ LOGISTICS	LOCAL			
COMMAND	REPEAT				STATUS/ LOGISTICS	REPEAT			
DIVISION/GROUP TACTICAL					GROUND TO AIR				

PREPARED BY (RESOURCE UNIT LEADER)	DATE	TIME

INCIDENT RADIO COMMUNICATIONS PLAN
ICS - 205

			INCIDENT NAME	PREPARED DATE TIME	OPERATIONAL PERIOD DATE TIME
SYSTEM/ CACHE	CHANNEL	FUNCTION	FREQUENCY	ASSIGNMENT	REMARKS

Notes:

PREPARED BY (COMMUNICATIONS UNIT)

MEDICAL PLAN **ICS-206**	INCIDENT NAME	DATE PREPARED	TIME PREPARED	OPERATIONAL PERIOD

INCIDENT MEDICAL AID STATIONS

MEDICAL AID STATIONS	LOCATION	PARAMEDICS	
		YES	NO

TRANSPORTATION

A. AMBULANCE SERVICES

NAME	ADDRESS	PHONE	PARAMEDICS	
			YES	NO

B. INCIDENT AMBULANCES

NAME	LOCATION	PARAMEDICS	
		YES	NO

HOSPITALS

NAME	ADDRESS	TRAVEL TIME		PHONE	HELIPAD		BURN CENTER	
		AIR	GRND		YES	NO	YES	NO

8. MEDICAL EMERGENCY PROCEDURES

ICS - 214

1. Incident Name:	2. Operational Period:	Date From:	Date To:
		Time From:	Time To:

3. Name:	4. ICS Position:	5. Home Agency (and Unit):	

6. Resources Assigned:

Name	ICS Position	Home Agency (and Unit)	

7. Activity Log:

Date/Time	Notable Activities		

8. Prepared by:	Name:	Position/Title:	Signature:

ICS 214, Page 1	Date/Time:		

1. Incident Name:	2. Operational Period:	Date From:	Date To:
		Time From:	Time To:

7. Activity Log (continuation):

Date/Time	Notable Activities		

8. Prepared by:	Name:	Position/Title: #	Signature: _____
ICS 214, Page 2	Date/Time:		

ICS 214   Activity Log

Purpose. The Activity Log (ICS 214) records details of notable activities at any ICS level, including single resources, equipment, Task Forces, etc. These logs provide basic incident activity documentation, and a reference for any after-action report.

Preparation. An ICS 214 can be initiated and maintained by personnel in various ICS positions as it is needed or appropriate. Personnel should document how relevant incident activities are occurring and progressing, or any notable events or communications.

Distribution. Completed ICS 214s are submitted to supervisors, who forward them to the Documentation Unit. All completed original forms must be given to the Documentation Unit, which maintains a file of all ICS 214s. It is recommended that individuals retain a copy for their own records.

Notes:
- The ICS 214 can be printed as a two-sided form.
- Use additional copies as continuation sheets as needed, and indicate pagination as used.

Block Number	Block Title	Instructions
1	**Incident Name**	Enter the name assigned to the incident.
2	**Operational Period** • Date and Time From • Date and Time To	Enter the start date (month/day/year) and time (using the 24-hour clock) and end date and time for the operational period to which the form applies.
3	**Name**	Enter the title of the organizational unit or resource designator (e.g., Facilities Unit, Safety Officer, Strike Team).
4	**ICS Position**	Enter the name and ICS position of the individual in charge of the Unit.
5	**Home Agency** (and Unit)	Enter the home agency of the individual completing the ICS 214. Enter a unit designator if utilized by the jurisdiction or discipline.
6	**Resources Assigned**	Enter the following information for resources assigned:
	• Name	Use this section to enter the resource's name. For all individuals, use at least the first initial and last name. Cell phone number for the individual can be added as an option.
	• ICS Position	Use this section to enter the resource's ICS position (e.g., Finance Section Chief).
	• Home Agency (and Unit)	Use this section to enter the resource's home agency and/or unit (e.g., Des Moines Public Works Department, Water Management Unit).
7	**Activity Log** • Date/Time • Notable Activities	• Enter the time (24-hour clock) and briefly describe individual notable activities. Note the date as well if the operational period covers more than one day. • Activities described may include notable occurrences or events such as task assignments, task completions, injuries, difficulties encountered, etc. • This block can also be used to track personal work habits by adding columns such as "Action Required," "Delegated To," "Status," etc.

| 8 | **Prepared by**
• Name
• Position/Title
• Signature
• Date/Time | Enter the name, ICS position/title, and signature of the person preparing the form. Enter date (month/day/year) and time prepared (24-hour clock). |

APPENDIX C

Additional Leadership Guidelines, Briefing and Debriefing Information

1. Planning

Is the plan as presented in the briefing and stated on the ICS Form 214 complete and clearly understood by all team members? Have potential dangers been adequately mitigated? Have contingency resources been identified? Are communications (and back up communications been addressed? Is the identification and description of the lost subject(s) adequate and correct? Have all questions been adequately addressed?

2. Preparedness

Is the team and its leader fully trained and prepared to accomplish the ICS 214 objective? Are all members physically and mentally prepared to accomplish the assigned tasks?

3. Environment

Has the team been properly briefed on all applicable environmental factors such as terrain, vegetation, weather and the myriad of other environmental factors that can affect the search and the team. Are contingencies in place to address environmental changes? Can the team continue to operate beyond the assigned time provided if the situation requires their continued presence?

4. Supervision

Is supervisory control adequately addressed? Is the chain of command clearly addressed? Are all members of the team in agreement of the supervision provided? This factor is doubly important if a team is formed during the incident.

5. Operational Factors

Is the team prepared to meet rapidly changing situations and operational hazards? Is the training and discipline adequate to complete the assigned objective in the time allotted?

BRIEFING AND DEBRIEFING

Briefing

People are most effective when they are well informed about all aspects of the situation at a search incident. Remember, people who feel they are not important enough to be given details about the operation are more likely to be less enthusiastic about a search especially after they have been under stress and are suffering from fatigue. Morale is important!

In addition to complete oral briefings, a written briefing serves as future reference for all personnel. The written briefing can be as detailed as necessary to provide complete and up-to-date information about the situation, past, present, and future.

The IC 204 briefing starts with a summary of the situation, past and present, which provides information that will help orient everyone on the search team to all facets of the incident.

The Operational briefings offer authoritative information and instructions to Task Forces and Strike Teams having primary involvement and assignment of a mission during a search. During the operational briefing crews and teams are given their mission assignments.

The briefing will include direction about the techniques a crew is expected to employ and an indication of how carefully they are to search their assigned areas. The POD for the mission should be an important part of a crew's assignment and crew briefing.

The leader normally should receive the operational briefing from the operations section chief and then, in turn, briefs the crew, task force or strike team about the mission. The crew members should be encouraged to ask questions about the assignment. If the leader needs additional information to answer crew's questions, the answers should be obtained and distributed *before* leaving camp to begin the assignment. The leader should then "brief back" the mission to the operations section manager so that it is clear to everyone that the mission is understood by all and it will be properly executed.

The following information needs to be known before beginning an assignment:

The crew should know how clues should be handled. Specific procedures or requirements for clue marking and /or retrieval must be defined in advance. Incorrect handling of evidence or waiting in the field for instructions can waste a lot of precious time or ruin the value of important clues.

The Crew leader must know what type of field assistance he/she can count on. If a victim is found and is in need of medical attention and transport, the crew leader must know what type of help and back up is available. In many situations it is just as likely that a member of the search team could be injured and need medical assistance and transport. The Crew leader must know exactly what resources are available to his/her own crew members, and he/she needs to know how to access that help.

If the search crew needs special equipment to either accomplish a mission or to facilitate the crew's comfort or safety, the crew leader needs to address these needs in the CP briefing. What safety considerations and hazards might a crew face? Safety needs must be anticipated.

Many times searchers need to be aware of certain external influences such as the media and relatives of the victim and how to respond to them or not respond as required by the Incident Commander.

Once the crew has returned from a mission the record of their activities will need to be prepared and presented. It is important to know what type of debriefing the Incident Commander expects to receives. If you don't know in advance what is expected you probably will not collect the type of information he/she is looking for. You also need to know how detailed your debriefing must be.

To insure that no important information is omitted from the briefing you give to your team, some uniform format is needed.

Rather than experiment with forms and formats, we recommend that you use the standard format used by the American military. The standard five part military operation order is well suited for this type of SAR briefing. This briefing style works hand in glove with the ICS type of information transfer used during a search. The reason the military order works so well with ICS is that ICS, itself is an adaptation of military command.

Situation – What has happened, what is happening and what is expected to happen?
Mission (Task assignment) – What the unit is assigned to do.
Execution – Detail plan of how the unit will accomplish the assignment.
Administration and Logistics – Equipment and support.
Communications and Command – Procedures and information.

Each of these parts can be broken down into subsections with each subsection containing detailed information about the assignment of the resource (team) and its members.

Situation

Subject Information – what we know about the person we are looking for.

Complete physical description of the person.
Clothing worn and equipment carried by the person.
Physical and mental condition of the person.
Behavioral traits of the person.
Circumstances surrounding the search. How it came about that this person is missing.
Medical/health problems of the person.
Photo if one is available.
Clue consideration.
Sole pattern of footwear.
Items he/she is believed to be carrying.

Subject's trip plans.

Missions and locations of search resources on the right or left as well as information on search resources in the search area prior to this mission.

Weather conditions forecast at present and anticipated during the mission.

Mission

Describes the unit's specific objective that is, what this unit is to accomplish, and the segment in which it is done.

Execution

Describes the overall plan to be used during the operation. Explains the overall assignments of individuals, and specific duties during the search mission. Provides details of the tactical assignment with explicit instructions about where and how to search. Such as:

Specific area to search. Boundaries of the assigned area.
Configuration, spacing of the searchers.
Where to start and stop.
Where the adjacent units will be.
Who will be responsible for:
Navigation
Tally
Documentation
Other specialized tasks.
Coordinating instructions. (Applying to all personnel).
Times of departure and return.
Transportation details.
Routes and navigation.
General information.
Organization of personnel.
Expected POD.
Method of *handling, marking, and reporting clues*.
How to handle external influences such as family and media.
Markings used to identify them.
Where to refer them for authoritative information.
Instructions for subject contact:
Dead
Injured
Well
Rescue/evacuation plan.
Scene protection.
Safety instructions.

Specific things to watch for.
Place and time for pre-departure inspection.

Administration and Logistics

Food and water.
Special equipment.
What specific equipment?
Carried by whom?
Where to obtain?
Location of medical assistance.
How to contact.
Estimated time it will take to get to the scene.

Communications and Command

Communications equipment
Radio frequency(s) to be used.
Call signs.
Codes.
Other type signals.
Hand and arm.
Light
Sound
Regular reporting times.
Command
Chain of command within unit(s).
Location of leader during various phases of this mission.

The team briefing should be given far enough advance to allow members to prepare themselves and their equipment and obtain and prepare any special equipment needed for their assignments.

The briefing should be given in an area that is free from distractions, sheltered from the elements, and large enough to comfortably accommodate the unit being briefed.

All visual aids, such as maps, terrain models, blackboards, aerial photos should be used to make sure each member understands the mission. If visual aids are not available, planned actions are sketched on the ground.

In order to minimize interruptions during the briefing everyone is expected to take notes and to ask his/her questions when the leader completes his/her explanation. And when the explanation has been completed it is important that the leader provide enough time to give thorough answers to the questions raised by the crew members.

When all members of the team fully understand the assignment and what responsibilities they, as individual members, have towards the assignment, the success of the mission is greatly increased. Therefore, it is very important to take the time to make sure everyone understands what he/she is supposed to do and to also understand where he/she fits into the mission. Don't assume a person understands just because he/she has not asked questions.

An accurate, thorough, and efficient briefing will greatly influence the outcome of the mission, the crew's ability to actually accomplish the mission, and the ultimate outcome of the search.

Debriefing

In order for the management team to make the most effective use of information gathered by field personnel during a mission, the field personnel must be given an opportunity to meet with management to tell them exactly what they were able to accomplish, what they saw, and what opinions they created.

Debriefing is a complete interview of a field search unit to gain a thorough understanding of all evidence and activities encountered during the mission. Always remember that the crew members themselves may not understand the full importance of what they are reporting. Therefore, encourage them to share all their observations. The more experienced management team may be able to draw conclusions which are not evident to the individual team members.

Debriefing is usually conducted by the Situation Unit of the Planning Section and done according to ICS guidelines. On larger incidents it may be that the leader of a Crew/Task Force/Strike Team is the only person from each team who is debriefed. However, when possible, the entire crew should attend the debriefing. Each person's observations are important.

Without thorough and accurate information, subsequent planning may be unrealistic, misdirected or incomplete. The crew leader needs to document as much detailed information as possible so that the following questions can be adequately answered.

> Without exaggerations, what exactly did the team members actually accomplish?
> What is the estimated probability of detection (POD)?
> What were the locations of any clues, regardless of how insignificant they may seem to the searcher?
> Were there any gaps in coverage or search difficulties encountered? It is critical to know what wasn't searched.
> Are there any hazards in the area?
> Were there any problems encountered with the communications?
> Are there any suggestions, ideas or recommendations from the searchers to consider during future missions?
> It is very important that all information be as precise as possible concerning:
> Areas covered.
> Any gap that occurred.

Estimated POD of the search.

Incomplete or inaccurate information in these areas will certainly cause inaccurate planning data for future efforts. Therefore, it is the responsibility of the debriefer to ask the right questions and to probe for meaningful answers. Remember that the individual searcher knows only what he/she has experienced and does not have the context of all the information that is coming in from many other searchers. The debriefer is in a position to put the clues together. Therefore, it is up to the debriefer to collect the facts by asking questions.

Debriefers may have to resort to actually "picking the brains" of the members being debriefed in order to ensure getting as much information as possible from them. The success of the entire mission may depend on some little fact that may seem totally irrelevant.

As many crew members as possible should attend the briefing to ensure that everyone feels that their input is important and to gather as many points of observation as possible. As much debriefing as possible should be done on an individual basis and as soon as possible after returning from the field.

In order to ensure accuracy and proper documentation, debriefings should be written. Try to confirm information by getting it from more than one source.

Searchers should bring to the debriefing their maps, sketches, photos, and a 214 form with notes. Use of these documents help to ensure the information gathered is objective, complete and accurate. It will also tend to jog memories so that the debriefings will contain information as complete as possible.

Don't try to depend on memory. As the search operation progresses and the number of missions accumulate, people tend to forget what happened and when it happened. Debriefing information should be written to ensure the accurate recording of this information.

Remember, an effective debriefing is *thorough*. It leaves no stone unturned. It is *timely, focused* on individual belief as well as the objective facts. It is *written* and *includes recommendations of the searchers and search leaders.*

APPENDIX D – Pack List

April 2015.

NASAR Consolidated Pack Guide

Note: This is the April 2015 version and should be compared to any lists posted on the NASAR web site for updated information and recommendations.

NASAR has had multiple pack lists (minimum equipment lists) and resource specific lists which cause confusion among members and make it hard to keep the lists updated and coordinated. This is the first publication of the Consolidated Pack Guide. This is the single publication that documents all NASAR program pack recommendations. It should be your first go-to document for all pack questions and guidance. All previous pack standards and guidance are superseded by this guide.

Developing a mandatory standard for something as complex as a SAR pack is nearly impossible. There is no way to reasonably take into account the different environments, legislation, circumstances, or team standards that members may encounter throughout the nation or other countries where NASAR is recognized. In the past the use of a "pack list" did not provide enough information regarding the expected pack contents or the their use for students, instructors or evaluators to make decisions regarding equivalent substitutions, or locally required modifications based on environment, circumstances or assignment.

This is a 24 hour SAR pack guide built using the ASTM 2209 standard as its foundation, and as such it is supposed to provide students, instructors and evaluators with enough information for them to evaluate a packs contents and determine if they provide the essential needs for the NASAR program, environment, circumstance and assignment they are being presented or used for.

The typical SAR 24 hour pack is designed to support a sole searcher on a field assignment for up to 24 hours without outside logistical assistance. Typically the searcher is with other searchers working on the assignment together, and is wearing clothes/uniform appropriate for the environment, circumstances and assignment. Although this is a 24 hour pack, there is no assumption that the 24 hour assignment includes a sleep period, that the searcher will be near their vehicle or any other vehicle, or have the opportunity to visit a cache to replace consumables, or swap out equipment due to darkness, changes in weather or other reasons. There is an assumption that the searcher may find and have to assist/support an injured victim (or injured searcher) for a portion of the 24 hour assignment.

The recommended equipment falls into several categories:

    Survival / First Aid / Signaling
    Self-Rescue

        Hygiene / Personal Items
        Navigation
        Communications
    Light Sources

    Clothing & Personal Protective Equipment
        Shelter
        Food & Hydration
        Load Bearing / Packs
        Search
        Resource Specific
        Mission Specific

It is more efficient if the items you select have multiple uses. Any item that has more than one use helps lighten and consolidate your pack. A lighter pack makes for a more effective search responder (as long as you still carry everything that you may reasonably need).

Setting up your 24 pack does not have to be overly expensive. You can save yourself some money by using the Pro Deals through NASAR (e.g. Promotive) or your local team. Look for sales and deals from local outdoor stores. Look at what your teammates carry, ask their advice and use online resources to find reviews of equipment so you buy the best that you can afford.

Standardizing your electronics on a single type of battery will also help you limit the weight you have to carry and provide power options. Remember to store your batteries so they won't short and drain prematurely, or worse, catch on fire.

Item Explanations

Each item has an expected function and capability. Items selected may have a specific design that lends them more towards SAR use or makes an alternative item incompatible with SAR. In order to utilize this guide to evaluate equivalent substitutions or even the requirement of an item for a specific environment or circumstance the background and explanation for each item is provided here. Instructors and Lead Evaluators are given some latitude in determining needs based on the environment, circumstances, agency requirements, assignment and their experience. NASAR expects that safety is always the priority when reviewing items.

Survival/First Aid Kit/Signaling

Plastic bag, zip-lock, quart size	This zip lock bag is intended to hold the first aid and survival kit. A heavy-duty version (freezer style not sandwich style) bag is preferred. The bag can also be used to carry water, as an ice pack, or a solar still.
Acetaminophen and/or Aspirin Tablets	

Survival/First Aid Kit/Signaling

Benadryl Tablets	These can be used to help counteract allergic reactions.
Antiseptic Cleansing Pads	Antiseptic pads can be used to clean small cuts and scrapes to keep them from getting infected. Alcohol based pads may sting when you use them, but they can also be used to assist you in starting a fire in a survival situation. Iodine type pads don't sting when you use them, but they have no fire starting capabilities.
Antiseptic Ointment/Cream	Helps prevent infection and promotes healing of small cuts and abrasions.
Band Aids, Various Sizes	SAR is a dangerous business and cuts or scrapes happen to everybody eventually. Being able to protect that small injury after it gets cleaned lets you continue searching and helps prevent infections from occurring.
Candle, Long Burning, Survival Type	Delete This...
Cotton Swabs, Non-Sterile	Otherwise known as Q-tips, these are used to help clean small wounds. Care should be taken when using them in ear or nasal canals.
Duct Tape	Duct tape comes in handy for so many things, from fixing holes in tents to field expedient splint work. The most functional is 3" wide, and can be wrapped around itself or some other pack item like a water bottle. At a minimum several feet should be carried since it is so multi-functional. Color doesn't really matter, but in keeping with the visibility needs of SAR the brighter the better.
Leaf Bag	Leaf bags make great expedient raincoats, or a mini-shelter from the wind and weather.
Fire Starting Capability	Waterproof matches in a protective case or a fire starter that uses a sparking striker. Fire can be used for signaling and for keeping warm, and for cooking. It makes sense that you have the ability to make a fire easily. Although the striker will work in most environments, the matches are typically easier to use.
Moleskin	Moleskin is used to help treat foot blisters.
Chemical Light Stick	Light sticks come in handy for a number of purposes, providing you light and signaling capability. A white or bright yellow/green light stick can help light the area immediately in front of you. A bright or contrasting color light stick tie to the end of a 3' string can be swung around in a circle quickly and makes an effective signal at night. A series of light sticks can show a evacuation path to a litter team in the dark.
Roller Gauze Bandage	
Safety Pins	Safety pins are small and light weight and handy for holding together broken zippers, missing buttons, and other cloth based connections. They can also be used as a field expedient fishhook in a survival situation.
Splinter Forceps, Tweezers	These come in handy for removing ticks or splinters.
Space Blanket / Emergency Reflective Sleeping Bag	
Hand Sanitizer	Hand sanitizer in a gel form or in a single use pad comes in handy keeping your hands and other body parts clean and sanitary. SAR is dirty work and whenever you handle a drink, food, or snack you should clean your hands first to prevent possible disease transmission. You should also try to clean your hands both before and after you glove up to treat an injury.
Whistle	A plastic chamber based (no ball) whistle is the preferred option. If you use a whistle with a ball in it, the ball could fall out, or freeze and render the whistle inoperable.

Survival/First Aid Kit/Signaling

Signal Mirror	A signal mirror is a powerful tool for signaling during the daylight (although it can be used with a flashlight in the dark, but less effectively). Glass mirrors have the best reflective properties, but plastic mirrors are less prone to cracking or breaking in your pack. A mirror that is specifically designed for signaling has a sight window built into it, which biases you towards successful use, and is highly suggested.
Strobe Light	A great signaling device, the government surplus models can be seen for a long ways but use a special battery. Many newer headlamps and flashlights have a flasher mode built in – a consideration when you buy a light. You could also get one of the laser based signaling devices as well.
Smoke Signal	Smoke signals are very effective signaling devices in the marine environment. In land based environments you need to be careful using them due to fire hazard potential. A signal mirror is more preferential to smoke signals for your pack. In some cases you won't be allowed to carry smoke signals or pyrotechnic devices on transport helicopters.
Para–Cord / Cordage (50')	Another really handy product, paracord can be used to help set up a shelter, secure a splint, or even replace a broken bootlace.
EMT Type Scissors	EMT style scissors are designed to cut through thick fabrics easily.
Sterile Dressings (3 or 4)	These are sterile 4" gauze squares.
Water Purification Capability	There are a couple of methods to purify water that you can select from depending on your environment and mission. There are filtration based systems that usually use a pump and are very effective in removing suspended solids from dirty water. There are chemical systems that purify the water but leave the suspended solids in the water, and finally there are UV systems that utilize a battery powered light to kill the bad stuff and leave the suspended solids. Some systems combine filtration with either UV or chemical which gives you the best chance at good clean water from that stinky cow puddle. Spend some time researching what works best in your area and what other members on your team carry.

Self-Rescue Equipment

Carabiners	
Knife or Multi-Tool	
Prusik Cords	Prusik cords are made from
Webbing	This is a single piece of 1" tubular climbing style webbing that is 25' long. A possible use is making a Swiss seat for you or a victim, so this should be protected from chemicals, sunlight and other things like towing cars. Other uses include securing a patient in a litter, quick leash for a dog, or even building an expedient shelter.

Hygiene/Personal Equipment

Personal Medications	You should include at least 72 hours' worth of your personal medications just in case you are delayed in getting back home.
Spare Prescription Eyeglasses and/or Contact Lenses	SAR involves lots of rough terrain and activity. It is possible to lose your glasses or a contact lens, as well as have your glasses damaged beyond use. Better to plan on a backup than be blind in the woods (or on a mountain, etc.). This includes carrying extra contact lens solution.

Hygiene/Personal Equipment

Sunglasses, 97% UV	These help prevent eye damage and strain in high light conditions (including snow). Polarized sunglasses are better but can be more expensive.
Hand Trowel / Shovel	One of the most important items you can carry, this is used to dig the field expedient latrine and cover it up once you have pottied.
Toilet Paper	Toilet paper (and feminine hygiene products) are essential hygiene items for a team member. Many outdoor stores sell compact rolls of toilet paper for backpacking. It is important to keep the your hygiene products dry, so keeping them in a Ziploc style freezer bag is a good idea. TP can also be used as fire tender in an emergency if kept dry.
Watch	An analog style watch with a second hand is preferable. It is easier to assess patients using a watch with a second hand.
Lip Balm	A lip balm with sun screen is preferable. Lip balm is just as useful in cold weather as it is in hot weather.
Sunscreen	A lotion that has UVA/UVB SPF of 50 or more is preferable. A higher or lower SPF is a personal preference based on your complexion, environment and cancer risk.
Insect Repellent	Depending on the part of the country you are in and the insects that you need to repel, you should get the appropriate formula. There are some urban legends about stuff that works on local critters that you might also look into (e.g. Avon Skin So Soft works on sand fleas in the South East).

Navigation

Compass	Orienteering type compass that is graduated in degrees, fluid filled, has a mirror and sighting system, and a clear baseplate.
Grid Reader / Map Ruler / Protractor	When working with maps, accuracy is very important. Using a grid reader or map ruler helps you navigate accurately.
GPS	GPS technology has become commonplace in SAR. There are many GPS models that will work for SAR, some are much more expensive than others. Talk to other members of your team, and see what they carry and use. Just remember that GPS technology uses batteries and has accuracy issues under certain environmental conditions. Do not allow yourself to become reliant on GPS to the point that your map and compass skills degrade or perish.
Altimeter	Altimeters are typically used in mountainous or hilly terrain and help you with determining how high you are on a slope. There are several styles, with most being barometer based and must be aligned with a known altitude point.

Communications

Radio	Some teams and agencies have radios. Make sure you know how it works, test it before you leave basecamp, and have a spare battery for it.
Cell Phone	Cell phones are commonplace, but cell service is not in many communities.

Light Sources

Light Sources

Primary Light Source	LED technology has changed flashlights and headlamps over the past few years. They are brighter and last longer than ever before. Your primary light source should be as bright as you can afford, and be hands free (i.e. a headlamp). By wearing your light on your head (or helmet) it keeps your hands free to climb, carry a litter, treat a patient, keep branches from hitting you in the face, manipulate your compass, etc. You should carry several spare sets of batteries for your lights as well.
Secondary Light Source	Light sources are technology and rely on batteries, so you should always carry a backup source or even two. Things to consider for the backup light source include common battery size with your other electronic devices, size and weight.
Chemical Light Stick	Light sticks come in handy for a number of purposes, providing you light and signaling capability. A white or bright yellow/green light stick can help light the area immediately in front of you. A bright or contrasting color light stick tied to the end of a 3' string can be swung around in a circle quickly and makes an effective signal at night. A series of light sticks can show an evacuation path to a litter team in the dark.

Clothing and Personal Protective Equipment

Cap / Headgear	Headgear is intended to keep sunlight and bugs off your scalp and neck. It can also keep your head warm (a lot of heat is lost through your head) in the winter, or cool in the summer (get it wet and let the evaporation cool your head). A wide brim that goes completely around the hat is preferable to a baseball style hat (a wide brim protects your neck from sun and is easier to hang a bug net from). If you are trying to stay warm, a wool or fleece type hat that is snug and can cover your ears is best. Don't forget that you might be wearing a helmet, and during the winter a fleece or wool hat underneath can go a long way towards keeping you comfortable and alive.
Clothing	Appropriate for the environment, weather, circumstances and assignment. This may be the uniform required by your agency, or team.
Clothing (Extra Set)	Appropriate for the environment, weather, circumstances and assignment. In case you or a fellow searcher or the victim is wet, cold, or contaminated. This gives you options to continue searching, protect someone from the environment, or prevent further contamination (like poison oak or other plants). You should at least carry extra socks to keep your feet dry. These should be kept in a zip lock style bag to keep them dry.
Footwear	Footwear is very dependent on your environment and mission. You want to select something that protects your foot, fits well, supports your ankle and wears well. You might also want to consider breathability, waterproofness, tread, and the type of sock you are going to wear.
Gloves	There are a couple of different types of gloves you will need to carry depending on your mission. You will always want to carry several pair of surgical style gloves for triaging and treating victims or collecting evidence (be considerate of people with latex allergies and use latex-free gloves). You will also want some leather style work gloves that will protect your hands when searching at night or doing USAR, or rope work, or other rough activities.

Clothing and Personal Protective Equipment

Eye Protection	Carrying and using eye protection is just common sense. There is night searching where you don't want to get a branch in the eyeball, working around helicopters where there is high speed dust in the air, and protecting yourself from body fluids while providing medical assistance. Eye protection should typically meet local safety requirements, and can be in glasses, or goggle form, and may also include tinting for UV protection (sunglasses).
ANSI/ISEA 207-2010 Compliant Vest	This is one of those blindingly bright reflective vests. If they are compliant with the ANSI/ISEA standard they will say so on the package. Not only are they required when working near traffic, they make you much more visible in the wilderness to helicopters, searchers and hunters.
Goggles, Clear	See eye protection.
Socks	Cotton kills – you need to select socks made from other materials (e.g. wool or synthetics) that will help wick perspiration away from your foot, and provide adequate cushioning based on your mission requirements.
Rainwear	A durable and breathable jacket and pants set with an attached hood. Goretex or similar material is preferable. Plastic or rubber coated material can cause sweating under the rain gear which can lead to life threatening conditions in cold weather. Armpit zipper vents help moisture escape and makes the jacket more efficient.
Trekking Poles	Trekking poles are very useful in many environments, especially when hiking hills. They can double as tracking sticks or a field expedient splint.
Gaiters	Gaiters are important in a number of environments, they keep thorns and weeds from getting into your laces, bugs from crawling up your pants leg, snakes from biting your ankles, and ice and snow from getting your lower pants all wet and crusty. Make sure you purchase the right gaiters for the purpose, because snake gaiters are not snow gaiters, etc.
Bandanna / Handkerchief	In hot environments you can wet the bandanna and use it to cool your neck or shade you from the sun. In cold environments you can use it like a mini-scarf to stay warm.
Zip Lock Bags	The gallon and quart size, heavy duty zip lock style bags come in handy for a lot of things like carrying water, keeping dirty or contaminated clothes separated from other stuff, collecting evidence, carrying extra food, carrying out trash, etc.

Shelter

Bivy Sack	A bivy sack is a great alternative to a tent for a single searcher. It is lighter than a tent, and can be made from a breathable water repellent fabric. Some even include a bug net for your face. A bivy sack can be used to help keep a victim warm and dry as well as yourself. In dire and austere circumstances it can be made into a field expedient litter, but you need to be pretty desperate to go there.
Ground Insulation	Being capable of insulating yourself from the ground so you can maintain body temperature and stay dry is important. Depending on the environment, weather, circumstances, and assignment this could be a self-inflating pad, a blow up pad, foam pad, leaf bags stuffed with leaves, etc. Remember that proper ground insulation may be the difference in comfort and survival for you or an injured victim you find.
Shelter Material	An 8' x 10' piece of waterproof or water resistant material. This combined with your paracord and items found in place should allow you to build a shelter that will protect you from the environment and weather.

Wire Ties / Zip Ties	These come in handy for so many things, building shelters, field expedient splints, closing off water containers, building a shelter, closing a broken zipper, etc. Carry a couple of different sizes because they are light and come in handy for so many things.
Leaf Bags	

Food and Hydration

Food	Let's be realistic, this is a 24 hour pack! You don't need a lot of food to survive for 24 hours. However, depending on your environment and assignment you will need to generate energy and fuel your body. Carrying some protein bars will go a long way in keeping you energized and may come in handy if you find a missing person that hasn't had food for a few days.
Water Bottle / Canteen / Hydration Bladder	You will have to hydrate, and that means carrying water, and water is heavy. You have many options for carrying water. Some searchers are carrying hydration bladders that are slipped into their backpacks, with a drinking tube that comes over their shoulder. Some searchers carry multiple water bottles or other canteens for their water.
Sports Drink	You can enhance your water with bringing along some sports drink like Gatorade or Powerade to help replace your electrolytes. Try not to load up on the ones with a lot of sugar.

Load Bearing and Packs

Pack	Pack selection is a very personal choice. First, it is important to realize that there are different sizes/designs that fit men and women differently. Second, there are many different pack options that make a pack SAR friendly. For example, a top loading pack really limits your access to what is in the bottom of the pack, but a zippered panel loading pack could suffer a zipper failure and you could leave all your stuff on the trail as you hike along. Remember that human nature predicts that if you buy a big pack, you will end up carrying all sorts of unnecessary stuff, a smaller pack forces you to be a better decision maker about what you are carrying.
Waist/Butt Pack	In some environments this is a better option than a full size pack. In many urban environments you don't need a full pack on your back because there are convenience stores close by, and you have access to your vehicle, or you have cell coverage or radio contact with your base and anything you need is just a call away. In this case it is important to carry your first aid and survival gear primarily.
Radio Chest Harness	A radio chest harness allows you to keep the radio near your hands, the speaker up near your ears, and your hands free. Chest harnesses may also carry your maps, notebook, writing instruments, etc.
Rain Cover (Pack)	Wet gear can compromise your mission; you need to keep it dry. Besides using waterproof gear bags you can use a rain cover for your pack.

Search Equipment

Picture Identification	The public expects to be able to identify you. I picture identification is very helpful.
Pad and Pencil	You should always have a couple of writing instruments and a notebook. You can use a pencil, or pen for writing. Notebooks come in different size and styles, and some are even made from waterproof paper.

Tracking Stick – 42" Length	If you are tracking or your assignment includes tracking, it is good to have an appropriately prepared tracking stick. If you are using trekking poles to assist you in hiking, one of them can be set up to act as a tracking stick.
Pacing Beads / Hand Counter	In many cases you will need to do pace counting during navigation. Pacing beads or a hand counter will help you navigate accurately.
Binoculars	Using binoculars can help you extend your search area, or can be used to staff an observation post assignment. There are several small folding models that are easy to carry and inexpensive.
Flagging Tape	Fluorescent (brightly colored) colored 1" flagging tape (either PVC or paper based) at least 100' in length. You use this to mark your trail, the area you searched, or an evacuation route for a rescue team. Some teams have a specific color coding so check with them before you buy.
Measuring Device	When you are tracking, you need to be able to measure and compare footprints and strides. Many trackers carry a 18" to 24" small retractable measuring tape. It also can be used for navigation and map work.

Resource Specific

Mission Specific

Glossary

The glossary contains the definitions of common and not so common SAR related words and acronyms (in alphabetical order).

Consolidated Pack Guide – this document, yes the one you are reading.

SAR – Search And Rescue

US&R or USAR – Urban Search and Rescue

APPENDIX E – GAR FORM

TEAM MEMBER RISK ASSESSMENT WORKSHEET

Green – Low Risk 0-11	Amber – Moderate Risk 12-19	Red – High Risk 20-25
Proceed with Mission	Proceed with Caution	Stop and Reassess

1. **Planning**
   Is the plan as presented in the briefing and stated in your team briefing complete and clearly understood by all team members? Have potential dangers been adequately mitigated? Have contingency resources been identified? Are communications and backup communications addressed? Is the identification and description of the lost subject(s) adequate and correct? Have all questions been adequately addressed?

2. **Preparedness**
   Is the team and its leader fully trained and prepared to accomplish the objective? Are all members physically and mentally prepared to accomplish the assigned tasks?

3. **Environment**
   Has the team been properly briefed on all applicable environmental factors such as terrain, weather and the myriad of other environmental factors that can affect the search and the team? Are contingencies in place to address environmental changes? Can the team continue to operate beyond the assigned time required if the situation requires their continued presence?

4. **Supervision**
   Is supervisory control adequately addressed? Is the chain of command clearly addressed? Are all members of the team in agreement to the supervision provided? This factor is doubly important if a team is formed during an incident.

5. **Operational Factors**
   Is the team prepared to meet rapidly changing situations and operational hazards?

6. **Team Mitigation**
   _____
   _____
   _____
   _____
   _____

APPENDIX F – SEARCH URGENCY FORM

Date Completed: _____

TIME COMPLETED: _____

Initials: _____

REMEMBER THE LOWER THE NUMBER THE MORE URGENT THE RESPONSE!

A. Subject Profile---
   Age: Very Young………1   Very Old………..1
                                        Other…………….2-3
   Medical Condition:
      Known or suspected injury or illness……………….. 1-2
      Healthy…………………………………………………………….3
      Known fatality……………………………………………………3

B. Weather Profile--
      Existing hazardous weather……………………………………..1
      Predicted hazardous weather (9 hours or less)…………..1-2
      Predicted hazardous weather (more than 8 hours)………2
      No hazardous weather predicted……………………………….3

C. Equipment Profile--
      Inadequate for environment…………………………………. 1
      Questionable for environment………………………………..1-2
      Adequate for environment……………………………………..3

D. Subject Experience Profile---
      Not experienced, not familiar with the area…………… 1
      Not experienced, knows the area………………………………2
      Experienced, not familiar with the area………………….3
      Experienced, knows the area……………………………….. 4

E. Terrain & hazards Profile---
      Known hazardous terrain or other hazards………………… 1
      Few or no hazards………………………………………………….2-3
                                        Total----------------

If any of the seven categories above are rated as a one (1), regardless of the total, the search could require an emergency response. The total should range from 7 to 21 with 7 being the most urgent.

8-11---Emergency Response   12-16---Measured Response   17-21---Evaluate & Investigate

APPENDIX G LOST PERSON QUESTIONNAIRES

NOTE: Use pencil/black ink, print clearly. Avoid confusing phrases/words and unfamiliar abbreviations. Complete and detail answers for future use. Answer ALL questions, if possible.

Incident Title: _____ Today's date: _____ Time: _____
Interviewer(s): _____ Incident number: _____

A. SOURCE(S) OF INFORMATION FOR QUESTIONNAIRE

Name: _____ How Info Taken: _____
Home Address: _____
Phone 1: _____ Phone 2: _____ Relationship: _____
Where/How to contact now: _____
Where/How to contact later: _____
What does informant believe happened: _____

B. LOST PERSON

Full Name: _____ DOB: _____ Sex: _____
Maiden Name: _____ Nicknames: _____ Other AKA's: _____
Home Address: _____ Zip: _____
Local Address: _____ Zip: _____
Home Phone: _____ Local Phone: _____ E-mail Address_____
Birthplace: _____ Ethnicity: _____ National Origin: _____ Language Spoken: _____

C. PHYSICAL DESCRIPTION

Height: _____ Weight: _____ Age: _____ Build: _____ Eye Color: _____
Hair: Color Current: _____ Natural: _____ Length: _____ Style/Binding: _____ Wig: _____
    Beard: ____ Style/Color _____ Mustache: ____ Style/Color _____ Sideburns: _____
Facial features shape: _____ Skin color: _____ Tone: _____ Complexion: _____
Color of fingernails: _____ Fake nails: _____ Color of finger nails: _____
Distinguishing marks (scars/moles/tattoos/piercing): _____
Jewelry (and where worn, incl. Medical bracelets); _____
Eyewear/Contacts (sunglasses, spares): _____ Eyesight w/out glasses: _____
Overall Appearance: _____
Photo Available: Y __ N __ Where: _____ Need to be returned: Y__ N __
Comments: _____
_____

D. TRIP PLANS OF SUBJECT

Started from: _____ Day/Date: _____ Time: _____

Going to: _____ Via: _____
Purpose: _____
For how long?_____ Exit date: _____ Alone? Y __ N ___ Group size: _____
Done trip before? Y __ N ___ Details: _____
Transported by whom/means: _____

Vehicle now located at: _____ Type: _____ Color: _____
    License #: _____ State: _____ Verified? Y __ N __ By whom: _____
Return time: _____ From where: _____
    By whom/what: _____
Additional names, cars, licenses, etc. for party: _____
Alternate   plans/routes/objectives   discussed:
_____
Discussed with whom: _____ When: _____
Comments: _____
_____

E. CLOTHING

	STYLE	*COLOR*	*SIZE*	*OTHER*
Shirt sweater:				
Pants (belt/suspenders):				
Outerwear:				
Under wear/socks:				
Head wear:				
Rain wear:				
Glasses:				
Gloves:				
Neck ware (scarf/neckerchief/tie):				
Extra clothing:				
Footwear:				
Sole type: _____ Sample available? Y __ N ___ Where: _____

Scent articles available? Y __ N __ What: _____ Secured?: Y __ N __
Where is scent article now? _____
Overall coloration as seen from air: _____

F. LAST SEEN

Time: _____ Where: _____ Why/how: _____
Seen by whom: _____ Location now: _____
Who last talked at length with person: _____
Where: _____ Subject matter: _____
Weather at time: _____ Weather since: _____
Seen going which way: _____ When: _____
Reason for leaving: _____
Attitude (confident, confused, etc.): _____
Subject complaining of anything: _____
Subject seem tired: _____ Cold/Hot: _____ Other: _____
Comments: _____
_____

G. OUTDOOR EXPERIENCE

Familiar with area? Y ___ N ___ How Recent: _____ Other: _____
Other areas of travel: _____
Formal outdoor training / degree: _____
    Where: _____ When: _____
Medical training: _____ When: _____
Scouting experience: _____ When: _____ Where: _____
    How much: _____ Scout rank: _____ Scout Leader? Y ___ N ___
Military Experience? Y ___ N ___ What: _____ When: _____
Where: _____ Rank: _____ Other: _____
Generalized previous experience: _____
How much overnight experience: _____
Ever lost before? Y ___ N ___ Where: _____ When: _____
Ever go out alone? Y ___ N ___
Where: _____
Stay on trail or cross country: _____
How fast does subject hike: _____
Athletic/other interests: _____
Climbing experience: _____
Comments: _____

H. HABITS / PERSONALITY

Smoke? Y ____ N ____ How Often: _____ What: _____ Brand: _____
Alcohol? Y ____ N ____ How Often: _____ What: _____ Brand: _____
Recreational drugs? Y ___ N ____ What: _____
Gum brand: _____ Candy brand: _____ Other: _____
Hobbies/Interests: _____
Outgoing / quiet: _____ Gregarious / loner: _____
Evidence of leadership: _____ Give up easy / Keep going: _____
Legal trouble (past I present): _____
Hitchhike? Y ____ N ___ Accepts rides easily: _____

Personal problems: _____
Religious? Y ___ N __ Faith: _____ To what degree: _____
Personal values: _____
Philosophy: _____
Person closest to: _____ In family: _____
Emotional history: _____
Education Highest grade achieved: ___ Current status: _____ College Education: _____
    School name: _____
    Teachers: _____
    Subject/Degree: _____ Year: _____
Local/fictional hero: _____
Comments: _____

I. HEALTH / GENERAL CONDITION

Overall health: _____
Overall physical condition: _____
Known medical/dental problems: _____

    Knowledgeable doctor: _____ Phone: _____
Handicaps/deformities/prosthetics: _____
Known psychological problems: _____
    Knowledgeable person: _____ Phone: _____
Medication: _____
    Dosages: _____
    Knowledgeable person: _____ Phone: _____
What will happen without meds: _____
Dentures/Partials: _____ Dentist: _____ Phone: _____
Comments: _____

J. EQUIPMENT

	STYLE	*COLOR*	*BRAND*	*SIZE*
Pack:				
Tent:				
Sleeping Bag:				
Ground Cloth/Pad:				
Fishing Equipment:				
Climbing Equipment:				
Light:				
Knife:				

Camera:				
Stove: _____ Fuel: _____ Starter Y __ N __ What: _____					
Drinking Liquid Container: _____ Liquid Amount: _____ Kind of Liquid: _____					
Compass: _____ Map: _____ Of Where: _____					
How Competent with Map/Compass: _____					

Food: _____
Brands: _____
Skis: Type: _____ Brand: _____ Color: _____ Size: _____
    Bindings: _____ Pole Type: _____ Length: _____
    How Competent: _____
Snowshoes: Type: _____ Brand: _____ Color: _____ Size: _____
    Bindings: _____ How Competent: _____
Firearms: Y __ N __ Brand: _____ Model: _____ Holster: _____
Money: Amount: _____ Credit/Debit Cards: _____
Other Documents: _____

Comments: _____

K. CONTACTS PERSON WOULD MAKE UPON REACHING CIVILIZATION

Full Name: _____ Relationship: _____
Address: _____ Zip: _____
Phone #: _____ Anyone Home Now? Y __ N __

L. CHILDREN

Afraid of the dark? Y N   Animals? Y N   Afraid of: _____
Feelings toward adults: _____ Strangers: _____
Reactions when hurt: _____ Cry: _____
Training when lost: _____
Active/lethargic/antisocial: _____
Comments: _____

M. GROUPS OVERDUE

Name/Kind of group: _____ Leader: _____
Experience of group leader: _____
Address/Phone of knowledgeable person: _____
Personality clashes within group: _____
Leader types in group other than leader: _____
What would subject do if separated from group: _____
Competitive spirit of group: _____
Intergroup dynamics: _____
Comments: _____

_____

N. ACTIONS TAKEN SO FAR

By: Family/Friends: _____
Results: _____
Others: _____
Results: _____
Comments: _____
_____

O. PRESS/FAMILY RELATIONS

Next of kin: _____ Relationship: _____
Address: _____ Zip: _____
Phone #: _____ Occupation: _____
Significant family problems: _____
Family's desire to employ special assistance: _____
Comments: _____
_____

P. OTHER INFORMATION (Use back of form)

_____

_____

MISSING PERSON (MP) QUESTIONNAIRE, INTERVIEW FORM/GUIDELINE

LOST PERSON QUESTIONNAIRE ---LONG FORM[25]

(v2 rev. 04/2014)

NOTE: *Use pencil/black ink, print clearly. Avoid confusing phrases/words and unfamiliar abbreviations. Complete and detail answers for future use. Answer ALL relevant questions, if possible.*

INTERVIEWER: *Introduce yourself, background, qualifications and explain purpose and process of the interview.*

IMPORTANT: *Take breaks during the interview to report important search and planning information to CP.*
Complete & report highlighted sections & item #s to CP ASAP.
Check with Search Management for any additional high priority items.

A. INCIDENT INFORMATION

1. Incident Name: _____ 2. Today's date: _____ 3. Time: _____
4. Interviewer(s): _____ 5. Location: _____
6. Incident number: _____

B. SOURCE(S) INFORMATION

1. Name: _____
2. How Info received: ❑ In Person ❑ Phone ❑ Other _____
3. Home Address: _____
4. Phone 1: _____ 5. Phone 2: _____
6. Relationship to MP: _____
7. Where/How to contact now: _____
8. Where/How to contact later: _____
9. What does interviewee believe happened: _____
_____

C. MISSING PERSON INFORMATION

1. Full Name: _____ 2. DOB: _____ 3. Sex: _____
4. Maiden Name: _____ 5. Nicknames: _____ 6. Other AKA's: __
7. Name to call: _____ 8. Safe/Password: _____
9. Who Knows Safe/Password:
10. Home Address: _____ 11. Zip: _____
12. Local Address: _____ 13. Zip: _____

---

[25] Courtesy of the Contra Costa County Sheriff's Search and Rescue Team, C. Young 2014.

14. Home Phone: _____ 15. Local Phone: _____ 16. E-mail Address:

17. 1st Cell Phone: _____ 18. 1st Cell Carrier: _____ 19. 1st Voice Mail PIN:

20. 2nd Cell Phone: _____ 21. 2nd Cell Carrier: _____ 22. 2nd Voice Mail PIN: _____

(Complete Section N with more Cell Phone data)

23. How long lived at this location/area? _____ 24. Previous addresses: _____

25. Facebook/Other Sites: _____ 26. Screen Names/Alias: _____

(See Section N for Details)

27. Birthplace: _____ 28. Ethnicity: _____ 29. National Origin: _____

30. Preferred language: _____ 31. Other languages: _____ 32. Spoken under stress (curse): _____

33. Work/Student: _____ 34. Contact Person: _____ 35. Phone: _____

36. Work/School Address: _____

37. Driver's License Number: _____ 38. State: _____ 39. Status (Current/Suspended): _____

D. PHYSICAL DESCRIPTION (Whole Section is High Priority)

1. Height: _____ 2. Weight: _____ 3. Age: _____ 5. Build: _____

6. Eye Color: _____

7. Eyewear/Contacts (sunglasses, spares): _____ 8. Eyesight w/out glasses: _____

9. Hair: Current Color: _____ Natural Color: _____ Length: _____ Style/Binding: _____

 Wig: _____ Bald: _____ Describe: _____

10. Facial hair: _____ Style/Color _____ Sideburns: _____

11. Facial features shape: _____ 12. Skin color: _____ Skin tone: _____

Complexion: _____

13. Color of fingernails: _____ Fake nails: _____ Length of finger nails: _____

14. Distinguishing marks (scars/moles/tattoos/piercing): _____

15. Overall Appearance: _____

16. Photo Available: ❏ Yes ❏ No Where: _____ Need to be returned: ❏ Yes ❏ No

 Any differences vs. current appearance: _____

17. Scent articles available? ❏ Yes ❏ No What: _____

Secured?: ❏ Yes ❏ No

 18. Collected by Whom: _____ 19. Where is scent article now: _____

20. Comments: _____

E. CLOTHING (Whole Section is High Priority)

	STYLE	COLOR	SIZE	BRAND / OTHER
1. Shirt/Blouse:				
2. Pants (belt/suspenders):				
3. Outerwear: Sweater/Coat				
4. Under wear/socks:				
5. Hat / Head wear:				
6. Rain wear:				
7. Glasses/sunglasses:				
8. Gloves:				
9. Neck ware (scarf/neckerchief/tie):				
10. Other Accessories:				
11. Extra clothing:				
12. Footwear:				
Shoe Sole type: _____ Sample available? ❑ Yes ❑ No Where: _____				
13. Purse:				
14. Backpack: (detail info Section L)				

15. Jewelry (and where worn, incl. Medical/Safe Return or Electronic bracelets (*see Section N*)):

16. Overall coloration as seen from air: _____

17. Money: Amount: _____ 18. Credit/Debit Cards: _____

19. Other Documents: _____

F. HEALTH / GENERAL & EMOTIONAL CONDITION

1. Overall health: _____

2. Overall physical condition: _____

3. Known medical/dental problems: _____

4. Knowledgeable doctor: _____ 5. Phone: _____

6. Medication (Prescriptions and OVC): _____

7. Dosages: _____

8. What will happen without meds: _____

9. What will happen if they OD on meds: _____

10. Knowledgeable person: _____ 11. Phone: _____

12. Hearing problems: ❏ Yes ❏ No   Hearing aids: ❏ Yes ❏ No Are they with him/her? ❏ Yes ❏ No
13. Knows Sign language: ❏ Yes ❏ No
14. Dentures/Partials: ❏ Yes ❏ No Dentist: _____ Phone: _____
15. Use cane, walker, wheelchair: ❏ Yes ❏ No
16. What would happen if lose it or fall down?
17. Able to walk distances, up/down stairs, around obstructions: ❏ Yes ❏ No
18. Known psychological problems: _____
19. Knowledgeable person: _____
20. Phone: _____
21. Handicaps/Deformities/Prosthetics: _____
22. Emotional/Mental Health History: _____
23. Current emotional state: _____
24. Any recent depression: _____
25. How does MP express depression: (turn in or out) _____
26. Desire for "own space": ❏ Yes ❏ No   Spending time alone lately: ❏ Yes ❏ No
27. Where does MP go to be alone / to seek solitude: _____
28. Any signs of dementia/confusion (*Complete Section T&W*): _____
29. Any history of suicidal tendencies (*Complete Sections U*): _____
30. Is the subject a danger to themselves or others? _____
31. Any specific fears or phobias: _____
32. Pain threshold? (low, medium, high, stoic) _____
33. How handles heat, cold, weather, darkness? _____
_____
34. Comments: _____
_____
_____
_____
_____
_____

G. LAST KNOWN LOCATION / POINT LAST SEEN

1. Last seen by whom: _____ 2. Their location now: _____

3. Time: _____ 4. Where: _____ 5. Why/how: _____

6. Who was last to talk at length with MP: _____

7. Where: _____ 8. Subject(s) discussed: _____

9. Weather at time: _____ 10. Weather since: _____

11. Seen going which way: _____ 12. When: _____

13. Reason for leaving: _____

14. Attitude (confident, confused, etc.): _____

15. MP complaining of and/or voiced concerned about anything: _____

16. MP seem tired?: _____ 17. Cold/Hot?: _____ 18. Other?: _____

19. Comments:

H. SUMMARY OF EVENTS LEADING UP TO AND FOLLOWING MP'S DISAPPEARANCE

1. When/How did you find out that he/she was missing? _____

2. What have you done to locate him/her? _____

3. Anyone see him/her leave? _____

    4. Which direction was MP headed? _____

    5. Did MP say where he/she might be going? _____

6. Did MP leave any notes? _____

7. Did MP take any money, credit cards, ATM, checkbook with them? _____

8. What would MP have in pockets/wallet/purse? (ID card, transit card, keys, medications, cell phone, etc.) _____

9. Has anything like this (or similar) happened before? ❑ Yes ❑ No

10. Describe prior events. Where was MP located last time? _____

11. Have you ever had to go out and find him/her? ❑ Yes ❑ No

12. Describe the events of the last few hours: _____

13. Describe the events of the last few days: _____

14. Describe the events of the last few months: _____

15. How long ago did MP eat (and what was it)? _____

16. Did MP take anything else with them (stuffed animal, favorite toy)? _____

17. Does MP keep a diary, journal, blog and/or an address book of friends (or relatives)? ❑ Yes ❑ No Where is it?

19. Does MP have own computer? ❑ Yes ❑ No (*Complete detail information in Section N*)

18. Does MP use any social networks ❑ Yes ❑ No Passwords? _____

(Complete detail information in Section N)

20. Any recent stresses or behavior changes: _____

21. Any recent changes in financial situation: _____

22. Any recent issues/problems at work: _____

23. Actions taken locate MP by family/friends/others:

24. Results: _____

I. TRIP PLANS OF SUBJECT

1. Started from: _____ 2. Day/Date: _____

3. Time: _____

4. Going to: _____ 5. Intended route: _____

6. Purpose: _____

7. For how long?: _____ 8. Exit date: _____ 9. Alone? ❑ Yes ❑ No

10. Group size: _____

11. Done trip before? ❑ Yes ❑ No 12. Details: _____

13. Transported by whom/means: _____

14. Vehicle now located at: _____ Type: _____ Color: _____

   Distinguishing details: _____ 15. License #: _____ State: _____

   Verified? ❑ Yes ❑ No By whom: _____

16. Planned return time: _____ 17. From where: _____

18. By whom/what: _____

19. Additional names, cars, licenses, etc. for party:

20. Alternate plans/routes/objectives discussed:

21. Resources used to plan trip (books/computer/maps/guides): _____

22. Available: ❑ Yes ❑ No

23. Discussed plans with whom: _____ 24. When: _____

25. Any animals with the party (horses, dogs) and number: _____

26. Comments:

J. OUTDOOR EXPERIENCE

1. Familiar with area: ❑ Yes ❑ No 2. How Recent: _____ 3. Other: _____

4. Other areas of travel: _____

5. Formal outdoor/survival training / degree: _____

6. Where: _____ 7. When: _____

8. Any 1st aid or medical training: _____ 9. When: _____

10. Scouting experience: _____ 11. When: _____ 12. Where: _____

13. How long: _____ 14. Highest Scout rank: _____

15. Scout Leader?: ❑ Yes ❑ No

16. Military Experience?: ❑ Yes ❑ No

17. What: _____ 18. When: _____ 19. Where: _____

20. Rank: _____ 21. Other: _____

21. Generalized previous experience: _____

22. How much overnight experience: _____

23. Ever lost before: ❑ Yes ❑ No 24. Where: _____ 25. When: _____

26. Ever go out alone: ❑ Yes ❑ No 27. Where: _____

28. Tends to stay on trails or cross country: _____

29. How fast does subject hike: _____

30. Athletic/other interests: _____

31. Climbing (technical or free) experience: _____

32. Comments:

K. HABITS / PERSONALITY / BEHAVIOR PREFERENCES

1. Smoke? ❑ Yes ❑ No 2. How Often: _____ 3. What: _____

4. Brand: _____

5. Alcohol? ❑ Yes ❑ No 6. How Often: _____ 7. What: _____

8. Brand: _____

9. Recreational drugs? ❑ Yes ❑ No 10. How Often: _____ 11. What: _____

12. Favorite foods (gum/candy): _____ 13. Brand: _____ 14. Other: _____

15. Person closest to: _____ 16. In family: _____

17. Other close friends (list in Section O).   18. Is MP close to friend's family members ❑ Yes ❑ No

   (list in Section O)

19. Hitchhike?: ❑ Yes ❑ No 20. Accepts rides easily: _____

21. Familiar with public transportation: ❑ Yes ❑ No 22. Does he/she use it? ❑ Yes ❑ No

23. Has bike, skateboard, scooter, roller blades: ❑ Yes ❑ No Description/location: _____

24. Goes on walks/hikes in area: ❑ Yes ❑ No 25. Where/favorite path: _____

26. Has good sense of direction: ❑ Yes ❑ No 27. Likes to explore: ❑ Yes ❑ No

28. Taken trips on own or with friends/relatives: ❏ Yes ❏ No

29. Reaction to strangers/police officers: _____

30. Will respond if called: ❏ Yes ❏ No

31. Knows how to use telephone/ dial 9-1-1: ❏ Yes ❏ No

32. Hobbies/Interests: _____

33. Favorite local places (shopping, parks, play areas, restaurants): _____

34. Describe daily routine: _____

35. Personal habits: (clean, neat, sloppy, dirty, etc.): _____

36. Who chooses MP's clothing & what is his/her response? _____

37. Personality: (outgoing, quiet, gregarious, loner, etc.) _____

38. Evidence of leadership: _____

39. Give up easy or keep going: _____

40. Any legal or criminal trouble (past / present): _____

41. Any personal problems or violent tendencies: _____

42. Does MP own any weapons: ❏ Yes ❏ No 43. Are they still in household? ❏ Yes ❏ No

44. Where: _____

45. What does he/she do for fun? _____

46. Able to swim / tread water: ❏ Yes ❏ No How long: _____

47. Attracted to water: ❏ Yes ❏ No

48. Afraid of any animals or birds: ❏ Yes ❏ No _____

49. Will he/she chase or try to follow animals? ❏ Yes ❏ No

50. Religious?: ❏ Yes ❏ No 51. Faith: _____ 52. To what degree: _____

53. Personal values: _____

54. Philosophy: _____

55. Education Highest grade achieved: _____   56. Current status: _____

57. College Education: ___

    58. School name: _____ 59. Subject/Degree: _____

    60. Year: ____

    61. Teachers: _____

62. Local/fictional hero: _____

63. Comments:

L. OUTDOOR EQUIPMENT

	STYLE	COLOR	BRAND	SIZE
1. Pack:				
2. Tent:				
3. Sleeping Bag:				
4. Ground				
5. Fishing				
6. Climbing				
7. Other				
8. Light:				
9. Knife:				
10. Camera:				

11. Stove: _____ Fuel: _____ Starter ❑ Yes ❑ No What: _____

12. Drinking Liquid Container: _____ Liquid Amount: _____ Kind of Liquid: _____

13. GPS: ❑ Yes ❑ No Compass: ❑ Yes ❑ No   14. Map: ❑ Yes ❑ No Of Where:

15. How Competent with GPS/Map/Compass/Orienteering skills:

16. Food: _____

17. Brands: _____

18. Firearms or Bow: ❑ Yes ❑ No 19. Brand: _____ 20. Model: _____

21. Holster: _____

22. Ski/Snowboard: Type: _____ Brand: _____ Color: _____ Size: _____

    Bindings: _____ Pole: _____ Length: _____

    23. How competent: _____

24. Snowshoes: Type: _____ Brand: _____ Color: _____ Size: _____

    Bindings: _____ How competent: _: _____

25. Comments: _____

_____
_____
_____
_____

M. CONTACTS PERSON MIGHT MAKE UPON REACHING CIVILIZATION

1. Full Name: _____ 2. Relationship: _____
3. Address: _____ 4. Zip: _____
5. Phone #: _____ 6. Anyone Home Now: ❑ Yes ❑ No
7. Answering machine?: ❑ Yes ❑ No
8. Who has access to messages: _____ Remote password: _____
9. Checked machine: ❑ Yes ❑ No

N. ELECTRONIC DEVICES

1. 1st Cell Phone: Type: _____ Model: _____ Provider: _____ Voice Mail
   PIN/Password: _____
         Battery Status: _____ Voice/Text Message Sent: _____ Received: _____
2. 2nd Cell Phone: Type: _____ Model: _____ Provider: _____ Voice Mail
   PIN/Password: _____
         Battery Status: _____ Voice/Text Message Sent: _____ Received: _____

(If cell phone(s) is/are available, check call history & phone book contacts)

3. Satellite Cell Phone: Type: ___ Model: _____ Provider: _____ Voice Mail
   PIN/Password: _____
         Battery Status: _____ Voice/Text Message Sent: _____ Received: _____
4. GPS: Model: _____ Default Setting: ___ Datum: _____ Can Set/Use Waypoints:
   _____
         Battery Status: _____ Download Routes: _____ Computer
         Available: _____
5. Radio: Model: _____ Freq.: _____ PL Tone: _____ Check Time/Interval: _____
         Battery Status: _____
7. Electronic Locator Device: Brand: _____ Freq: _____ Where Worn on
Subject: _____
         Company contact: _____ RDF or cell phone/GPS: _____ Battery Status: _____
6. Beacon (PLB, ELT, EPERB): Model: _____ Number: _____ Registered: _____
         Battery Status: _____ Web Password: _____
7. SPOT type device: Brand: _____ Service Provider _____
Registered to: _____
         Last message received: _____ When: _____ By whom: _____
         Plan if "Emergency" notice is received: _____

8. Laptop/Computer Model: _____ Location: _____ Password: _____

   Battery Status: _____ Screen Name: _____

   Recent internet usage, browser history, emails, etc.: _____

9. Tablet Device: Model: _____ Location: _____ Password: _____

   Battery Status: _____ Screen Name: _____

10. Does MP use any social networks (Facebook, Twitter, etc,)? ❏ Yes ❏ No

    (list all site and multiple names on same site)

    1st network: _____ User name: _____ Password: _____

    List of online friends: _____

    Recent logon, status, location tags, blogs and/or comments: _____

11. Are there any CCTV cameras available at the PLS (or residence) ❏ Yes ❏ No

12. Where can the recordings be obtained: _____

13. Does MP have an, tablet, or laptop with WiFi capability or with a data plan? ❏ Yes ❏ No 14. What is the associated phone number: _____

15. What service: _____

16. Does MP use any gaming or animation sites? ❏ Yes ❏ No

17. What sites: _____ 18. What is their user name(s): _____

18. Do they use apps. to locate their phone(i.e. find my phone, find my iPhone, find my friends, etc.): _____

    (Note: To preserve batteries on the target devises. Instruct the family and friends not to call the phone unless requested. Utilize text messages from the search team/law enforcement to contact the target device.)

O. FAMILY, FRIENDS AND PRESS RELATIONS

1. Next of kin: _____ 2. Relationship: _____

3. Address: _____ 4. Zip: _____

5. Phone #: _____ 6. Occupation: _____

7. Other Family/Friend Contact: _____ 8. Relationship: _____

9. Address: _____ 10. Zip: _____

11. Phone #: _____ 12. Occupation: _____

13. Other Family/Friend Contact: _____ 14. Relationship: _____

15. Address: _____ 16. Zip: _____

17. Phone #: _____ 18. Occupation: _____

19. Other Family/Friend Contact: _____ 20. Relationship: _____

21. Address: _____ 22. Zip: _____

23. Phone #: _____

24. Occupation: _____

25. Significant family problems: _____

26. Family's desire to employ special assistance: _____

27. Comments:

P. OTHER INFORMATION

1. Where do you think he/she might be? _____
_____

2. Anything else about MP we should know about or that might help us? _____
_____
_____
_____
_____

Q. GROUPS OVERDUE / DYNAMICS

1. Name/Kind of group: _____ 2. Leader: _____

3. Experience of group leader: _____

4. Address/Phone of knowledgeable person: _____

5. Personality clashes within group: _____

6. Leader types in group other than leader: _____

7. What would MP do if separated from group: _____

8. Competitive spirit of group:

9. Intra-group dynamics: _____

10. Comments:

Supplemental Questions – Specific Subject Types

R. CHILD / ADOLESCENT SUBJECT

1. Afraid of dark?: ❑ Yes ❑ No   Animals?: ❑ Yes ❑ No   2. Which ones?
3. Feelings toward adults: _____ 4. Strangers: _____
5. Reactions when hurt: _____ 6. Cry: _____
7. Training when lost: _____
8. Active/lethargic/antisocial: _____
9. Does MP act mature or immature for their age? ❑ Yes ❑ No _____
10. Understand social and personal relationships? ❑ Yes ❑ No _____
11. Has MP been disciplined lately? ❑ Yes ❑ No _____
12. How does MP accept punishment (run or stay and take it)? _____
13. Does MP attend school? ❑ Yes ❑ No
14. Where? _____

    15. Grades, attendance, problems? 16. Contact info? _____

    17. Teacher's Name and Phone _____

    18. How does he/she do in school (grades, get along with the teacher, discipline problems)? _____

19. Who does MP play with? _____
20. Have you noticed any "strangers" lately? _____
21. MP mentioned any strangers/new people lately? _____
22. Does MP get an allowance? ❑ Yes ❑ No   Able to handle money? ❑ Yes ❑ No
23. Has MP reached puberty? ❑ Yes ❑ No   24. How are they handling it and are they sexually active? _____
25. Where is the mother/father now? _____
26. What games does MP play with his/her friends and where? _____
27. Does MP play hide and seek and where? (Is there a "fort" or "clubhouse")? _____
28. Comments:

29. List close friends, school mates, boyfriends, girlfriends & contact info.

_____   _____
_____   _____
_____   _____

S. AUTISTIC SPECTRUM

1. Is MP considered low-functioning, moderate-functioning, or high-functioning? _____

2. What cognitive age is MP functioning at? _____

3. Ever wandered away before? ❑ Yes ❑ No   4. Circumstances: _____
_____

5. Has a tracking device? ❑ Yes ❑ No   6. If so, has it been activated? ❑ Yes ❑ No

7. Asked to go to a particular type of area recently (water, school, family, neighbor, or friend's house): ❑ Yes ❑ No

8. Did he/she go there? ❑ Yes ❑ No

9. Likes to go to water areas, streams, pools, lakes? ❑ Yes ❑ No Any local sources: _____

10. Does MP have any specific "likes" that they're drawn to that may help search effort? (types of vehicles, music, sounds, favorite characters, toys, locations, etc.) ❑ Yes ❑ No _____

11. Any dislikes, fears, or sensory issues that may hinder search effort? (dogs, sirens, lights, shouting, aircraft, uniforms, etc.) ❑ Yes ❑ No   12. How he or she will typically react to negative stimuli: _____

13. Likes to hide in small spaces. ❑ Yes ❑ No

    14. Past hiding spots in the house? _____

    15. Any past hiding spots in other locations (school, park, etc)? _____

    16. Other likely hiding spots: (e.g. freezers, refrigerators, storage areas, closets, cabinets, under beds and small hiding spots in the house, garage, yard and outbuildings.) _____

17. Will respond if strangers are calling his/her name? ❑ Yes ❑ No _____

18. Will hide from searchers. ❑ Yes ❑ No _____

19. Will respond better if searchers "sing" his/her name. ❑ Yes ❑ No

20. Is there a song or a phrase (maybe from a game or a frequently watched movie, TV program) that the MP might respond to when searchers call out? ❑ Yes ❑ No   21. What is it: _____

22. Insists upon a particular route for going to school, to the store, to a relative's or family friend's house. ❑ Yes ❑ No

23. Describe route: _____

24. Has an aide or tutor at school or at home. ❑ Yes ❑ No   25. Name, contact, description of role of aide or tutor:
_____

26. Has a resource specialist at the school whom we may contact. ❑ Yes ❑ No

27. Contact information: _____

28. What does the MP do under stress? _____

29. What kind of "stimms" (repetitive stimulation actions) does the MP do? _____

30. Under what circumstances does the MP stimm? _____
   (i.e. autistic child may rock and bang head against the car headrest only when the car is moving, or may flap his fingers directly in front of his eyes when there is "visual noise".)

31. What routines does the MP person insist upon?   30. Frequency? _____
_____

32. Sensory or dietary issues, if any: _____

33. Calming methods, and any additional information First Responders may need: _____

34. Atypical behaviors or characteristics of the Individual that may attract the attention of Responders: _____

35. Method of Preferred Communication. (If nonverbal: Sign language, picture boards, written words, etc.): _____

36. Method of Preferred Communication II. (If verbal: preferred words, sounds, songs, phrases they may respond to): _____

37. Is the MP attracted to active roadways/highways: _____

38. Does the MP have a sibling with special need: ❏ Yes ❏ No 39. Has that sibling wandered away before ❏ Yes ❏ No

40. Where was the sibling found: _____

41. Where does the MP like to go? Does the child have a favorite place: _____

42. Is the MP nonverbal? ❏ Yes ❏ No 43. How will the MP likely react to his or her name being called: _____

44. Will the MP respond to a particular voice such as that of his or her mother, father, other relative, caregiver, or family friend: ❏ Yes ❏ No 45. Whom: _____

46. Does the verbal MP know his or her parents' names, home address, and phone number: ❏ Yes ❏ No

47. Does the MP have any sensory, medical, or dietary issues and requirements ❏ Yes ❏ No 48. List: _____

49. Does the MP rely on any life-sustaining medication: ❏ Yes ❏ No 50. List: _____

51. Does the MP become upset easily: ❏ Yes ❏ No 52. What methods are used to calm them down: _____

T. COGNITIVELEY IMPAIRED / MENTALLY CHALLENGED

1. Learned to sit up, crawl or walk later than other children? ❑ Yes ❑ No _____

2. Learned to talk later or have trouble speaking? ❑ Yes ❑ No _____

3. Has trouble communicating? ❑ Yes ❑ No   Describe _____

4. Finds it hard to remember things? ❑ Yes ❑ No _____

5. Has trouble understanding how to pay for things? ❑ Yes ❑ No _____

6. Has trouble understanding social rules? ❑ Yes ❑ No _____

7. Has trouble seeing the consequences of his/her actions? ❑ Yes ❑ No _____

8. Has trouble solving problems? ❑ Yes ❑ No _____

9. Has trouble thinking logically? ❑ Yes ❑ No _____

U. DEPRESSED / DESPONDENT / POSSIBLY SUICIDAL (VERBAL OR NON-VERBAL)

1. Has sleep been disrupted lately? ❑ Yes ❑ No _____

2. Has there been a stressful event or significant loss (actual or threatened) in his/her life? ❑ Yes ❑ No

3. History of serious depression or mental disorder? ❑ Yes ❑ No _____

4. Significant anniversary date(s) (e.g. the passing of a loved one): _____

5. Expressed feelings of guilt, hopelessness or depression? ❑ Yes ❑ No _____

6. Has been expressing great emotional and/or physical pain or distress? ❑ Yes ❑ No _____

7. Has been putting things in order, e.g., paying up insurance policies, calling friends, giving away possessions?
❑ Yes ❑ No

8. Has talked about committing suicide, or said he/she is tired of living? ❑ Yes ❑ No _____

9. Has attempted suicide in the past? ❑ Yes ❑ No   10. If so, how? _____

11. Any history of being committed for 72hour metal evaluation (5150 Cal W&I): _____

11. Has shown efforts to learn about means of death or rehearse fatal acts or methods to avoid rescue? ❑ Yes ❑ No

12. Has the means (e.g., gun, pills, rope) to complete their intent? ❑ Yes ❑ No _____

13. Are any weapons, kitchen knives, etc. unaccounted for? ❑ Yes ❑ No _____

V. EXHIBITING PSYCHOTIC BEHAVIOR

1. Shows signs of sedation, depressed respiration, a semi-hypnotic state, contracted pupils, depressed reflexes and/or intoxication? ? ❏ Yes ❏ No _____

2. Shown lack of feeling, pain or fatigue? ? ❏ Yes ❏ No _____

3. Showing signs of lack of coordination, restlessness, excitement, disorientation, confusion and/or delirium? ❏ Yes ❏ No

4. Experiencing hallucinations, pupil dilation, increased blood pressure and body temperature, depressed appetite, and on occasion, nausea and chills? ? ❏ Yes ❏ No _____

W. EXHIBITING SIGNS OF DEMENTIA OR ALZHEIMER'S

1. Has aides or caregivers. ❑ Yes ❑ No 2. Names / contact info. _____

3. Has memory or other cognitive losses that affects job skills or daily life. ❑ Yes ❑ No 4. What: _____
_____

5. Ever wandered away before? ❑ Yes ❑ No 6. Circumstances: _____
_____

7. Has difficulty performing familiar tasks. ❑ Yes ❑ No 8. Explain:_____

9. Has problems with speech or language. ❑ Yes ❑ No 10. Explain: _____

11. Has problems recognizing once familiar people ❑ Yes ❑ No 12. Who: _____

13. Has problems with motor skills (dressing/eating) ❑ Yes ❑ No 14. Explain: _____

15. Is sometimes disorientated to time and place. ❑ Yes ❑ No 16. How often _____

17. Sometimes slips back to an earlier time/place. ❑ Yes ❑ No 18. When and where? _____

19. Obtain prior addresses going back many years. _____
_____

20. Shows signs of poor or decreased judgment. ❑ Yes ❑ No 21. Explain: _____

22. Has problems with abstract thinking. ❑ Yes ❑ No 23. Explain: _____

24. Places items in inappropriate places. ❑ Yes ❑ No 25. Explain: _____

26. Exhibits rapid changes in mood or behavior. ❑ Yes ❑ No 27. Explain:_____

28. Exhibits violent behavior. ❑ Yes ❑ No 29. Explain: _____

30. Having any problem with incontinence. ❑ Yes ❑ No 31. Explain: _____

32. Exhibits dramatic changes in personality. ❑ Yes ❑ No 33. Explain: _____

34. Shows a loss of initiative. ❑ Yes ❑ No 35. Explain: _____

36. Are problems or issues consistent, or do they vary from day to day or at different times of day (sundowning)? _
_____

37. Is MP still driving? ❑ Yes ❑ No 38. Access to vehicle? ❑ Yes ❑ No 39. Is vehicle still there?
❑ Yes ❑ No

40. Is there any history of taking a vehicle that does not belong to them? ❑ Yes ❑ No

41. Explain:

42. Work history, locations and mode of transportation: _____

43. Additional notes: _____
_____
_____

APPENDIX H – ROPE ANCHORS

Wrap 3 – Pull 2 Tie Off

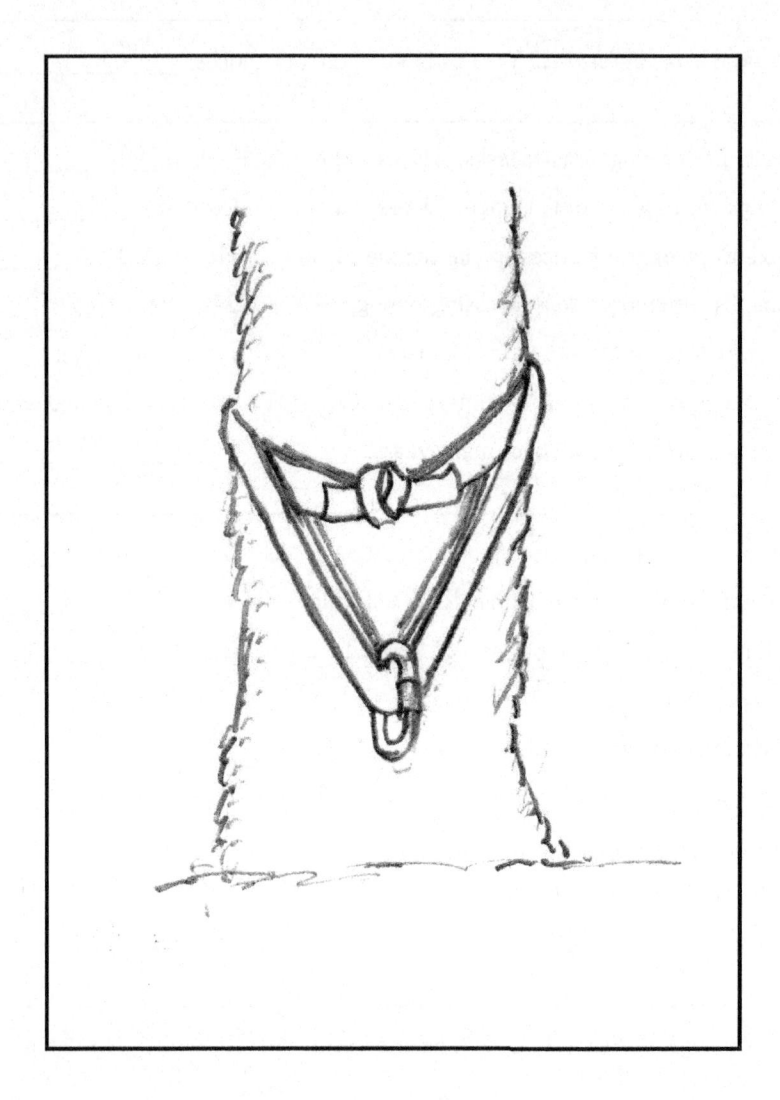

What is wrong with this picture? (answer on next page)

A Wrap 3 turns webbing around an anchor and tie off as illustrated with a water knot. Pull two turns out and attach a locking carabineer as an anchor.

Answer: No overhand safety knot.

Tensionless Rope Anchor

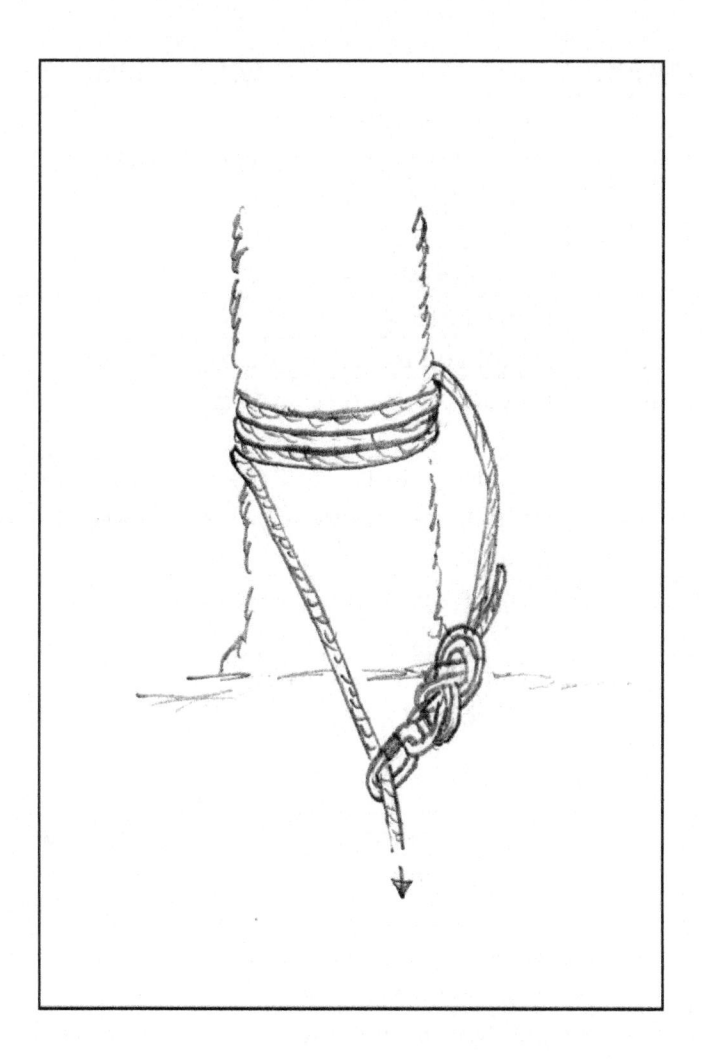

FIGURE 8 ON A BIGHT.

Wrap three turns around anchor wrapping upward for a downhill load as shown. Do not let the wraps cross. Use a figure eight on a bight and a locking carabineer to connect the running end to the standing end.

BASIC DYNAMIC BELAY COMMANDS[26]

SIGNALLER	COMMAND	MEANING
Climber	On belay.	I am tied securely into rope.
Belayer	Belay On.	I am in belay position, ready to belay.
Climber	Ready to Climb.	I am preparing to move.
Belayer	Climb.	I am expecting you to move and will begin hauling the rope or letting in slack.
Climber	Climbing.	I am climbing.
Climber	Up Rope.	I want you to pull up the rope and remove any slack.
Belayer	No Response or OK.	Adjusts the rope accordingly.
Climber	Slack.	I want you to pay out the rope, thus releasing the tension. Often necessary to afford the climber the freedom to make a move.
Belayer	No Response or OK.	Provide the necessary slack.
Climber	Tension	I want you to pull the rope tight.
Belayer	No Response or OK.	Pulls the rope tight preparing for a possible fall.
Climber	Falling.	Obvious.
Belayer	Fall.	Catches fall in prescribed manner, saving the life of the fellow climber.
Climber	Off Belay.	I am detached from the rope and have moved to a safe place out of the rock fall zone, away from the lip or away from any similar danger.
Belayer	Belay Off.	Ok, I can relax. The rope is free for the next person to tie in.

---

[26] Padgett, Allen & Smith, Bruce. <u>On Rope; North American Vertical Rope Techniques; For Caving....Rapellers.</u> Revised edition, National Speleological Society, Huntsville AL, 1996. Print. P. 262.

APPENDIX I URBAN SEARCH FORMS

Note: All BASARC forms are courtesy of the Bay Area Search and Rescue Council (BASARC). All of the BASARC and MP forms are available online at www.basarc.org .

BASARC FORM 132 – URBAN INTERVIEW LOG

URBAN INTERVIEW LOG	1. INCIDENT NAME	2. DATE/TIME	3. TEAM IDENTIFIER

STREET ADDRESS	RESIDENT CONTACTED	RESIDENT'S NAME	OTHER'S AT HOME	PHONE #	HOW LONG HOME	RESIDENT TO CHECK HOME AND YARD	SAR CHECKED YARD	PLACES TO HIDE IN AREA	COMMENTS	SUGGEST FOLLOW UP VISIT
	Y N		Y N			Y N	Y N			Y N
	Y N		Y N			Y N	Y N			Y N
	Y N		Y N			Y N	Y N			Y N
	Y N		Y N			Y N	Y N			Y N
	Y N		Y N			Y N	Y N			Y N
	Y N		Y N			Y N	Y N			Y N
	Y N		Y N			Y N	Y N			Y N
	Y N		Y N			Y N	Y N			Y N
	Y N		Y N			Y N	Y N			Y N
	Y N		Y N			Y N	Y N			Y N
	Y N		Y N			Y N	Y N			Y N
	Y N		Y N			Y N	Y N			Y N
	Y N		Y N			Y N	Y N			Y N
	Y N		Y N			Y N	Y N			Y N
	Y N		Y N			Y N	Y N			Y N
	Y N		Y N			Y N	Y N			Y N

SAR 132 BASARC | 5. PREPARED BY

BASARC FORM 134 --- CLUE LOG

CLUE LOG	1. INCIDENT NAME	2. DATE	3. INCIDENT NUMBER

CLUE #	ITEM FOUND	TEAM	DATE/TIME	LOCATION OF FIND	INITIALS
	SAR 134 – BASARC 3/98				

BASARC FORM 135 --- CLUE REPORT

CLUE REPORT	1. INCIDENT NAME	2. DATE	3. INCIDENT NUMBER
4. CLUE NUMBER	5. DATE/TIME LOCATED	6. TEAM THAT LOCATED CLUE	

7. NAME OF INDIVIDUAL THAT LOCATED CLUE

8. DISCRIPTION OF CLUE

9. LOCATION FOUND

10. TO INVETIGATIONS
- ☐ **URGENT REPLY NEEDED**, TEAM STANDING BY TIME _____
- ☐ INFORMATION ONLY

11. INSTRUCTIONS TO TEAM
- ☐ COLLECT
- ☐ MARK AND LEAVE
- ☐ DISREGARD
- ☐ OTHER _____

CLUE & SEGMENT PROBABILITIES TO BE COMPLETED BY PLANS

11. CLUE PROBABILITY	13. SEGMENT PROBABILITY SEGMENTS	LIST
☐ VERY LIKELY A GOOD CLUE ☐ PROBABLY A GOOD CLUE ☐ MAY BE A GOOD CLUE ☐ PROBABLY NOT A GOOD CLUE ☐ VERY LIKELY NOT A GOOD CLUE ☐ DON'T KNOW	VIRTUALLY 100% CERTAIN CLUE MEANS SUBJECT IS IN THESE SEGMENTS	
	VERY STRONG CHANCE THAT CLUE MEANS SUBJECT IS IN THESE SEGMENTS	
	STRONG CHANCE THAT CLUE MEANS SUBJECT IS IN THESE SEGMENTS	
	BETTER THAN EVEN CHANCE THAT CLUE MEANS SUBJECT IS IN THESE SEGMENTS	
	NO INFORMATION FROM THE CLUE TO SUGGEST SUBJECT IS OR IS NOT IN THE SEGMENT	
	BETTER THAN EVEN CHANCE THAT CLUE MEANS SUBJECT IS NOT IN THESE SEGMENTS	

COPIES			
☐ PLANS ☐ INVESTIGATIONS ☐ DEBRIEFING	☐ ATTACHED TO CLUE ☐ OTHER _____	STRONG CHANCE THAT CLUE MEANS SUBJECT IS NOT IN THESE SEGMENTS	
		VERY STRONG CHANCE THAT CLUE MEANS SUBJECT IS NOT IN THESE SEGMENTS	
		VIRTUALLY 100% CERTAIN CLUE MEANS SUBJECT IS NOT IN THESE SEGMENTS	

SAR 135 BASARC 3/98	14. PREPARED BY:	15. CLUE & SEGMENT PROBABILITIES PREPARED BY

INDEX

Abductions 82, 83
About the Authors 201
Activity Log 16
Administration Ready Pack 9
ADSAR 1
aimable orienteering compass 41
Air Communication Plan 156
Air Operations, Obstacles 158
air scent dog 113, 114, 115, 177
Air Scent Dogs 177
Air Space Plan 156
Air transport 187
Aligning the Compass 41
Alzheimer 72, 85, 89, 168, 170
AMBER alerts 88
AMBER conditions 24
AMDR 57, 58, 62, 147, 148, 149, 150
Anchor 132
antivenin 28
APPENDIX A 212
APPENDIX B – Selected ICS Forms 215
APPENDIX C 226
APPENDIX D 233
APPENDIX D – Pack List 233
APPENDIX E – GAR Form 242
Appendix G --- Lost Person Questionnaires
 249
APPENDIX H --- Rope Anchors 268
APPENDIX I --- Urban Search Forms 271
area search 55, 56
Attraction 52
attraction, containment, hasty and grid searches 49
Attractive Nuisances 170
Avalanche Dogs 109
Avalanche Search 75
Average Maximum Detection 147

Average Maximum Detection Range (AMDR) 147
Aviation 155, 164
azimuth 32, 40, 41, 42, 44
Azimuth 38
Backtracking 80
Baseline 56
Bauman bag 162
Bearing .... See Leadership
Behavior .... See Leadership
Behavioral Symptoms 197
belay 134, 135, 137
bezel ring 41
Briefing and Debriefing 176
BRIEFING AND DEBRIEFING 227
brownout 155, 159
building searches 167
Building Searches 174
Calculating POS 152
Camper (Car camper) 83
Canine Typing according to the Department of Homeland Security 111
Carabineers 132
Care .... See Leadership
carry crew 139
caterpillar method 140
Cave Dogs 109
characteristics of a successful leader 5
CISD 195, 198
Clue Aware 94
clue awareness 91
coagulopathy 28
Coggins Test 122
cognitive level 72
Cognitive Symptoms 196
Command 2, 9, 14, 15, 17, 19, 24, 40, 46, 49, 155, 185, 187, 199, 205, 228, 230

command functions 14
Communications Unit 17, 19, 215
Compass 41
Computer Generated Maps 46
containment49, 50, 51, 52, 126, 128, 170, 171, 175, 176
Containment 50, 51, 171
Contouring 81
Councils or State Emergency Management Agency Standards 118
Courage .... See Leadership
Crew Leader 91, 105, 140, 157, 158
Critical Incident Stress Debriefing 198
critical separation 147, 150
Critical Separation (CS) 147
critical spacing 56, 143, 144
Critical spacing 144
Critical Spacing 150
cross trained dogs 106
Cross-Trained Dogs 110
Ddogs, types of search and rescue dogs. 105
decision making 7, 13, 196
Declination 39, 40
Deductive Reasoning 145
Dementia 82, 85, 86
dementia with Lewy bodies 85
demobilization 15, 18
Department of Homeland Security 111
derig 136, 137
Detection57, 60, 93, 105, 106, 109, 146, 147, 148, 149
detection training 60
direction of travel41, 50, 52, 74, 80, 86, 97, 100, 113, 114, 115, 120, 177, 178
Direction of Travel 54
Direction Sampling 78
Direction Traveling 77
Disaster search dogs 105
Documentation 18, 122, 177, 191
Doing Nothing,lost person behavior 82
door to door canvassing 167
Door-to-door canvassing 172
Door-to-Door Canvassing 171

drones 164
Electronic Distance Measuring 46
Electronic Navigation Aides 44
Enthusiasm .... See Leadership
Environmental Safety 25
Equator 32
Equine Certification and Readiness 122
Equine Required Equipment 123
Equine Safety 122
Equine Scent Training 125
Equine Training Sessions 123
Extraction 183, 188, 191
Facilities Unit 17, 224
FEMA 12, 13, 105, 108, 111, 196
Field Operations 170, 176, 199
Field Team Tasking 171
figure eight on a bight 134, 136
figure eight stopper knot 136
Finance/Administration 18
First Responder Dogs 108
five priority assessment patient categories 181
five steps of an initial patient assessment 181
FLIR 164
Flyers 174
Folk Wisdom 81
Food Unit 17
Forward Looking Infrared Imaging 164
foveal field 61
FROSTBITE 26
FUNSAR 31, 96, 182
Gaining Access 185
GAR Model 10, 24
Gear Sherpa's 139
global positioning system 31
Global Positioning System (GPS) 44
Gordon, Ross 52
GPS 31, 33, 37, 44, 46, 157, 191, 237
grid azimuth 40
Grid Naming 56
Grid Reader 36
Grid Systems 32

Ground Support Unit	17, 20
Guide Person	56
Guideline	56
hasty non-area linear search	55
Hasty Search	170
Hasty Teams	54
Hazardous Terrain Safety	131
hazardous terrain	131
hazards	23, 28, 29, 116, 136, 184, 226, 228, 231
Hazards	27
heat cramps	26, 27
Heat Exhaustion	27
heat stroke	26
Heat Stroke	27
hemotoxic venom	28
high angle system	131
high-angle operations	131
Hiker	84, 89
HMS carabineer	133
hoist	155, 161, 162
Hoist	161
How to Find and Request SAR Dog	119
Human Remains Detection dogs	105
Human Remains Detection Dogs	109
human remains detection/cadaver dog	105
Humility	See Leadership
Humor	See Leadership
Hyperthermia	26
Hypothermia	25, 26
IC	See Incident Commander
ICS courses	14
ICS Courses	9
ICS five major organizational functions	14
ICS Form 214	9, 16, 19, 40, 49, 60, 152, 226
ICS Forms	9, 19, 20, 215
Immovable Object	42
Incident Action Plan	15, 17, 18, 20
Incident Action Plan (IAP)	18
Incident Command Systems	14
incident commander	105, 106, 112
Incident Commander	2, 14, 49, 52
initial assessment	185
Initial Call-Out	170
Initial Planning Point	50, 52, 69, 71, 145
Initial Planning Point (LKP/PLS)	50
Initiative	See Leadership
Institution Check	171
Integrity	See Leadership
International Dateline	32, 34
International Search & Rescue Incident Database (ISRID)	73
interviewing	50, 144, 167, 169, 170, 178
Investigation	17, 71, 169, 191
IPP	See Initial Planning Point
ISRID	73, 80, 81, 82, 207
ISRID database	73, 81
K9 Do's and Don'ts	115
kernmantle nylon rope	133
Knowledge	See Leadership
Koester, Robert	iii, 52, 71
landing zone	155, 156, 157, 158, 159, 160, 161, 189
Landing Zone	157, 159
Landing Zone Selection	157
last known point	49, 114, 157
Last Known Point	50, 170
Latitude	32, 33
latitude/longitude	33, 34
Leader	5, 9, 10, 16, 55, 111, 112, 113, 114, 115, 120, 215
leadership	5
Leadership	1, 5, 10, 13, 21
Leadership Theories	10
lensetic compass	41
Lensetic compass	40
Lewy bodies	85
Litter handling	139
litter movement	131, 140
litter to transport a patient	137
Litter Wheel	139
live find dog	105
Live Find Dogs	106
LKP	17, 50, 69, 71, 97, 143, 144, 145, 146, 170
Logistics	14, 17, 228, 230

Logistics Section Chief	17
Longitude	32, 33, 34
Loose Grid	56
Lost Person Behavior	69, 71, 73, 82, 144, 145, 146
Lost Person Questionnaire	66, 71
Lost Person Strategies	76
low angle rigging	133
low angle rope system	132
low angle system	131
low-angle operations	131
lower a litter	135
Management by Objective	11
Managing Stress	197
Map Reading	31
MBO	11, 13
Medical evaluation	185
Medical Unit	17, 19
micro management	14
Military Version of the 7.5 Minute Map	32
Missing Person Questionnaire	9, 50, 60
Missing Person Report (MPR)	144
Mobility and Responsiveness	75
Mounted Equipment	123
Mounted Responding to a Search	123
Mounted SAR teams	126
Mounted Unit	121, 122, 128
Mounted Unit – Using Equines in SAR	121
Mounted Units	66, 124, 127
Move a Crew across a Slope	136
Move a Crew Down	134
Move a Crew Up	135
MPQ	50, 51, 55, 60
MPR	144, 145
Munster hitch	132, 134, 137
Munter hitch	135, 136
National Incident Management System	9
Navigation	31, 44
Night Navigation	44
Non-Scent Discriminating	106
North Georgia Mounted Search and Rescue Team	124
Northumberland Rain Dance	147, 148
On lead trailing dogs	114
operational period	49
operations chief	106
Operations Chief	15, 16
Operations Section	15
Operations Section Chief	15
Orienteering	40
overhand knot	140
Overhead Team	52
Packaging	183, 187, 188, 191
Parkinson's disease	85
Participative Management	13
path of least resistance	54
Patient assessment five priorities	185
Patient Assessment	183, 185, 191
patient care and litter	137
Patient Transport	137
pear-shaped carabineer	133
Perception, Recognition and Detection	60
Perceptions	20
Physical Symptoms	197
pick-up zone (PZ)	156
place last seen	49, 69, 105, 107, 113, 114, 157
Place Last Seen	50, 52
Planning	9, 14, 17, 19, 20, 40, 50, 52, 55, 66, 69, 71, 144, 145, 151, 168, 226, 231
planning chief	106
Planning data	71
Planning Section	9, 17, 19, 55, 144, 151
PLS	17, 50, 52, 69, 71, 97, 98, 113, 114, 145, 146, 170, 175
POA	54, 55, 113, 143, 144, 145, 146, 151, 152
POD	43, 55, 143, 144, 146, 147, 151, 152
POS	55, 143, 151, 152, See Probabillity of Success
power line right-of-way	54
Preplanning	190
Pre-planning	183
Prime Meridian	32
Probability and Critical Spacing	143

probability of area	113, 143
Probability of Area (POA)	146
probability of detection	43, 55, 143
probability of detection (POD)	43, 55
probability of success	55, 143
Probability of Success	See POS
probability theory	143, 145
Profiles, lost person behavior	82
prussic knot	136, 137
Psychological Symptoms	196
purposeful wandering	150
Random Traveling	76
Rattlesnake	27
rattlesnakes	28
Recommended Reading	199
Recovery	190
References	199
reflector	53
reflex tasking	2
Reflex Tasking	49, 50, 52
reflex tasks	49
Resource Unit	18, 19
Risk assessment	24
Rope	133, 138, 139, 200
rope system	131, 132, 137
Ropes, Hardware	132
Route Sampling	78
Route Traveling	76
Safety	2, 10, 23, 25, 122, 128, 131, 138, 139, 172, 177, 185, 188, 189, 191, 200
SAR teams	2
Scenario Lock	75
scene safety	184
scent article	100, 105, 106, 107, 114, 116, 117
scent articles	114, 115, 116, 175
Scent Articles	117
Search Lane	56
Search Manager	52, 97
Search Probability	143
search strategies	167
Search Tactics	49, 55
Search Techniques	59
Searching data	71
Section Chief	17, 19, 169, 224
SeniorAlert	88
sign-cutting	100, 115
Silver Alert	88
single person rescue load	133
Single Resource	16
Situational Management	13
Size up	49, 184, 185, 191
Size Up	24, 183
SKED	162
SMARTER	5, 11, 12, 13, 19
SMARTER Approach	12
snakes	27, 28
Spatial Model	69, 74
spatial models	74, 75
Spinal immobilization	188
spokes and reflectors	53
Stabilization	183, 186
staging area	16, 18, 50, 115
Staging Area Manager	16
Statistics, missing person	72
stokes basket	162
STOP, ASSESS and MITIGATE	24
Strategy	55
stress	192, 195, 196, 197, 198, 199, 227
Stress	195, 196, 197, 198, 199
Stress Management	195
Stressors, Environmental	196
Stressors, Personality	196
Stressors, Psychosocial	196
stressors, three types	195
strike team	56, 60, 65, 126
Strike Team	14, 16, 49, 55, 152
Strike Team Leader	14, 49, 152
subject category	71
Subjective Reasoning	144
Supply Unit	17
Sweep Width	147
Tact	See Leadership
Tactical Briefing	82
tactics	2, 49, 50, 55, 60, 75, 92, 161, 167, 175

Tactics 55, 93
tactics, indirect 50
Tag lines 163
Task Force 16, 55, 65
Task Lists 155
Taylor, Ab 91
TEAM BRIEFING OUTLINE 212
Team Work .... See Leadership
Technical Rescue 25
Technical Search Teams 24
tensionless hitch 132, 136, 137
Theory 144
Think Tank Function 17
Tight Grid 58
topo map 32
Topographic (TOPO) Maps 32
Track Aware 96
track awareness 91, 96
trackers 50, 52, 65, 92, 93, 100, 115
Trackers 10, 91
tracking ability 91
Tracking Ability Levels 94
Tracking dogs 105
Tracking Dogs 107
tracking log 97
Tracking Skill Sets 92
Tracking Tasks 97
Tracking Tips 92
Tracking, Combining a K9 Asset with a Tracking Asset on your Team 100
Tracking, Moving Forward on a Track Trail and Marking Found Tracks 98
Tracking, PLS Approach and Identifying Tracks 97
Tracking, Step-By-Step 99
trailing dog105, 107, 113, 114, 115, 117, 177
Trailing dogs 105
Trailing Dogs 107, 177
Trained, Reliable and Certified Dog Handler Teams 118

Types of Search and Rescue Dogs 106
Types of Stressors 196
Unit Log Form 19
United States Geological Survey 36
United States Geological Survey (USGS) ... 32
Universal Transverse Mercator 32, 33
Universal Transverse Mercator (UTM) System 33
Unmanned Aircraft 164
urban2, 25, 32, 52, 53, 72, 83, 85, 87, 88, 108, 167, 168, 169, 170, 175, 177
Urban / Disaster search dogs 105
Urban Interview Log 173
Urban Reflex Tasking 50
urban search 23
Urban Search / Disaster Dogs 108
Urban Searches 167
Urban searches, Planning and Strategies 168
USGS map 32, 36
UTM 32, 33, 34, 35, 36, 37
UTM Coordinate Numbering 35
UTM Grid Reader 36
vascular dementia 85
venom 27
View Enhancing/Cell Signal Seeking 78
Vulnerability Assessment 167, 168
Water search dogs 110
Wheel Model 52
When to Request and Deploy a Search Dog 112
whiteout 155, 159
Whiteout 159
Wilderness Air Scent Dogs 105
Wilderness Air Scent Live Find Dogs – Scent Discriminating 106
Wilderness Air Scent Live Find Dogs 106
wilderness search 50, 53, 168
wind information 157
Working with a Search Dog 112

Figure 96 Finding a Clue.

Printed in the United States of America.

Printed in Great Britain
by Amazon